Friends at the Bar

Friends at the Bar

A Quaker View of Law,
Conflict Resolution, and Legal Reform

NANCY BLACK SAGAFI-NEJAD

SUNY PRESS

Published by State University of New York Press, Albany

For information, contact State University of New York Press, Albany, NY
www.sunypress.edu

Production by Eileen Meehan
Marketing by Michael Campochiaro

Library of Congress Cataloging-in-Publication Data

Sagafi-nejad, Nancy Black, 1937–
  Friends at the bar : a Quaker view of law, conflict resolution, and legal reform / Nancy Black Sagafi-nejad.
       p. cm.
  Includes bibliographical references and index.
  ISBN 978-1-4384-3413-1 (hardcover : alk. paper)
  1. Quakers—Legal status, laws, etc.—United States.   2. Religion and law—United States.   I. Title.

  KF4869.Q83S24 2010
  342.7308'52—dc22   2010020730

10 9 8 7 6 5 4 3 2 1

To Tagi, Jahan, and David with love and respect

Contents

List of Figures   ix
Foreword   xi
Preface   xv
Acknowledgments   xvii

Introduction   1

Part One

Chapter 1
About Friends   9

Chapter 2
Friends' Beginnings in England   29

Chapter 3
Penn's Holy Experiment in Pennsylvania and His Changes to Its Laws   47

Part Two

Chapter 4
Quakers as Plaintiffs and Defendants in Court and as
"Divine Lobbyists"   69

Chapter 5
Quaker Lawyers and Lawyer Ethics   121

Chapter 6
Mediation and Arbitration: Past and Future   177

Epilogue 199
Appendix 203
Notes 207
Glossary 231
Selected Bibliography 235
Index 241

List of Figures

Figure 1   A Lawyer and His Client   54

Figure 2   Length of Time Practicing Law   123

Figure 3   Reasons for Becoming a Lawyer   124

Figure 4   Size/Kind of Practice with Use of Alternative
Dispute Resolution (ADR)   127

Figure 5   Strength of Identification as Quaker with Quaker
Influence on Practice   128

Figure 6   Type of Law Practice   131

Figure 7   Quaker Influence on Practice with Experience of Tension   137

Figure 8   Strength of Identification as Quaker with Experience
of Tension   139

Figure 9   Strength of Identification as Quaker with Use of ADR   188

Figure 10   Quaker Influence on Practice with Use of ADR   191

Foreword

When I was becoming a Quaker, some of my most influential mentors were conscientious objectors to World War II, to the peacetime draft, and to the then-current Korean Police Action. Most had served in Civilian Public Service camps. Others had served one or two prison terms for their opposition to war. They were lawbreakers for conscience's sake, asserting obedience to a "higher law." One important mentor was an elderly Quaker lawyer who had refused to register when the Roosevelt administration tried to extend draft registration for men into their sixties. He and his wife were tax resisters. In fact, some of my first Quaker models were also women my grandmother's age, who spoke easily of civil disobedience and being arrested. (This was a surprise to me, since where I grew up, people who got arrested and jailed preferred not to discuss the matter.) When I appealed my draft board's refusal to grant my conscientious objector status, a nice draft board member asked me, "Paul, how did you get yourself into this fix?" Well might he wonder.

My first Quaker brushes with the law help frame my reading of *Friends at the Bar: A Quaker View of Law, Conflict Resolution, and Legal Reform,* Nancy Black Sagafi-nejad's careful, insightful and multilayered study of how Quakers, and especially Quaker lawyers, have negotiated, reconciled, or lived in tension with their professional and spiritual lives. The Friends she studies are on both sides of the bar: as defendants, plaintiffs, lawyers, judges, and prosecutors. To be a lawyer today requires detailed knowledge of law and statute, as well as the protocols of the courtroom; how to represent, to litigate, to reach a settlement, and to work effectively in a system adversarial by design. It also requires maintaining one's own integrity and living by what Quakers call our "testimonies," the word we use exactly as it is used in a court of law–a promise to tell the truth, whole and nothing but.

The book is divided into two parts. The first gives us a history of the origins of Quakerism in the aftermath of the English Civil War, the Puritan Commonwealth, an age of life-and-death competing Christian communions— primarily Catholic, Anglican, Presbyterian, and Baptist, as well as a host of "dissenting" sects, for example, Seekers, Ranters, Levelers, Diggers, Fifth Monarchy

Men, Muggletonians, and of course "the people in scorn called Quakers." Those
sects differed widely in theology, but they had in common being targets of
judicial oppression. Friends even got their nickname in court, from a judge
who sneered at George Fox's assertion that Friends "quaked" before the Lord.

This first period of Quakerism, from the mid-seventeenth century through
the Commonwealth, the Stuart Restoration, the founding of Pennsylvania, the
Glorious Revolution and down to when Quakers withdrew from control of the
Pennsylvania legislature rather than vote approval of war tax for the French and
Indian War, lays the foundation for a rich legal history. The first Quakers were
either in court or in prison, or getting ready for either, much of the time. In
response, Friends created several institutions to challenge the laws and defend
themselves assertively in court and in petitioning parliament. The Meeting for
Sufferings became the instrument for documenting Quakers' battles with the
law, for supporting families while the parents were in prison, and for engaging
wherever possible with parliament, Lord Protector, and King to change unjust
laws. Fox traveled with a book on the common law with him and was a stickler
for proper process such as the reading of charges aloud and the exact wording
of warrants. He was a self-taught lawyer, as were virtually all the Quakers
entangled in the law at that time. The incidents he recounts in his journal are
exciting, serious, and sometimes comic, and they virtually always ended with
Fox going back to prison.

Friends at the Bar gives us an overview of such pivotal court contests as the
Penn v. Mead trial, which ultimately established the independence of juries. Had
space allowed, the book might also have explored many other ingenious Quaker
responses to legal oppression, from the passive resistance of Isaac Penington, who
on principle never defended himself in court, to the assertiveness of Thomas
Elwood, who at his own expense brought witnesses from a distance to prove in
court that an informer had lied about the defendants' being at a specific Quaker
meeting. Or the noncooperation of groups of Friends who stopped traveling to
distant courts at their own expense, instead requiring that the authorities pay
for transporting them. Suddenly indulging in legal oppression became expensive
for the taxpayers, so harassing Quakers for unlawful assembly or preaching in
public declined substantially.

These Quakers helped bring down many unjust laws or practices, helped to
achieve notable victories for civil liberties. And as part proprietor of West Jersey
and later governor of Pennsylvania, Penn the scholar, statesman, and conscientious
lawbreaker, creates a model legal charter for preserving individual liberty.

In her explication of key Quaker testimonies, Nancy Black Sagafi-nejad
cites Howard Brinton's explanation of the Peace Testimony as a commitment
to harmony, which underlines why Quaker lawyers would be committed to
negotiation, mediation, and arbitration as tools for avoiding adversarial conflict.
Brinton emphasizes two aspects of harmony—peace and justice—confirming the

practical truth that there can be no peace without justice, nor justice without peace.

The second part of this book closely explores how individuals as well as local and yearly meetings, and the American Friends Service Committee have played direct roles as plaintiffs and defendants in landmark First Amendment, liberty of conscience and equal rights cases, and challenges to immigration policy. The examples remind us that our only way to challenge a law's constitutionality in court is by showing that it directly harms us. That means that "proving an interest" may require disobeying a law and thus risking a conviction and punishment. Many individuals and Quaker institutions today challenge laws directly or in amicus curiae coalition with the American Civil Liberties Union and civil rights organizations. Nancy Black Sagafi-nejad also focuses usefully on the work of the Friends Committee on National Legislation, the "Quaker lobby," which has been so instrumental in developing both civil rights legislation and in challenging abuses of civil liberties.

All this valuable discussion prepares us for what seems to me the heart of the book, its concluding chapters, which take us deeply into the ethical choices and conflicts Quaker lawyers experience. The author solicited responses to a series of questions (found in the Appendix) and analyzes the replies of one hundred practicing or former Quaker male and female lawyers. These lawyers record the difficulties of telling the whole truth in adversarial proceedings, of dealing with pressure to generate billable hours, and keeping their integrity while performing professionally. They emphasize the inadequacy of law school curriculum to address ethics adequately. Quaker lawyers are idealists who enter the profession to do good and serve real needs for people. Many of them report disillusionment, isolation from colleagues, and lack of support within their group practices. Out of this discussion the book offers some valuable recommendations about how the law school curriculum and the in court norms might be changed.

Any good book leaves its readers wanting to know more and with questions implied. And this is a very good book. Reading it sets me considering the substantial Quaker responses to the civil rights movement as well as to the widespread assaults on civil liberties we usually call McCarthyism. The Yearly Meeting of the Civil Liberties Committee of Philadelphia, which grew out of a national Quaker conference on the issues in 1954, and the Rights of Conscience Committee created by the American Friends Service Committee, are only two examples of Quaker work for civil liberties with which I had personal acquaintance, but of course Quakers were deeply engaged in legal challenges and civil disobedience and in supporting the civil rights movement. Undoubtedly other yearly meetings and Quaker organizations have their own histories of engagement with the law. The Friends Committee on National Legislation has a prominent part in that history. Official Federal Bureau of Investigation files show that the American Friends Service Committee was under surveillance for many years, going back to the 1930s, and in the Vietnam War era some of its files were actually stolen and some of its offices broken into. The Service Committee has reasons to believe that surveillance in the name of Homeland Security has also occurred since September 11, 2001.

Friends at the Bar is an excellent and timely study. It frames important questions about how religious and political dissenters, specifically Quakers, can live their witness with integrity in "the century of total war" that is still ongoing. It shows us the tensions for Quaker lawyers between the expectations of their professional lives and their commitment to truth-telling. It gives us encouragement to think of ways to replace adversarial approaches to conflict with mediation and arbitration.

Paul Lacey
Professor Emeritus
Earlham College
Richmond, Indiana

Preface

This book had its genesis in this Quaker lawyer's recognition that truth-telling and other important Quaker beliefs seem to conflict with the "successful" practice of law. This realization came as I began, in my early forties, to practice law. As I learned more and became engaged in actual practice, I wondered how long I could be truly comfortable with it. Most Friends (and I) take truth-telling seriously, and are occasionally, even often, quite literal in their speaking and in the interpretation with that of others. I sensed that being relentlessly truthful in the practice of law could place a client in jeopardy, especially if opposing counsel were not.

As I puzzled over this, I thought of other Quaker beliefs that seemed inapposite to a lawyer's actions and behavior. The Quaker testimonies of harmony, equality, and community can be at odds with the adversarial nature of law as practiced in the United States at the turn of the third millennium. I began to wonder if other Quaker lawyers shared similar musings and, furthermore, if something inherent in Friends' history and beliefs made certain of these conflicts inevitable.

In the spring of 1991, I had the good fortune to be awarded the Henry J. Cadbury Scholarship at Pendle Hill, the Quaker center for study and contemplation in Wallingford, Pennsylvania, founded in 1930. For the academic year 1991–1992, I resided at that tranquil place, conducted research at the excellent Friends Historical Collection housed at nearby Swarthmore College, and devised and distributed a survey to Quaker lawyers whose responses to it form a central and important part of this book.

Although their answers and comments came from their particular vantage point as Quaker lawyers, some scholars, whose work is discussed in chapter 5 and who are not members of the Society, share similar views on law and truthfulness. I hope these respondents' and scholars' perspectives will be of interest to those outside the small coterie of Friends and the even smaller circle of Quaker lawyers.

Acknowledgments

I owe gratitude to many:

To Pendle Hill for awarding me the 1991–1992 Henry J. Cadbury Scholarship to begin this study. There I lived, studied, worked, and shared meals in fall, winter, and spring with the friendly Friends who comprise that community and who made it not only a productive, but warm, experience.

To the Quaker lawyers, who so painstakingly and thoroughly answered the survey questionnaire, I give special thanks. I am indeed indebted to them.

To the Friends Historical Collection at Swarthmore College and to others who deserve my appreciation for suggestions on the manuscript or Quaker lawyer survey or for help in other ways: Hugh Barbour, Kathleen Brandes, Pam Burrell, Nancy Frommelt, J. William Frost, Tom Hamm, Heleodoro Lozano, Deborah Patton, Karl Peter Sauvant, Joanna C. Scott, Barbie Selby, Donald Smith, and the late Richard Franke, Helen Hollingsworth and Eleanor Webb. To Paul Lacey, special thanks for his Friendly help and encouragement and to Craig Horle for being willing to share his extensive knowledge of early English citation styles.

To the editors at SUNY Press: Nancy Ellegate, my gratitude for her discovery of something worthy in the manuscript and her gentle and easy manner, and to Eileen Meehan, my thanks for her kind understanding and patience with my near-endless tinkering.

To our sons Jahan and David, with love, who began their college years as I became the Cadbury Scholar at Pendle Hill, and who have encouraged me by just being who they are, and

To my husband of forty-three years, Tagi Sagafi-Nejad, along with my gratitude, my heartfelt love and admiration, who, during this endeavor, was forgiving of my foibles and ever-steadfast in his help, support, and encouragement.

Introduction

"There is an essential 'parasiticality' ('intertextuality,' . . .) involved in the production of any text whatsoever, . . ."[1]

It seems presumptuous for authors to stress the significance of their work because they owe so much to those who wrote and researched in the field before. The most that many, including this author, can do is to explore new connections among already well-researched areas and make educated guesses, not definitive conclusions, about their meaning and significance. These are then presented to the reader for further consideration and reflection.

By elucidating historical and sociological connections between Quakers and their many and varied encounters with law and legal systems, this book may provide a better understanding of the religious tensions between Quakers and the law, which continue to this day. After providing a relevant exposition of Friends' beliefs, their historical beginnings in England and America, and cases they brought or defended in court, this book's main task is to present the views of 100 Quaker lawyers on practicing law as they also practice their faith. Other lawyers, too, may feel similar tensions between their faith or conscience and what is required of them as zealous advocates of clients' causes in today's legal environment.

Suggestions and insights on present-day shortcomings and future possibilities may initiate or reintroduce a discourse on the need for change in our legal rules and institutions so that practicing law might be more fulfilling and less tension-producing. Quakers who have had a rich communal experience with law for more than three centuries, especially those who are lawyers, may add ideas to such a dialogue. Perhaps this powerful historical tradition and Quaker lawyers' own talents can contribute to new initiatives and give renewed thrust to extralegal dispute resolution, a matter of some significance to the Quaker lawyers.

The reading experience might be enhanced if some queries are kept in mind: Are there lessons to be learned from early Friends? If so, can these be helpful in today's world, beset as it is with conflict and tension between individuals, cultures, religions, and nations? On a smaller but still important scale, can these lessons speak again to Quakers and Quaker meetings as well as to various larger communities? Can law be successfully practiced so there is less of a dichotomy between one's "personhood" and one's "lawyerhood"? If so, how? Is the legal profession effectively foreclosed to persons who want their personal and professional lives to be in harmony? Can Quaker lawyers contribute to ideas on how law practice can be more fulfilling and less conflict-producing? Can Quakers' early use of mediation and arbitration to resolve disputes be appropriate today? Can it be beneficial within Friends meetings? Within the larger community? Are Quaker lawyers especially capable in practicing the various methods of alternative dispute resolution? Are mediation and arbitration more humane and gentle ways of solving disputes? Do they foster and promote community? Harmony? Equality? Simplicity? Are these peculiarly Quaker values, or are they more widely honored? In pondering these, readers may discover new questions.

I hope some ideas and findings in the book can contribute to a renewed dialogue on legal ethics and legal reform and that, notwithstanding the emphasis on Friends' thoughts about laws and legal systems, the book will interest readers who are neither Quakers nor lawyers. The thoughts, ideas, and opinions advanced may hold relevance for dispute resolution professionals and others generally interested in matters of ethics, law reform, social justice, and peace and cause them to participate by adding their own ideas and proposals to the discourse.

The book is divided into two parts, each containing three chapters. The first part is historical and the second part is future-oriented, but both are linked by Quaker testimonies, which remain common and germane to both.

Part 1, chapter 1, "About Friends," provides an elucidation of Friends' most important beliefs within the context of the original, silent, or "unprogrammed," worship, which George Fox, William Penn, and other early English Friends brought to America. This primer on the testimonies, thought, and practices of Quakers will likely be of little interest to readers already familiar with Friends. But for those who are not, the chapter provides an overview and brief explanation of the "testimonies," concepts, and language, their genesis in scripture, and their place in the thought of George Fox, the Society's founder. A glossary provides definitions of words and phrases distinctive to Quaker parlance as well as definitions of some pertinent legal words or phrases. Thus, while superfluous for Friends and others knowledgeable about the Society, this chapter provides a base for the understanding and deeper meaning of subsequent chapters.

Chapter 2, "Friends' Beginnings in England," explores the prevailing climate and Friends' and others' thoughts on the law, lawyers, and legal system of mid-seventeenth-century England, the time of the Society's founding. It follows the English course of Quakerism up to William Penn's founding of Pennsylvania in the early 1680s. The chapter discusses early Friends' conflict with English laws they considered antithetical to their beliefs and the resultant birth of their peculiar brand of civil disobedience—a willingness to suffer the punishment of laws they considered unjust with direct petitions for change to those in positions of power. Some of Fox's suggestions for legal reform have been echoed by late-twentieth-century U.S. legal commentators and by the Quaker lawyers who responded to the survey reported in chapter 5. For instance, Fox urged that the language of legal documents and the legal system itself be more accessible and less costly to laypeople. He also railed against capital punishment, the bribery of judges, and judges' dictating verdicts to juries. The chapter also discusses the famous trial of Quakers William Penn and William Mead, who were charged with preaching in the streets of London.

Several factors contributed to Fox's largely negative view of the law—the prevailing social climate in England, persecution of Quakers under English law, and their frequent contact with English legal procedure in the course of defending themselves in court. Friends took seriously New Testament admonitions against taking oaths and thus chafed under laws requiring them. Since truth-telling was, and is, the lodestar of the faith, they believed that swearing to tell the truth on certain occasions when they always did so was unnecessary. This chapter explains Friends' past in the context of their interaction with the laws and legal system of mid- to late-seventeenth-century England. The story then traverses the Atlantic Ocean to Quaker William Penn's "holy experiment" in the American province of Pennsylvania.

Chapter 3, "Penn's Holy Experiment in Pennsylvania and His Changes to Its Laws," explores Friends' experience with the laws and legal system in America, especially in the late seventeenth and early to mid-eighteenth century. Penn's large grant of land from England's King Charles II allowed him as Proprietor to create a colony of Quakers who embodied the Society's beliefs and to promulgate new laws that incorporated legal reforms Fox and others in England had long sought. Penn had himself been a victim of England's draconian legal rules and practices during his 1670 trial, and so the legal reform he instituted in Pennsylvania was born both of religious principle and bitter personal experience.

Although this account travels with Penn to America, many Quakers remained in England and collectively charted their own course. Understanding how the interaction of Quakers and the law in England did, or did not, diverge from that in America would no doubt be interesting, but that story will have to await another time.

After the first three chapters of part 1 sketch the history and experience of early Friends in England and America within the context of the original silent or "unprogrammed" meetings, part 2 shifts toward the recent past, present, and future. This part explores U.S. laws, lawyers, and legal system and the traditional resolution of disputes within the conventional legal system, that is cases in court, and the alternative resolution of disputes outside it. It also examines thoughts and ideas of contemporary Quaker lawyers and legal scholars on the current legal system and law practice.

Chapter 4, "Quakers as Plaintiffs and Defendants in Court and as 'Divine Lobbyists,' " examines mostly twentieth-century U.S. court cases that directly implicate Friends' testimonies and are actions that involve both Quaker defendants and, despite historic admonitions against "going to law," Quaker plaintiffs. The former, often prosecuted by the government for acts of civil disobedience, mostly relate to the peace testimony. Quaker plaintiffs brought actions regarding abridgment of constitutional rights including freedom of religion and association. The U.S. Supreme Court decided one such case brought by an interviewee and respondent to the Quaker lawyer survey described in chapter 5. This discussion of Quaker-involved court cases is not intended to be an exhaustive survey throughout U.S. legal history, but rather is a story of the interface of Quakerism and the Anglo-American system of jurisprudence and a combination of factors within each that have caused discord.

In chapter 5, "Quaker Lawyers and Lawyer Ethics," this discord resurfaces in the survey of Quaker lawyers' views, the centerpiece of this work. Stemming from the author's original research, the survey details the responses of 100 Quaker lawyers to a 30-part questionnaire regarding the intersect of their law practice with Quaker faith (and practice). Their responses are the basis for examining if, or to what extent, there are discontinuities between the two practices. The men and women lawyers and a few judges were wonderfully forthright in explaining their thoughts and concerns. Some of the concerns Quaker lawyers voiced are most likely shared by others who are neither Friends nor lawyers, but who might like to join a discourse on legal ethics and thereby strengthen a thrust toward legal reform.

This chapter also reviews some of the literature on legal ethics and the "role" or the persona of the "Lawyer" and some effects of this current legal practice on clients, society, and the lawyers themselves. Like Fox and Penn, these scholars suggest some measure of legal reform. In this chapter the small but hardy band of Quaker lawyers, the core of whom were respondents to the survey, are encouraged to initiate a dialogue with other interested persons or groups, a first step toward a broader discussion of lawyers' ethics and legal reform in the United States.

Chapter 6, "Mediation and Arbitration: Past and Future," the final chapter, contains both past and future in describing early Quaker alternatives to court-based dispute resolution and alternative dispute resolution today. Part 2 concludes by calling for renewed use of these alternatives both within the Society of Friends and beyond. It discusses how early Quakers' use of mediation and arbitration enabled many to adhere to the scriptural admonition against "going to law." The author suggests that these finely tuned dispute resolution procedures constitute an important Quaker legacy that might be resurrected for use in today's Friends meetings. Alternative dispute resolution, increasingly of interest today, is particularly compatible with Friends' peace and community testimonies and may provide an antidote to the discomfort many Quaker lawyers feel.

This last chapter suggests contributions that Quaker and other lawyers might make to the current practice of law in addition to their support of alternative dispute resolution. They might concentrate on framing aims of achieving justice more broadly both through the legal system and outside it. Friends' long history of activism on issues of peace and social justice make them particularly well-suited to impact U.S. legal institutions and the practice of law. Friends might indeed lead a friendly "revolution" to help effect change within the legal system to ensure that its various components—lawyers, judges, rules, and practices—are infused with a greater concern for truthfulness and peacefulness to effect a greater measure of justice in our courts.

Part One

1

About Friends

Be obedient to the Lord God . . . be valiant for the Truth . . . be examples . . . that your . . . life may preach. . . . Then you will come to walk cheerfully over the world, answering that of God in every one. . . . [1656][1]

George Fox and the Founding of the Religious Society of Friends

George Fox (1624–1691), the English founder of the Religious Society of Friends, began to "profess the Truth" in the mid-seventeenth century during a period of political and religious turmoil in England. Fox wanted to recapture the original purity and spirit of early Christianity that he believed had been clouded by later accretions and try to recreate a New Testament way of life in his place and time. Although he did not intend to establish a new religious sect, by midcentury one had formed. Originally, it was called Friends in the Truth; later it became known as the Religious Society of Friends, still its formal name. The sobriquet "Friends" had its origin in scripture: "Henceforth I call you not servants; for the servant knoweth not what his lord doeth; but I have called you friends. . . ."[2] The term "Quaker" is said to have been first used in 1650 by an English judge Gervase Bennet of Derby. When George Fox was charged with a violation of law, he told officials that they should tremble before the word of God; Judge Bennet reportedly replied that it was Fox who was the "quaker."[3] Throughout this book, the Quakers will be variously referred to as Friends, Religious Society of Friends, Society of Friends, or the Society.

"There was a man sent from God, whose name was John . . . sent to bear witness of the Light. That was the true Light, which lighteth every man that cometh into the world."[4] Fox stressed this inner light—that of God in every human being—and held that everyone should seek to "answer" this light in each other. The primacy of truth and truth-telling was central as was Friends' refusal to fight, either in war or in their relations with others. Quakers were originally cautioned not to go to law against Quakers, but later this was expanded to anyone.

Fox established a rather simple organizational structure for the Society, which continues to this day—a system of Monthly, Quarterly, and Yearly Meetings divided by geographical regions. The Monthly Meeting, the smallest unit, is part of a larger Quarterly Meeting, which is contained within a Yearly Meeting, the largest in terms of members and encompassed geographical area. The Monthly Meeting (there may be one or more in a city) gathers every First Day (Sunday) to worship and again once monthly to transact business. Despite its structure, the Society of Friends is more akin to a fellowship than to an institution.

Truthfulness and Integrity

"Justice is truth in action."[5]

The critical importance of truth and truth-telling to Quakers is germane to an inquiry into the nature of any tension between their testimonies[6] and the practice of law, the primary focus of this book. In theory there is no conflict because the purpose and goal of the English legal system, and its later derivative in America, was justice through a search for and discovery of truth. The system's basic premise is that, ideally, truth will emerge from adversaries' spirited advocacy for their respective positions—justice as truth in action. While truth may be the *ideal* and ultimate goal of our Anglo-American jurisprudential system, abuse of any of the myriad steps in the legal process could compromise truth in seventeenth-century legal practice, as it can still in the United States today.

Over the centuries, various philosophers and scholars have wrestled with the concept and meaning of truth. Plato, the great Greek philosopher, wrote in *Phaedrus,* "In the law courts nobody cares . . . for the truth about what is just or good, but only about what is plausible."[7] Some of his dialogues attack the Sophists, ancient Greek teachers known for their clever and sometimes fallacious and deceitful arguments. The "role of the advocate became more absorbing than that of the adherent, conquest more important than truth."[8]

Lucius Annaeus Seneca, the Roman stoic philosopher who lived during the time of Christ had views on truth that sound startlingly similar to those of Friends. For instance, he believed that speech devoted to truth should be plain and straightforward, that truth is everlasting and never perishes, and the language of truth is simple. Like Fox's "so say and so do" seventeen centuries later, Seneca drew a correlation between one's language and one's life. Another interesting parallel between the latter's thinking and Friends' was the dwelling of the spirit within each person.[9]

Hugo Grotius, the early–seventeenth-century Dutch lawyer, magistrate, and ambassador is considered the founder of international law. Contrary to Seneca's belief that speech should be devoted to truth, he believed that falsehoods are sometimes justifiable and so, from a moralist's viewpoint, should not be considered lies.

The name some gave the earliest Quakers—Friends in Truth—is significant because integrity and truthfulness were then hallmarks of Quaker belief and life and remain today a pivotal tenet of the faith and a steadfast goal of its practice. "He that walketh uprightly, and worketh righteousness, and speaketh the truth in his heart" shall dwell in the Lord's holy hill.[10] In fact, earlier Friends' passion for all truth-telling even caused some to shun theater and literature because actors necessarily expressed feelings that they did not truly feel, and novelists wrote about events that did not actually occur.[11] Some Quakers leaned over backward to tell only exact and verifiable truth and, in doing so, resorted to careful understatement. There is a story, probably apocryphal, of two Quakers walking together along a country lane. One remarks to his companion that the sheep in the adjacent field have recently been shorn. His friend replies that yes, they had indeed been shorn, *at least* on their sides that faced the lane,[12] that is, the sides of the sheep they could clearly observe from their vantage point!

To Friends, a critical component of truthfulness is consistency. Even as a boy, Fox was disturbed by the divergence of precepts and behavior he noticed among members of his English church. Perhaps for that reason, his writings were replete with the advice, "So say and so do."[13] And, perhaps due to Fox's strong early influence, Friends have consistently attempted to conform belief to conduct, that is, what one is in words, he or she should also be in life. This Quaker effort at a convergence of belief and action is particularly germane to discussions of some common legal practices that conflict with Friends' beliefs.

The exhortations of Fox and other Quakers over past centuries have produced in Friends a substantial awareness of this unity of thought and action—the essence of integrity. Integrity derives from the Latin *integritas,* "wholeness," which derives from *integer* or "whole." A person who has integrity is of one piece, entire, and relatively unbroken by inconsistencies and contradictions. The truth spoken should be consistent with acts performed. Truth and "testimonies" are to be lived.

For example, this single standard resulted in Friends' refusal to swear to tell the truth in a court of law or to swear oaths of allegiance to the sovereign. The standard for truthfulness was the same; whether testifying in court or conversing with a friend, a Quaker was bound at all times to tell the truth. Therefore, a simple affirmation should suffice to show that statements in court were only part of the usual integrity of their speech. Fox wrote in a 1656 epistle, "And ye all walking in this Light, it will bring you to all plainness and singleness of speech which will make the Deceit to tremble."[14] The great Greek playwright Sophocles wrote similarly about oaths; Theseus speaks to Oedipus, "I will not bind thee . . . with oaths." Oedipus replies, "Oaths were no stronger than my simple word."[15]

Over the centuries Friends, like other imperfect beings, have tried to attain integrity or wholeness with varying degrees of success. The influential Friend John Woolman wrote of the less successful: ". . . Where men profess to be so meek and heavenly minded, and to have their trust so firmly settled in God that they cannot join in wars and yet by their spirit and conduct in common life manifest a contrary disposition, their difficulties are great. . . ."[16] Nevertheless, most Friends *persistently aim* to achieve this wholeness of belief and action, a powerfully significant and distinguishing attribute of Quaker faith.

The issue of integrity becomes important in regard to the professions Friends choose. To be consistent, the practice of a chosen career should be consonant with how they are led by faith. Relatively early in its history, the Society of Friends recognized the possibility of conflict between its beliefs and members' professions. A 1795 extract from London Yearly Meeting's Minutes and Epistles states, "Circumscribed even as we are more than many, it is not unusual, in our pursuit of the things of this life, for our gain and our convenience to clash with our testimony." Thus Quakers' attempt to live united in belief and action also extends to their life occupations.

An 1851 Advice similarly cautioned:

> In conducting your outward affairs, whether in agriculture or trade or as professional men . . . scrupulously avoid doing anything that may compromise our Christian testimonies, or lessen their excellence in the sight of others. Maintain strict integrity and plain dealing, marked by Christian courtesy and respect to all. . . . In transacting his business, and in providing things honest in the sight of men, the true Christian may, in his daily work, exalt his profession and commend his principles to others.[17]

For early Friends, the office of magistrate was incompatible with Quaker testimonies because it required the administration of oaths and organizing of the militia in times of civil unrest. A central question explored in this book is whether practicing law in the United States around the turn of the twenty-first century is likewise incompatible with Quaker testimonies. Can one maintain "strict integrity" and "scrupulously avoid doing anything that may compromise our Christian testimonies" and practice law today?

The Quaker Testimonies

The primary Quaker testimonies are harmony or peace, community, simplicity, and equality with truth-telling infusing all. Quakers' use of "testimonies" to indicate their beliefs is significant. The word "testimony" is derived from Latin *testis*—witness, which means giving evidence, being present, or seeing personally. "Testimony," then, connotes active participation; in the language of Quakers, "letting one's life speak." It transcends "belief," which implies a certain acceptance, trust, and passiveness.

The four primary testimonies comprise the essence of Quaker "theology" and are usually mutually reinforcing with one exception, which will be discussed later. For instance, simplicity is related to individual peace because a pursuit of material wealth can entail competition with and exploitation of others, and material goods can contain and nourish the seeds of war. A Quaker has explained the testimonies as the "ways we understand God has called us to *live* our social, political, and economic lives as aspects of our spiritual lives."[18] James, the New Testament epistle encapsulates each testimony: "And the fruit of righteousness is sown in peace of them that make peace."[19] (harmony, peace); " . . the wisdom that is from above is . . . without hypocrisy"[20] (simplicity); . . . the wisdom that is from above is . . . without partiality . . ."[21] (equality); and "Thou shalt love thy neighbor as thyself"[22] (community).

These testimonies together with the belief that there is that of God, the Light or Inward Spirit in every person form the wellspring of Quaker activism. "But be ye doers of the word, and not hearers only, . . ."[23] "What doth it profit, my brethren, though a man say he hath faith, and have not works? . . ."[24] "For as the body without the spirit is dead, so faith without works is dead also.[25] Matthew also lauds the activist spirit: "Let your light so shine before men, that they may see your good works, and glorify your Father which is in heaven."[26]

The Golden Rule, "Therefore all things whatsoever ye would that men should do to you, do ye even so to them . . ."[27] figured prominently in early Quaker thought and practice. If followed, this rule obviates the need for other rules because it not only calls for empathy to consider the effect of one's actions on others, but it also expands one's perspective to include a concern for the greater good.

Friends' concern for service gave rise to the American Friends' Service Committee (AFSC), founded in 1917. The AFSC's original purpose was to provide Quakers and other conscientious objectors an opportunity to perform alternative service in wartime. Its goals subsequently broadened to include the protection and promotion of civil rights and liberties. Its work reflects and embodies Friends' testimonies: equality, by the impartiality of its aid and relief efforts to persons and groups of all political, social, and economic persuasions; simplicity, by the standard of living necessarily required of its workers; community, by its efforts to unite the world's people into an interdependent community; and harmony, through its main objective, the promotion of peace.[28]

Testimony of Harmony/Peace

"Blessed are the peacemakers; for they shall be called the children of God."[29]

Early Friends arrived at their position of pacifism as they did their other testimonies—by following the Light and writings from scripture. One of Fox's deservedly famous statements, "I lived in the virtue of that life and power that takes away the occasion of all wars,"[30] is valuable because it suggests, albeit vaguely, a way of living that would prevent wars in the first instance.

On January 21, 1661, Friends set forth their pacifist stand to England's King Charles II in *A Declaration from the Harmless and Innocent People of God, called Quakers, against All Plotters and Fighters in the World*:

> [W]e . . . do utterly . . . deny all outward wars and strife and fightings with outward weapons, for any end or under any pretence whatsoever. And this is our testimony to the whole world . . . [T]he spirit of Christ, which leads us into all Truth, will never move us to fight and war against any man with outward weapons, neither for the kingdom of Christ, nor for the Kingdoms of this world. . . .[31]

Friends have enduringly held fast to opposition to war because they believe it contrary to the spirit and will of God. Moreover, a focus on the Inner Light in every person empowers them to resolve disputes—even those between nations—without resort to the machinery of war.[32] In fact, many Quakers look and work toward a time when arms and other military machinery will no longer be part of any government.

A Maryland Monthly Meeting once discussed Friends' peace witness in terms of both its individual and communal aspects. The individual peacemaker is called on to deal with violence and aggression within himself or herself and to find ways of living in harmony with one another. The community too can engage in positive peacemaking by promoting peaceful methods of conflict resolution, international exchanges, and peace education and research, as well as bearing witness to peace through public demonstrations. Its members can also support conscientious objectors and those who refuse to pay taxes when such revenues are used to pay for war. The Quaker peace testimony then is broader than the refusal to participate in war because it includes answering that of God in others and attempting to remove wars' *causes*.

Friends' peace testimony encompasses a negative refusal to participate in war as well as a positive affirmation of the power of peace and good to overcome evil. Countless Friends have undertaken preemptive affirmative acts to remove the seeds of war, and, when war occurs, to repair its damage. In the twentieth century, the AFSC has led this effort and, with Quaker Peace and Service, shared the 1947 Nobel Peace Prize. In his speech awarding the prize, the chairman of the Nobel Committee quoted a young Quaker worker who said that he and others tried to rebuild "in a spirit of love what had been destroyed in a spirit of hatred." The chairman added that religion means little until it is translated into positive action.[33]

Harmony in Relation to Other Friends' Testimonies

A discussion of harmony in the context of other Quaker testimonies is bound to raise some important queries as activism in the latter may present hard choices. Should the testimony of harmony ever be suspended so that those of community or equality or truthfulness can be more fully realized? If so, under what circumstances? Or should there be harmony at any cost? And if so, how is the cost measured? Dissecting the principle of harmony might seem intellectual hairsplitting, but for Quakers who have attempted from the time of George Fox's "so say and so do" to live their beliefs, the meaning of harmony in the nitty-gritty of daily living deserves scrutiny.

Harmony can be at odds with speaking the truth and acting against injustice. Justice, tolerance, and other good qualities exemplified in the life of Christ are models against which many Friends measure their lives. What are Friends to do then when a powerful intransigent injustice appears? Do they passively preserve harmony or actively and inharmoniously protest against it?

The premise underlying a view that harmony should always be maintained is that lack of it is worse than injustice or oppression. But one can challenge that. An insistent pursuit of neutrality in a conflict can be a way of siding with the oppressor. Hitler's viciously inhumane treatment of Jews is an example. Must those who live in the light seek harmony by silence in the face of such evil and at the expense of equality that would have allowed the Jewish oppressed to keep dignity and indeed their very lives?

In spite of what moral relativists might think, the way is often quite clear: justice is as clearly discernible from injustice as are the oppressed from the oppressor. It is not invariably true that all conflicts are based on misunderstandings, and blame is always to be found on both sides. Nor is it invariably true that Quakers will always choose harmony. Suspension of harmony may, in fact, be necessary to speak against tough problems of systemic injustice. As we will see in chapter 4, several Quakers sued in court to rectify wrongs despite the traditional injunction against going to law. The vindication of rights in cases decided by the U.S. Supreme Court set precedents that subsequently aided others in similar situations.

Simplicity

For Friends, simplicity includes avoiding self-indulgence, keeping material goods proportionate to needs, and speaking and acting without hypocrisy, the latter also related to truthfulness. The Philadelphia Yearly Meeting's 1955 *Faith and Practice* stated:

> Friends are watchful to keep themselves free from self-indulgent habits, luxurious ways of living and the bondage of fashion. . . . Undue luxury often creates a false sense of superiority, causes unnecessary burdens upon both ourselves and others and leads to the neglect of the spiritual life. By observing and encouraging simple tastes in apparel, furniture, buildings and manner of living, we help do away with rivalry and we learn to value self-denial.[34]

Of the Quaker testimonies, simplicity is the least salient among modern Friends and is a relatively rare example of a difference in the teaching and practice of early vis-à-vis contemporary Friends. In earlier times, Friends' practice of simplicity was more patent with a distinctive lack of adornment in dress. Quakers' clothing was plain—black hats and jackets such as those depicted on a Quaker Oats box, plain breeches for men, and simple black dresses and white caps for women. Although some Friends may strive for simple living today by resisting the frenzied accumulation of material goods, relatively few are able to attain truly simple living. Religious practice is not immune from society's influence, and in today's America, simplicity can be an elusive goal.

And because Friends place great importance on sincerity and genuineness, speech in earlier times was likewise simple, unadorned, and without obsequiousness. Truth-telling and simplicity overlap when elaborate language designed to flatter is avoided in favor of more truthful plain speaking. A cogent example of Fox's literalness and desire to avoid flattery was his conversation with Major Ceely who interviewed Fox in Launceston jail in 1656. Doffing his hat, Ceely greeted Fox, "your servant, Sir." Fox replied, "Major Ceely, take heed of hypocrisy and a rotten heart, for when came I to be thy master and thee my servant?" and then asked if it was usual for servants to put their masters in prison.[35]

Moreover, simplicity is evident in the interiors and exteriors of Quaker meetinghouses, and even those that have been renovated remain plain and without ornamentation. There are no altars, stained glass, elaborate pulpits, or soaring arches usually found in other houses of worship. For unprogrammed Friends, the name of their place of worship is "meetinghouse" rather than "church." The plain benches in the meeting rooms are often oriented toward the center.

The worship that takes place in such meetinghouses is itself simple, especially in "unprogrammed" meetings where the worship is silent and contains no set program, sermon, or music.[36] And because these Friends believe that a sincere and inwardly attentive worshipper can commune with and try to ascertain the will of God without an intermediary, there is no officiating minister or priest, "no outward expression except the prophetic voice which had been heard in the New Testament Church at the beginning."[37] Neither do these Friends uphold the sacraments of ordination, baptism, or communion. For them, the inward experience renders such outward rites unnecessary and even distracting. In the silent "waiting," all formal ritual is subtracted, making possible a direct undiluted reception of the Spirit. This permits "a fresh and direct facing of facts under conditions in which the conscience becomes sensitized."[38]

Equality

"Let the brother of low degree rejoice in that he is exalted;
But the rich, in that he is made low: because as the flower of the grass
he shall pass away."[39]

Friends' testimony of equality embraces respect for all persons and a corresponding absence of racial, class, or hierarchical distinctions in speech or conduct. Friends' refusal to pay "hat honor," doffing one's hat as a sign of social deference, meant that Early Friends would not remove their hats before a king or other high-ranking official but would do so only when addressing God in prayer. Like many Quaker practices, the origin of this refusal was scriptural: "Uncover not your heads, neither rend your clothes; lest ye die, and lest wrath come upon all the people. . . ."[40] "David went up by the ascent of mount Olivet, . . . and had his head covered . . . and all the people that was [sic] with him covered every man his head. . . ."[41] This same standard of respect for all, regardless of their station in life, caused Friends to use full names, but no titles.

They also exhibited equality in speech by using second-person singular pronouns in addressing others. Although it was customary to speak to "inferiors" familiarly as "thou" and to "superiors" more respectfully as "you," Friends would speak to everyone in the singular, manifesting a single standard of respect for all persons[42] equal before God. Even Quaker children would address their parents as "thou."[43]

In matters of race the testimony of equality was manifest by Quakers' belief that God is in all persons. Francis Daniel Pastorius protested slavery of Negroes as early as the 1680s. In his address to Germantown Monthly Meeting in 1688, Pastorius noted:

there is a saying that we shall doe [*sic*] to all men like as we will be
done ourselves; making no difference of what generation, descent,
colour they are . . . to bring men hither, or . . . sell them against
their will, we stand against. . . . Pray, what thing in the world can
be done worse towards us, than if men should . . . steal us away,
and sell us for slaves to strange countries; separating husbands from
their wives and children.[44]

As other Friends gradually evolved to realize that slavery of a person was
wrong, they began to work toward its abolition. Quakers defied the 1793 Fugitive
Slave Law[45] by helping slaves escape, harboring or concealing them, or helping
prevent their recapture and return; doing this subjected them to a $500 penalty.
A popular avenue of escape was by the Underground Railroad, which was neither
underground nor a railroad; Levi Coffin, a Friend, was called its "president."
In 1850 Congress amended the 1793 statute to authorize the appointment of
new commissioners to aid slaveholders in reclaiming their "property."

In the course of 80 years, Friends Advices became progressively less tolerant
toward slaveholding. In 1696, they advised against the importation of Negroes;
in 1730, against buying imported Negroes; in 1754, against buying any slaves. In
1758, Friends visited with all Quaker slaveholders to persuade them to set their
slaves free, and in 1762 the Advices suggested Friends should "labor with" those
who still held slaves. By 1776, meetings could disown Quaker slaveholders.[46]
Quakers formed a Free Produce Association, which boycotted products made by
slave labor.[47] Just as their testimony against war has sometimes caused Friends
to become adversaries of the state, so too did their witness of equality. For
instance, they objected when blacks, Native Americans, or Japanese Americans
in the 1940s were treated unequally and as if they were innately inferior. Again,
some Friends chose the path of civil disobedience in their resolve to obey God's
law over man's when the two were opposed.

Equality is also evident within the internal structure of the Quaker
meeting. The administration of the meeting *and* its worship was, and remains,
in unprogrammed meetings a corporate responsibility. No individual has special
religious duties or is literally or figuratively elevated above others. Mostly in
earlier times, elders or overseers and wise and "weighty" Friends, did exercise
an advisory function "not *over* the meeting, but *under* it, as the instruments
of its will."[48] Members also share and participate equally in the "meeting for
worship with a concern for business," held once every month.

Community

Community is reflected in Quakers' concern for others—in widening circles
from the smallest group—the Monthly Meeting, outward to the larger Friends'

communities, Quarterly and Yearly Meetings—and still further to non-Quaker communities from the smallest to the largest, the world. The testimony of community embodies care for others' welfare because Friends believe that all persons are children of God who share alike in his Light. Working toward the alleviation of human suffering and injustice is in political, social, and economic terms the equivalent of the command to love God and one's neighbor as oneself.[49] The Golden Rule,[50] too, emphasizes empathy and responsibility toward others.

The use of mediation and arbitration as early Friends' preferred means of solving disputes figured importantly in the nurture and preservation of community. "The success of non-legal dispute settlement has always depended upon a coherent community vision. How to resolve conflict, inversely stated, is how (or whether) to preserve community. Only when there is congruence between individuals and their community with shared commitment to common values, is there a possibility for justice without law."[51] Friends not only regard community as worthy of preservation but as central to their faith.

Light

"Ye are all the children of light. . . ."[52]

Children of Light was another name given to early Friends. Fox believed that Friends must learn how to understand scripture in "that Light and Spirit which was before Scripture was given forth, and which led the holy men of God to give them forth. . . ."[53] For Friends, Light is powerful as both symbol and reality and, like many spiritual ideas, it defies precise definition. English Quaker lawyer William Braithwaite wrote about such human-divine words in the early 1900s. He, for instance, could give no full definition of the word "spiritual," "which ranks high among the elusive words of the language." He hoped that it would always escape capture and definition because he thought we should have some words that belong both to earth and heaven.[54]

Light is beyond conscience because it shines through conscience to instruct, sensitize, and transform it. "If we are faithful to our measure of Light, we shall be guided up toward God, and up to a greater measure of the Truth"[55] in a process of enlightenment and evolvement. Light can also refer to Christ and can connote truth and love. Because Friends' faith is not a series of static tenets but an evolving process, Light may have various gradations of meaning for Quakers. Many Friends have written about the Light. Isaac Penington in *Naked Truth* (1674) wrote, "The same light which discovereth the darkness, also chaseth away the darkness, . . . and purifieth the mind; for the light hath not only a property of enlightening, but also of cleansing and sanctifying."[56]

Another view of Light is found in a legal brief written for Friend Rosa Packard who sought to avoid paying her portion of federal taxes used for war: "Quakers believe each individual can know God directly by experience because . . . [according to] John . . . 1:6–9, the Light is placed in us as a birthright, a capacity and potentiality. But direct experience alone is not enough; it must be tested for its truth-bearing value and, if found trustworthy, lived by. . . . [T]he 'Inner Light' has long been a dominant Quaker image to describe how God works in us."[57] Another view of the light is the truth, God's own goad and probe, as described by Margaret Fell: "let the Eternal Light search you . . . for this will deal plainly with you"[58]

Friends' believe that persons evolve in moral consciousness. If Friends are true to their "measure of light," they will be guided up toward God and to a still greater measure of truth. For instance, we have seen that Quakers have always rejected war as against God's will. However, if a person's conscience urges him to fight, he must be faithful to the measure of light he has. If he continues his faithfulness and "waits upon the Lord and sensitizes himself to the reception of more Light, a greater measure will be given him. He will then see the wrong in fighting. In his first state, he would be a coward if he did not fight; in the second, he would be a coward if he did. . . ."[59] Both courage and patience play a part in this Quaker process of spiritual evolvement.

This quintessential Quaker spiritual principle—the Light of God within every person—is closely related to the testimonies. The Light is a source of unity and community for Quakers because it is shared by all persons, a bond that brings them together with God and each other.[60] For Friends, the best way to interact with others is to "answer" that of God, or the Light, in them. Put in graphic terms, "[t]he vertical relation to God and the horizontal relation to man are like two co-ordinates used to plot a curve; without both the position of the curve could not be determined."[61]

Friends' social concern stems from this belief in the interconnectedness of all persons sharing the light. Connectedness engenders compassion, which strengthens Friends to help others afflicted by poverty, conflict, and injustice. New York Yearly Meeting's 1995 *Faith and Practice* describes the Quaker process of individually and communally testing a "concern" or social action "in the light," another part of Friends' "gospel order":

> Individual concerns can become the means by which the community can bring the power of the Spirit into social action; the method Friends have developed to do this involves the progression and deepening of concerns from monthly to Quarterly to Yearly Meetings. This process is another part of our gospel order, by which we wait with a concern and test it individually, then with a friend or family member, then with a group of Friends and the monthly meeting itself, and finally with quarterly and yearly meetings. Friends are thus available at each step to 'test the concern in the Light,' to consider

the concern in relation to all they know about the situation and the persons involved and, most important, to hold the concern up to the light of the Inward Teacher, although we do not need to share, agree with, or endorse each other's concerns in order to support them.[62]

In a broader way, the Light can be viewed as a kind of sieve through which concerns, ideas, thoughts, and prayers are sifted, cleansed, and clarified. In such a sifting process, what remains salient is probably the truer, better, and clearer course. The Light is often spoken of in connection with leadings: "The Inner Light does not lead men to do that which is right in their own eyes, but that which is right in God's eyes."[63] Friends "hold in the Light" persons immersed in sickness, grief, or difficulty so that God may support and uplift them.

Friends further believe that the Light within every person generates an unquestioned capacity for goodness and that its power can redeem and transform those who falter. "[I]f we feel that even in the most evil of men there is that of God, we can appeal to it, and we may . . . reach it and set in motion a process of transformation from within."[64] This belief in a person's potential for rehabilitative transformation will resurface in a discussion of a reason for Penn's reduction of capital crimes in the early laws of Pennsylvania.

Friends' Relationship with God and Others

Unlike most religious groups, the Society of Friends does not have a theology in the sense of a body of doctrine or dogma for its members' adherence. It is a noncreedal religion with no formal doctrinal statements issued from a religious hierarchy. Indeed, unlike virtually all other Western religions, Friends' "concept of authority and doctrine flows upward from the individual to the group, rather than down from an ecclesiastical authority . . . to the laity."[65] A Quaker has suggested that "our theology is our testimonies and how we live them; our theology is in our hands."[66] For Quakers, the Spirit of God is the ultimate authority in governing the individual.

Addressed "to the Children of Light," a 1656 statement on Quakers' lack of dogma accompanied the 20 Balby Yorkshire [England] Advices, these stated, "Dearly beloved Friends, these things we do not lay upon you as a rule to walk by, but that all with the measure of light which is pure and holy may be guided, and so in the light walking and abiding these may be fulfilled in the Spirit—not from the letter for the letter killeth, but [from the Spirit which] giveth Light."[67] Friends believed that to have unity in their search, they had to forego any desire to impose unity on each other. For instance, Friends have no single view vis-à-vis the Bible or the state.

More than 250 years after the Balby Advices, *The True Basis of Christian Unity* was presented to London Yearly Meeting in 1917. It noted that formulated statements of belief tend to crystallize thought on issues that are beyond embodiment in human language, hamper the search for truth, and erect barriers that may exclude seekers who would otherwise gladly come in.[68] New York Yearly Meeting's 1995 *Faith and Practice*[70] explained that instead of imposing rules of conduct, the Society lays upon its members the responsibility to live by the Spirit of Light and Truth. The 1972 Philadelphia Yearly Meeting *Faith and Practice* explained that Quakerism is rooted in an increasing experience and appreciation of God and his creation, inwardly felt.

Instead of formulated statements, Friends refer to *Faith and Practice*,[69] an evolving guide to individuals and meetings on various aspects of faith, subject to revision as the spirit of truth and new experience shed further insight through a continuing process of discernment and revelation. Each Yearly Meeting's *Faith and Practice* also includes thoughts and spiritual insights of Friends over the centuries and can vary slightly from one meeting to another.

Common principles are defined and expanded in simple declarative "Advices," the first, the Balby series written in 1656. The Advices are well-suited to Quakers' practice of divining their own "leadings" from God or the Light. In addition to "Advices," Friends use "Queries," sets of questions, to challenge and guide them in self-examining the extent to which their lives are expressions of what they profess. Examples are: Do you show a forgiving spirit and a concern for the reputation of others? Where differences arise, do you try to speedily end them? Are you just in payment of debts and honorable and truthful in all your dealings? Do you encourage efforts to overcome racial prejudice and antagonism?[71] Both advices and queries grow out of Friends' collective experience in attempting to live in the Light.

The Society of Friends shares some beliefs with the descendants of the Anabaptists[72]—pacifism, no infant baptism, no swearing of oaths, and little if any interest in formal theology. Descendants such as the Mennonites are active in social service and have joined Friends in efforts to support conscientious objection to war and other forms of peacemaking. Although the Church of the Brethren is also active in social service, other pacifist groups or subgroups have tended to withdraw from the world rather than live in its midst. In this respect, the latter differ from Friends who lobby Congress through Friends Committee on National Legislation (FCNL), bring and defend court actions, file amici curiae briefs, and are active in peace and social justice issues through the AFSC and Yearly Meetings. Friends believe that one's life cannot be compartmentalized into various areas. This holistic approach with its infusion of faith into all aspects of life has remained a distinguishing characteristic of the Society since its beginnings.

A distinctive Quaker process is one by which members seek and discover guidance by listening for a "leading" from God, the Light. "Each [Friend] is responsible for discerning how she or he is called to act, but each person is also part of a fellowship of faith, responsible to and supportive of one another."[73] The initial responsibility is the member's own, then his or her individual discernment followed by communal support for the "leading." "A significant Quaker contribution is the ethic by which individual discernment is blended into the group. It is a staged process, rather than a theory, that leads to "openings" or revelations both for the individual and the community and might be said to begin with quieting impulses, addressing concerns, gathering consensus, finding clearness, and, finally, bearing witness.[74]

Friends and the State

". . . We ought to obey God rather than men."[75]

Obedience to the state is secondary to Friends' primary allegiance to God. A 1915 London Yearly Meeting statement explained Friends' stance on conflicting claims between God's law and that of the state: "Christ demands of us that we adhere, without swerving, to the methods of love, and therefore, if a seeming conflict should arise between the claims of His service and those of the State, it is to Christ that our supreme loyalty must be given, whatever the consequences." A half-century later, the 1972 Philadelphia Yearly Meeting *Faith and Practice* reconfirmed this in the context of the peace testimony:

> Since our first allegiance is to the god of love, we must obey the law of God rather than the law of man when this allegiance is challenged by the demands of the state. We support both the young men who oppose war by performing work as conscientious objectors and those who resist any cooperation with the military. . . . Since our peace testimony is not only opposition to active participation in war but a positive affirmation of the power of good to overcome evil, we must all seriously consider the implications of our employment, our investments, our payment of taxes, and our manner of living as they relate to violence.[76]

The often-quoted exchange between George Fox and William Penn illustrates how the Light works through the individual's conscience and how the testimonies are "lived." After Penn became a Quaker in 1667, he still wore regalia, including sword, of a gentleman who frequented the English court. One day he asked Fox whether he, now a Quaker, should continue to wear his sword. Fox simply advised, "Wear it as long as thou canst."[77] Fox meant that at some point, the inner Light would sensitize Penn's conscience so that he could no longer wear the sword. Not long after this conversation with Fox, Penn was without his sword; he had worn it as long as he could.

This strong and individualistic conscience has animated Friends' actions throughout their history and continues to do so. Howard Brinton explains this by reference to Paul's letter to the Galatians. Paul noted that Christianity was neither the old Mosaic law nor the new law but freedom from law, a liberty of conscience, not the command of external law but one's own "internal guidance" based on the love of God.[78]

Friends respect the state as an instrument for the maintenance of an orderly society and give it loyalty and cooperation, but when it acts coercively, for example, to force citizens to participate in violence, which is contrary to divine law, Friends seek to protect liberty of conscience by engaging in civil disobedience or actively encouraging a change in laws that violate God's law against killing, or both. Quakers are, and have often been, civil disobedient activists who speak truth to power in order to better align laws toward God's law and the greater good. In 1678 William Penn wrote to the "Children of Light" that true godliness does not turn men from the world but excites their endeavors to mend it.[79] And, in fact, Friends see their refusal to accede to the state's unjust demands as a measure of loyalty to the government and may reach others' consciences so they might together improve society. In their view their civil disobedience is not an oxymoron.

This civil disobedience derives from a deep and rich tradition within the Society. For centuries, Friends have presented demands for justice to those in positions of authority with the power and ability to effect change, reasoning that if we are to achieve peace and justice, the habit of implicit obedience to authority must be broken, especially when the authority becomes evil.[80] Quakers also spoke or wrote to heads of state, legislatures, and courts to make them aware of specific injustices and attempt to persuade them to take remedial action. During George Fox's imprisonment in Worcester in 1674, his wife Margaret Fell traveled to London to speak with King Charles II and ask for Fox's release by "laying before him [his] long and unjust imprisonment, with the manner of [his] being taken, and the justices' proceedings against [him], . . ."[81] Friends' numerous petitions and tracts indicate little diffidence; it was similarly so when, as defendants, they spoke directly to jurors during trial. Friends believed that confronting persecutors or jurors would prick their consciences and cause them to discover the Light within themselves. Speaking against injustice, rather than silently suffering it, had a twofold advantage: it helped their own immediate situation and could help others by resulting in positive change in the future. For example, Elizabeth Fry expressed her concern about English prison conditions directly to Queen Victoria and AFSC representatives later urged the Nazi Gestapo to implement emergency feeding programs and faster emigration of Jews. Although the concept and practice of speaking concerns directly and truthfully to those in power dates to Friends' beginnings, the phrase itself—"speaking truth to power"—is a twentieth-century Quaker construct subsequently adopted by others.

As we will see in chapter 4, Friends continue this tradition by bringing civil rights actions in the courts and by lobbying Congress through the FCNL.

Friends' Gospel Order

Friends' testimonies of harmony and community are particularly pertinent to gospel order, one aspect of which was the Society's early and extensive use of such as mediation and arbitration to resolve disputes in a gentler and more private way. "[I]n corners of our [American] historical experience are intriguing experiments that testify to a persistent counter-tradition to legalism."[82] One "corner" included the Quakers' use of extralegal alternatives and William Penn's provision of an arbitration statute in the early laws of Pennsylvania province. He may have been influenced by Friends meetings' internal system of dispute resolution, initially created to resolve intra-Quaker disputes outside the public eye and to heed the scriptural caution against "going to law."

Friends generally preferred this extralegal means of settling differences and restoring peace and harmony. This early brand of communitarian justice is traceable to Matthew:

[I]f thy brother shall trespass against thee, go and tell him his fault between thee and him alone: if he shall hear thee, thou hast gained thy brother. But if he will not hear thee, then take with thee one or two more, that in the mouth of two or three witnesses every word may be established. And if he shall neglect to hear them, tell it unto the church. . . .[83]

This sequence of steps became a part of Friends' gospel order—in England and America. Gospel order was recommended in a 1681 minute[84] adopted by Philadelphia Yearly Meeting: "It's Agreed if any Differences Arise between any Persons professing the Truth that they do not go to Law One with Another, before Endeavours have been made and Used for the Ending thereof, by the Particular Monthly Meetings they belong to." The phrase "between any Persons professing the Truth" referred to Quakers. Although initially gospel order was used only among Friends, it was later expanded to include all persons with whom Friends had differences.

Suing a Friend without necessity and without the meeting's consent was strongly discouraged and could, in certain meetings and times, lead to disownment by the Society. Even now, some Friends discourage suits, although despite this,

Quakers did (and sometimes do) take disputes to court. This was especially true if mediation or arbitration had been tried. Some sued on ordinary matters such as trespass or debt, but later they also brought actions to maintain the integrity of the testimonies and rights to freedom of religion and conscience. A Quaker's liberty of conscience became an issue in *Elfbrandt v. Russell* when the plaintiff refused to take an oath of loyalty required of Arizona schoolteachers. Racial equality was litigated when some Pennsylvanians were denied club membership *because* they were black.[85]

Traditions and Practices Unique to Friends

Meeting for Worship

Early Friends gathered regularly to worship in silence as unprogrammed Friends do today. In this kind of worship, each person focuses inwardly toward direct communion with the divine Spirit. As worshippers expectantly wait in God's presence, the sense of fellowship with God and each other becomes strengthened. Whereas the worship does not rely in unprogrammed meetings on preplanned words, neither is it silence qua silence. Robert Barclay, a learned seventeenth-century Friend, likened the gathering in communal silence to the augmentation of light by many glowing candles. Barclay wrote: "when I came into the silent assemblies . . . I felt a secret power among them, which touched my heart."[86] He described silent worship as consisting "not in words, so neither in silence, as silence; but in a holy dependence of the mind upon God, from which dependent silence necessarily follows in the first place, until words can be brought forth which are from God's Spirit."[87]

All who attend meetings actively participate and share equally in the responsibility to listen, to be receptive to continued silent waiting, and to be open to a leading to stand and speak. Usually when persons speak in meeting, they try to be brief and plain and keep "close to the root." Out of a worshipper's words or out of the silence, a "concern" may develop, a sense of a direct intimation of God's will to do something or to demonstrate sympathetic or empathetic interest in some individual or group.[88]

Some may wonder about the value of gathering as a group and waiting in silence, but many who have experienced this have found that group devotion heightens insight and increases awareness of the Inward Light. In Quaker parlance, a "gathered meeting" is "awake, and looking upwards. . . . In the united stillness . . . there is a power known only by experience, and mysterious even when most familiar."[89] At the close of worship or "rise of meeting," Friends greet each other and shake hands.

Meeting for Worship with a Concern for Business

Friends' business meetings are meetings for worship with a focus on matters such as finance, social action, meetinghouse upkeep, and care of members. Those who attend do not vote but reach a unified consensus by communal discernment and deliberation. After consensus is reached, the clerk rephrases the "sense of the meeting," and then it is approved and recorded. The clerk tries to be sensitive to the search for truth and unity, but if there is a thorny issue on which opinions diverge, he or she may ask for silence during which members can discern, through divine "leading," that which corresponds with God's will. Alternatively, a difficult matter may be "laid aside" to be reconsidered later when a sense of unity may be more likely to emerge.

Examples of queries related to meeting for business are: Are these meetings for held in a spirit of worship, understanding, and forbearance? Is the meeting aware that it speaks not only through its actions, but also through its failure to act?

Marriage

The Quaker marriage ceremony has remained essentially unchanged through the centuries, and as in earlier times, the meeting gives its approval to the marriage in advance of the wedding day. Held as a silent meeting for worship, a marriage "after the manner of Friends" has no official to administer vows. The bride and groom enter the meeting room together and sit where all can see them. After their entrance, any person may stand to share a memory or prayer. Then in the presence of God and the community, the bride and groom promise to each other to be loving, caring, and faithful. An appointed Friend reads the marriage certificate aloud to the gathering, and the couple signs it; after the rise of meeting, each guest also signs. A Meeting Committee is responsible for legal recordation of the marriage.

The Clearness Committee

A process unique to Friends is the clearness committee, which helps members achieve a measure of "clearness" on an important decision, change, or challenge in their lives, another example of Quakers' individual and communal discernment. The Friend who seeks clearness on a matter convenes a meeting of several chosen members to help discern whether a leading toward a resolution or new direction is consonant with the Spirit and to help the Friend clarify what, if any, action to take. The meeting also uses such a committee when a member seeks to marry under the care of the meeting or a person seeks membership in the

Society. In the latter case, members can explore with applicants their spiritual journeys, familiarity and agreement with Friends' principles and practice, and commitment to assume responsibilities of membership.

Careful listening and honest feedback are important to this process. Clarity can, and often does, emerge through a sequence of searching, listening, and responding. A Friend has spoken of "prophetic listening" as a way to draw from others the seed of their own highest understanding. Thomas Shaffer, a law professor at the University of Notre Dame, has also written about communal discernment: "what is important [to this process], after one assumes the presence of God in the discussion, is that everyone be allowed to speak, and that everybody else feel bound to pay attention."[90] Chapter 6 highlights certain parallels in the processes of clearness committees and mediation and in the attributes important to each.

Conclusion

In addition to the testimonies, Quaker faith and practice emphasizes truthfulness and integrity and the congruence of belief and action. Friends hold the enduring hope that the world's people will realize their collective capability to create a world without war and, in living the peace testimony, they work toward that end. In simplicity, they attempt to lead simple lives and avoid a cycle of acquisitiveness. In witnessing community, Friends' concern for the common good encourages them to extend help and care to all of the world's people. And, in the witness of equality, they attempt to treat all persons with equal dignity and respect without regard to artificial distinctions of race, class, wealth, or power because there is that of God within all persons. Like Fox, they try "to walk cheerfully over the world, answering that of God in every one."[91]

Friends' faith and practice includes some apparent incongruities. The Society discourages going to law,[92] and yet Friends do. Harmony is a primary testimony yet many Quakers practice civil disobedience by refusing to follow laws of the state that contravene God's law. Friends are relatively individualistic in their worship yet they reach decisions by communal consensus, and work both individually and communally to discern God's leadings. They are gentle yet they speak plainly and are persevering and forthright. They worship in silence yet they let their lives speak.

2

Friends' Beginnings in England

". . . if anything be commanded of us by the present authority which is
not according to equity, justice, and a good conscience toward God . . .
we must in such cases obey God only . . . and deny active obedience for
conscience's sake, and patiently suffer what is inflicted upon us for our
disobedience to men."[1]

From their earliest beginnings in mid-seventeenth-century England, Quakers were
mavericks, often in conflict with established law, and moreover, for religious
and sociocultural reasons, had a marked irreverence toward the legal system.[2]
Friends such as George Fox, Edward Burrough, and others believed that law
should be based solely on commands of the Spirit. Because Quakers disobeyed
English laws they believed conflicted with these commands, hundreds died and
thousands were jailed.

Early Friends' Civil Disobedience of English Laws

Early Friends' refusal to swear an oath placed them at odds with a fundamental
requirement of English common law procedure and left them vulnerable to
charges of obstruction of justice. In early 1659, Yorkshire justices sent a petition
to Richard Cromwell, Lord Protector, "these populous Places and Parts adjacent,
now are, and for a long Time have been miserably perplexed, and much disettled
by that unruly Sect of People called Quakers, whose Principles are to overturn,
overturn, overturn Magistracy, Ministry, Ordinances. . . . These will not know
nor acknowledge any Subjection they owe to any Powers upon Earth."[3] The
genesis of Friends' refusal to swear can be traced to Matthew:

> . . . Thou shalt not forswear thyself, but shalt perform unto the
> Lord thine oaths; But I say unto you, Swear not at all; neither by
> heaven; for it is God's throne; Nor by the earth, for it is his footstool;
> neither by Jerusalem; for it is the city of the great King. Neither shalt

thou swear by thy head. . . . But let your communication be, Yea, yea; Nay, nay: for whatsoever is more than these cometh of evil.[4]

Fox contended that the refusal to swear oaths was not from obstinacy but from obedience to this scriptural command. Friends believed that yea and nay were all that need be offered their government, and the saying, "Let your yea be yea and your nay, nay," is occasionally spoken by modern Quakers, regarding their efforts to be forthright and speak the truth.

Another important reason for Friends' refusal to swear was that they sought to tell the truth at *all* times, not only on particular occasions. Friends believed that one who truly and uprightly feared God would no more speak falsely than swear falsely and so would testify from his good conscience as truly as if he had sworn. Oath-taking was a futile redundancy for Friends because truthfulness was a compelling element of their faith and a basic part of their lives. The words of Margaret Fell forcefully imparted the importance of plain speaking and truthfulness: "Now, Friends deal plainly with yourselves, and let the Eternal Light search you . . . for this will deal plainly with you; it will rip you up, and lay you open . . . naked and bare before the Lord God, from whom you cannot hide yourselves . . . Therefore give over deceiving of your Souls. . . ."[5] Margaret, Judge Thomas Fell's widow, later became George Fox's wife.

However, because oaths had been the "immemorial core and sanction of English jurisprudence,"[6] this attitude was an abiding source of friction between Quakers and the English legal establishment. The Quaker Act of 1661–1662[7] specifically targeted them because legal officials believed their civil disobedience obstructed the administration of justice. On September 7, 1664, Justice John Kelyng denounced their refusals to swear: "without swearing we can have no Justice done, no Law executed, you may be robbed, your Houses broke open, your Goods taken away, and be injured in your Persons, and no Justice or Recompense can be had, because the Fact cannot be proved."[8] The first Conventicle Act, passed that year, formalized this rationale into law.[9]

During Fox's imprisonment at Worcester, Friends delivered to King Charles II, his Council, Members of Parliament, and other officials "People Called Quakers Relating to Oaths and Swearing,"[10] complaining about the imprisonment of 130 Yorkshire Quakers for refusing to swear oaths and charging that magistrates in York who had known for years about this stand of conscience had nevertheless imprisoned them for it.[11] Court officials would often ignore the original cause of a Quaker's indictment and, knowing of their refusal to swear, would deliberately administer oaths of allegiance and supremacy and then prosecute them for it.[12] From 1660–1669 in Lancashire alone, more than 250 Quakers refused to swear the Oath of Allegiance.[13] Such refusals had repercussions such as banning them from government employment, from recovery of their stolen goods, and from prosecuting suits against their debtors.

In addition to laws requiring oaths of allegiance, trade and property laws required sworn affidavits. For example, the 1678 Act for Burying in Woolen[14] required a sworn statement that the material used to wrap a corpse was woolen. Wills and estates probated in ecclesiastical testamentary court also required oaths, but in this court, weaker enforcement generally caused Friends to suffer less. Occasionally, officials allowed proxies to swear for them, although, some Quakers rejected this as a matter of principle. Moreover, oaths were customarily required of men who matriculated at the English Inns of Court,[15] so Quakers who refused to swear were barred from a legal education and admission to the bar.[16] This, together with the scriptural injunction against suits, helps to explain the paucity of Quaker lawyers in seventeenth-century England.

After Friends' decades-long struggle against oaths, Parliament finally passed the Affirmation Act of 1696, which provided "that the solemn Affirmation . . . of the People called Quakers shall be accepted instead of an Oath in the usual Form." Although the law's lobbyists had agreed to the language, some Lancashire Friends objected to inclusion of the phrase "in the presence of almighty God" because of the required invocation of God to sanction their words, believing that yea and nay were sufficient in lieu of an oath.[17] A perpetual affirmation law passed in 1722 omitted this reference, requiring only that the speaker "solemnly, sincerely, and truly declare and affirm." The allowance of affirmation in lieu of swearing continues to the present day.

Early Friends disobeyed other English laws. Officials arrested William Penn for disobeying the Five-Mile Act of 1665,[18] which prohibited a person who would not swear, or who was convicted of preaching in an unlawful assembly, from coming within five miles of any town or borough that sent representatives to Parliament. This arrest resulted in his and William Mead's trial in Old Bailey in 1670. Although this law ostensibly applied to "holy orders," officials considered Quakers to be within its ambit. It empowered justices to sentence one who refused an oath to six months' imprisonment.

Early English Friends also disobeyed Sunday Observance Acts. One, enacted in 1677,[19] provided that no tradesman, workman, or laborer should do any labor nor should any drover, waggoner, or butcher travel or come to an inn or lodging on the Lord's Day. Despite the commandment to keep the Sabbath holy,[20] many Friends did not respect laws forbidding travel or work on Sundays because they considered every day to be holy; however, the commandment calls the Sabbath seventh day while Quakers called Sunday first day. Nor did some Friends obey laws requiring the observance of holidays, even working or opening shops on "the day called Christmas." In Norwich on Christmas Day, 1676, people threw snowballs, ice, and bones through the doors and windows of Quaker-owned shops open that day.[21]

Most Friends also disobeyed English marriage laws because they believed that marriage was the work of God, not man. This view, together with a desire for a direct relationship with God, led them to stand as witnesses to marriages in their meetings without the presence of an official intermediary designated by the Crown. Judges were usually, but not invariably, lenient about this practice. Three Friends—Christopher Rowth, Anthony Carr, and Richard Woodmansey—suffered draconian enforcement of the law requiring the presence of a Church of England intermediary. Because their marriages did not follow prescribed form, the judge convicted Rowth, Carr, and Woodmansey of cohabiting with women who were not their "legal" wives and sentenced them to prison.[22]

Quakers refused to attend mandatory services in the Church of England in defiance of two English laws enacted during the reign of Elizabeth I.[23] One law authorized fines for anyone older than age 16 for each Sunday's absence from the parish church, and the other authorized confiscation of absent offenders' goods and land. Sixteen men and women were committed to Peter Prison in York for refusing to pay fines imposed for their absence from the parish church.[24]

Friends who gathered in meetings for worship violated the Quaker Act of 1661–1662:[25]

> whereas said Persons [Quakers] under a pretence of Religious Worship do often assemble themselves in great numbers in several parts of this Realm to the great endangering of the Publick Peace and Safety and to the terror of the People . . . if the said persons comonly called Quakers shall . . . assemble themselves . . . under pretence of joyning in a Religious Worship not authorized by the Lawes of this Realm . . . for his or her third offense . . . [it] may bee lawfull . . . to cause him . . . to be transported . . . to any of his Majesties Plantations beyond the Seas.

Soon after the restoration of King Charles II to the throne, Edward Burrough presented a declaration to him with an account of the sufferings of "the People of God in Scorn called Quakers," complaining that they were being punished for liberty of conscience and for obeying and confessing to the Truth.

Under the Corporation Act of 1661[26] and the Test Act of 1673,[27] Quakers and other nonconformists out of communion with the Church of England were barred from employment in certain posts. Mandatory tithing was also a sore point with Quakers who defied a century-old law enacted during the reign of Henry VIII that required the payment of tithes. For such noncompliance, magistrates, upon a sworn complaint, could distrain their property[28] or fine or imprison them until the tithes were paid. Quaker Stephen Lorrimore was imprisoned in York Castle for two years for this offense.[29]

English officials viewed early Friends' persistent refusals to cease meeting, swear oaths, give recognizance for good behavior, pay tithes, or remove their hats in court as undermining the authority of the realm. This was, in some sense, true because Quakers then, and many now, regarded themselves as subjects of God, not of a king or an authority of the state. However, Quakers regarded civil disobedience differently—some held that one who submits to a law's punishment actually fulfills it. The "principle of 'loyal opposition' . . . was a puritan and, above all, a Quaker contribution."[30] Loyalty was, and is, not incompatible with civil disobedience as persons can help in improving a system, law, or procedure by forthrightly exposing its flaws. Early Friends' civil disobedience coupled a certain acceptance of suffering with a clear demand for correction.

The writ of praemunire[31] facias was a legal writ charging an offense of procuring translations, processes, excommunication, bulls, or other actions or benefits from the pope against the king or generally obeying an authority other than the Crown by introducing a foreign power into the kingdom. This process, created by statutes initially passed during the reign of Edward I, was interpreted to apply to Friends, and under it, officials had the power to seize their estates. If convicted, Friends could be punished by forfeiture of inheritance rights, loss of the king's protection, or life imprisonment.[32] Margaret Fell suffered under the praemunire laws[33] as did Yorkshire Quakers John Leavens, Samuel Poole, and Christopher Hutton, who were sentenced in 1662.[34]

Friends' refusal to doff their hats as a sign of respect for a king, judge, or other high-ranking person placed them in defiance of an important English custom and frequently resulted in contempt of court citations.[35] For example, when summoned to serve on a York jury, Philip Chatt of Skipsea came into court wearing his hat. For that officials fined him for contempt and confiscated two oxen.[36]

During their 1670 trial in London's Old Bailey,[37] William Penn and William Mead one day entered court bareheaded. The Lord Mayor directed a court officer to place hats on their heads. When an official asked Penn whether he felt he owed the court respect, he acknowledged that he did, but he did not regard doffing his hat as a sign of it. When the court fined him for contempt, Penn defiantly, but reasonably, noted that he and Mead had entered court without hats, and since the Bench had ordered hats placed on them, the Judge himself should bear the fine![38]

Quakers' peace testimony was another source of civil disobedience, their refusal to pay militia charges. In 1683 Richard Robinson of Countersett, Yorkshire, was fined three heifers for this infraction.[39] Although it is not widespread, Friends' refusal to pay taxes for military purposes continues today, and several such cases will be discussed in chapter 4.

English officials' enforcement of laws transgressed by Friends was sporadic and not consistently oppressive. Enforcement often depended on individual attitudes that might differ from decade to decade and from place to place. The kindness of friends and neighbors also alleviated Quakers' suffering; some would refuse to buy their distrained goods, or, would buy at a very low price and return to the Friends.[40] Some ship captains and crews also refused to carry out orders banishing them to places such as Barbados or Jamaica.

Although enforcement against Friends was most severe toward the end of Charles II's reign, prosecutions diminished on the accession of James II in 1685. Friends' practice of petitioning the Crown, the Parliament and others in power with descriptions of their sufferings may have had some impact. In April 1687 the new king issued a Declaration of Indulgence that enabled hundreds of Quakers to be released from prison, permitted greater religious toleration and liberty of conscience, and suspended penal laws related to ecclesiastical matters. It even allowed religious dissenters the right to recover fines that had been levied against them.

Threatening and Intimidating Jurors

During the late seventeenth century, English judges often threatened and intimidated juries. Contemporary observers did not consider the "twelve men in scarlet" who manned the courts of King's Bench, Common Pleas, and Exchequer to be independent arbiters of the law, but rather civil servants of the Crown, charged with implementing the royal will.[41] This practice directly affected Friends because their repeated acts of civil disobedience caused their frequent appearance before juries. Many English judges of that time were ill-disposed toward Quakers, so judges directing the verdicts of juries posed a significant problem for Friends.

In a 1664 trial of 16 Quakers in Old Bailey, some jurors questioned whether the silence of a Quaker meeting was, *in fact*, contrary to the liturgy of the Anglican Church or law of the land.[42] The jurors' persistence so annoyed the judge that he called them as disorderly as any he had ever seen. When the jury subsequently acquitted the Friends, the judge argued against the verdict and succeeded in changing some jurors' minds. Other jurors refused to indict the Quakers after finding they had met to worship according to the scriptures. For that, each juror was fined £100.[43]

When a grand jury once refused to return an indictment against four Quakers, the judge rose from the bench in a great rage and insisted that he be sworn as a witness against one of them.[44] In *Wagstaffe's Case* (1667), the judge directed the jury to convict the defendants. When it nevertheless refused, the judge fined the jurors and ordered them committed to Newgate Prison until they paid the fines.[45] This kind of manipulation was no doubt why Friends originated the practice of speaking directly to juries whom they considered the true "judge." By describing their sufferings, they directly appealed to jurors' consciences to enable them to see their own inner Light. One Quaker defendant addressed the jury:

You by the Court are made our Judges, and the matter of Fact, for which we are called in Question this Day, is not criminal, nor any matter of Dishonesty, but only for our meeting together in the Worship and Service of God . . . That which you are chiefly to consider . . . is, Whether or not we were met together in Manner and Form . . . as is declared in the Indictment. As to the manner of our Meeting, it was not with Force and Arms, as you your selves in your own Consciences know, but we met together in the Fear of the Lord . . . and it is not in the Power of any Creature to prescribe to his Maker, how he shall be served and worshipped.[46]

Thomas Speed, who was also indicted for unlawful assembly "with Force and Arms to the Terror of the People," spoke to jurors:

You have Families, Relations, and Estates; we have Families, Relations, and Estates: Weigh well out of all Prejudice, and consider what you are about to do as touching us. Suppose with your selves, that the Verdict you are now going to consult of, may be the last that ever you may give in this World; and that when you have brought in your Verdict on us, you your selves should immediately appear before the high Tribunal of the God of Heaven: Go therefore, and do that wherein you may have Peace with your Maker. . . .[47]

The legislature disapproved of the practice of fining and imprisoning juries for rendering a judge's undesired verdict. In 1667 the House of Commons summoned a justice to defend this treatment of jurors who had acquitted Quaker defendants in a 1665 trial.[48] Several years later Edward Bushell, a juror in the Penn-Mead trial, squarely appealed the legitimacy of the practice in *Bushell's Case*. This appeal resulted in a decision that finally curtailed judges' power to direct a jury to bring in a particular verdict or to fine or imprison its members if they refused.

During this time, the king also intimidated and controlled the judiciary through his officials, often by giving judges specific instructions before they visited various English counties. Even local officials and justices of the peace might pressure judges; they would occasionally write letters to Parliament praising a judge who pleased them or condemning one who did not.[49] Fox and others seem to have been correct about the need for legal reform.

The Trial of William Penn and William Mead

The well-documented case of the Crown against William Penn, "gentleman," and William Mead, "linen-draper," is a prime example of early Friends' conflict with the English legal system and its laws. The trial took place in London on September 1, 3, 4, and 5, 1670.[50] The indictment charged that Penn and Mead had unlawfully and "tumultuously" congregated with about 300 people at 11 o'clock on the morning of August 14, in the 22nd year of the King, "with force and arms" in "Grace-church-street." Having been shut out of a meetinghouse, Penn had preached to the gathering in the street "to the great terror and disturbance of many" and to "the ill example of all others." An element of the indictment was the alleged use of swords and staves although the prosecution presented no evidence of this. Penn believed that the Crown had proved very few facts at the trial.

When trial commenced, Penn appeared pro se and requested a copy of the indictment. When court officials told him that he must first plead before he could receive a copy of the charges, he protested that he could not defend against an indictment he could not see and read. Moreover, if he could not read the law on which charges were based, the proceedings were arbitrary and illegal. Mead appeared pro se and pled not guilty; he exercised his right against self-incrimination by refusing to acknowledge his presence at the street gathering at which Penn preached.

Penn persisted in asking under what law he was being prosecuted; Sir John Howell, the court recorder, answered that it was the "common law." Dissatisfied with that vague answer, Penn further pressed him. Howell said he could not answer because there had been too many cases over too many years. Penn retorted that if the law was common, it should be easy to produce; moreover, if the jury did not have access to the law, it could not reach a just determination as to whether the defendants had violated it or not.[51]

With apparent sarcasm, Howell asked Penn if he would like to instruct the court on the law, reminding him that most lawyers had studied it for decades. Exhibiting the Quaker penchant for literalism, or perhaps merely being playful, Penn replied that if the common law was so difficult to understand, it was far from common.[52] This repartee continued. The court called Penn a "troublesome fellow"[53] and directed an official to stop his mouth or put him out of court. Howell stated that if Penn were allowed to ask questions until the next morning, he still would not be the wiser. Penn retorted that would depend on the answers he had been given.[54]

Penn argued that continued denial of *oyer*, a reading of the law he allegedly violated, would be an abridgement of the rights and privileges given him and all Englishmen by the Great Charter (Magna Carta). Penn stated that he had broken no law and that arresting him for an act of religious worship constituted another violation of the Great Charter. Tired of his relentless arguing, the court ordered Penn hauled away to the bale dock, leaving Mead to carry on alone. Then, the court declared Mead an enemy of the laws of England and ordered him to the dock as well. In defendants' absence, the court delivered its charge to the jury:

it was to render a guilty verdict if it found that Penn had been preaching and Mead had allowed it. Penn shouted from the bale dock that charging the jury in his and Mead's absence violated their rights, and furthermore, he had not been fully heard and wanted to speak to the jury again.[55]

Although the jury declared Penn guilty of preaching in the street, it rendered a not guilty verdict on all other charges. The court considered the verdict unsatisfactory and warned jurors that they would be locked up without meat, drink, fire, or tobacco until they reached an acceptable verdict. Naturally, Penn objected to the court's intimidation, saying that justice should be done regardless of the judge's arbitrary intentions. The jury was polled, but it held fast. The judge rejected its verdict again and again until he fined the jurors and ordered them to prison until they paid the fines.

Due to the jury's partial acquittal, Penn asked to be freed, but officials denied this request because he was fined for contempt. Although Penn quoted the Magna Carta,[56] "No Freeman ought to be amerced, but by the Oath of good and lawful Men of the Vicinage,"[57] nonetheless he and Mead and the jury were imprisoned for nonpayment of fines. Due to Penn's high social status, while awaiting the start of his trial he had been allowed to stay at the Black Dog Inn instead of Newgate Prison. But now he was finally incarcerated there.

This imprisonment caused jurors Edward Bushell, John Baily, John Hammond, and Charles Milson to bring an action, *Bushell's Case*, in the Court of Common Pleas, which they won the next year. Thus, the Penn-Mead trial had led to an important change in English law after the court recognized the inviolability of juries' independence. Other Quaker protests have led to changes in U.S. laws. We will see this in chapter 4 where several Supreme Court precedents were established from cases brought or defended by Friends.

George Fox's Thoughts on Law and Lawyers

"I beheld the Lawyers black, their black robes as a puddle, and like unto a black pit, almost covered over with blackness."[58]

Fox's view of lawyers, so forcefully stated, emanated in part from the persecution he and other Friends experienced under Charles II. Their close encounters with the English legal system made them acutely aware of its flaws and the need for legal reform. The wretched prison conditions they experienced impelled their efforts to effect prison reform as well. Fox, like others in the Society of Friends, showed a "basic concern for Social evil, and a constant testing of social life by consciences made sensitive by personal experience of ethical combat and victory."[59]

In 1654 Quaker John Camm sent Lord Protector Oliver Cromwell the paper "Some Particulars Concerning the Law," and a few years later in

1659–1660, Quakers published at least three tracts advocating legal reform:
George Fox's "To the Parliament of the Comon-wealth of England: Fifty-Nine
Particulars laid down for the regulating things and taking away of oppressing
Laws and Oppressors and to Ease the Oppressed"; Thomas Lawson's "Appeal
to the Parliament Concerning the Poor that There may not be a Beggar in
England"; and Edward Billings [Byllynge] "A Mite of Affection, Manifested
in 31 Proposals."[60] In these tracts, Friends advanced several proposals: that all
statutes be published in English, law procedures be decentralized and shortened,
persons be allowed to plead their own causes, prison conditions be improved,
tithes be abolished, and imprisonment for refusing oaths and "hat honor" be
ended. Fox called lawyers terrible and lawless and believed that the whole nation
smarted under their oppression.[61] Quaker Robert Barclay echoed this sentiment
when he called lawyers "that deceitful Tribe . . . who by their many Tricks
and Endless Intricacies have rendered Justice in their Method burdensome to
honest men and seek not so much to put an end, as to foment Controversies
and Contentions."[62]

One source of Fox's drive for legal reform was the social, political, and
religious milieu of seventeenth-century England. The 1640s was a period of
upheaval and vigorous opposition to the powers that be. This impetus for
greater equality of rights and opportunity yielded antilegal sentiment from
Puritan radical thinkers such as George Wither, Gerrard Winstanley, and John
Warr who clearly perceived the need for legal reform and joined the chorus of
those demanding it.

George Wither, a seventeenth-century poet and author of the 1646
Justitiarius Justificatus (*Justice Justified*), was familiar with law, having entered
Lincoln's Inn in 1615. His dislike for lawyers and the legal system was evident
in his complaints about legal "mumbo-jumbo," the incomprehensibility of "law
French," delays, and corruption.

Gerrard Winstanley, another writer of the same period, likened the law
to a fox and poor people to the geese the fox feeds on. In his 1652 *Law of
Freedom*, he stated that there was no need for lawyers in society and in the
ideal commonwealth he envisioned, there were none.

John Warr advocated legal reform in his 1640s work *The Corruption and
Deficiency of the Laws of England*. He believed that the epitome of all laws
should be an equal and speedy distribution of rights and thus advocated that
law be returned to its ideal and original state—toward the protection of the poor
rather than an instrument of the poor's oppression. His work is a "remarkable
application to legal philosophy of the radical protestant emphasis on the religion
of the heart—a legal theory based on the inner light."[63]

An important reason for Fox's own advocacy of legal reform was the critical
importance of truth-telling to Friends.[64] The common use of exaggerated claims
and untruths in pleadings and other legal documents was unpalatable to Fox

and, more important, were antithetical to Friends' commitment to truth-telling. The desire for a direct relationship with the Divine, without intervention, was paralleled by the conviction that neither should there be intermediaries in the legal system. William Penn wrote about this in a November 15, 1671, letter: ". . . so all things may be done, worthy of the blessed unchaingable [*sic*] Truth & our immovable Foundation, the Law of the Spirit of Life, which makes free from the Laws & Lawyers of Sin, & gives the Tongue of the Learned into every mouth, wherewith to plead his own righteous Cause, & so a good conscience become an able & bold Advocate."[65]

Penn's words presage allowance of pro se representation in the courts of Pennsylvania province where he established many of its laws. The letter's postscript reemphasizes truth-telling and conscience, and criticizes lawyers: "And how can we imploy those Lawyers to plead against Oathes, who are maintained by them, & who maintain them, & for money could plead as heartily for them & so their ground of the Plea is not Conscience, but Covetousness, the Root of all Evill [*sic*]. Christ, that lead us not to swear, is an only Advocate for not swearing, & there Truth leaves it."[66]

Several of Penn's writings followed similar themes: *Truth Exalted* (1668), *Truth Rescued from Imposture* (1671), *The Spirit of Truth Vindicated* (1672), and *Plain Dealing* (1673).

Like John Warr, George Fox espoused a legal theory built on the inner light. Although he regarded law, along with medicine and theology, to be one of the three great professions, he believed that lawyers were "out of the equity . . . true justice, and . . . the law of God." He asked: "Is it not contrary to the Law of God and equity and reason, for such as are [im]prisoned for the truth, for speaking the word of God, to be brought into the court . . . and there have an Indictment drawn against him? . . ."[67]

Nevertheless, Fox believed that lawyers could be reformed and brought into the law of God, and his writings exemplify his tireless efforts to effect this. He stated that the law of God brings one to love one's neighbor as himself and answers that of God in everyone. He believed that the converse was true, that if a man wrongs his neighbor he wrongs himself.

In his 1655 *Instruction to Judges and Lawyers*, Fox wrote that God gave the law not for the righteous but for sinners,[68] and he believed that law should be restored to the Mosaic code. Sir Edward Coke shared Fox's view of the primacy of fundamental law "which [the] holy church hath out of Scripture . . . for that is the common law, upon which all lawes [*sic*] are founded.[69] The "law of God" was to Fox and Coke the essential scriptural commands of the spirit to love one's neighbor as oneself and to do unto others as you would have them do unto you. Fox and Friends such as George Bishop often referred to the Golden Rule. In a speech to a jury deciding his fate, Bishop said: "Friends, you have Consciences of your own, according unto which you would worship God, and you would not take it well, if some such Thing as hath been done . . . to us, should be done to you for worshipping God according to your Consciences: Now, what saith the Judge of all, Whatsoever ye would that Men should do unto you, do ye even the same unto them, for this is the Law and the Prophets. . . ."[70]

Fox's interest in law and legal matters was reflected by his personal library, which contained Edmund Wingate's "The Bodie of the Common-Law of England" and a copy of the Magna Carta. In 1659 Fox sent specific proposals for legal reform to the English Parliament: "Let no men or women be summoned up two hundred miles or upward to the Court at London because they cannot give the Priest Tithes, who doth no work for them, and when they appeared they will [im]prison them, because they did not appear by an Attorney, and swear to their answers. . . ."[71]

Fox and Penn advocated increasing access to the legal system by letting people plead pro se. Like George Wither, Fox urged that legal documents be written not in law French or Latin but, rather, in people's common language. "Let all laws in England be brought into a known tongue, that every Countryman may plead his own cause, without Attorney or Counsellour or for Money."[72] Fox was relentless in this advocacy for he believed that people knew their own business better than anyone and could plainly speak to it with fairness, reason, and common sense.

Fox's belief that lawyers should not charge fees or receive stipends, gifts, or rewards may have been controversial even in his day. He thought that because God was a free God, one who read the law should do it freely. "[L]et not the Law be sold nor bought, and let . . . none of them be handlers of the Law that will not do Justice without money;"[73] he cautioned lawyers not to charge great fees" because the high rates paid lawyers for a day's work were many times higher than the wages of a poor man. Shakespeare too wrote of "lawyers' fingers, who straight dream on fees."[74]

Fox noted that if a client's criminal case was lost, the lawyer would neither go to prison for the client nor refund his money. He illustrated this by an analogy: if a furniture maker built a bed for a customer and it turned out badly, the joiner would either refund the customer's money or make him a new bed.[75] He thought that lawyers should do likewise; when a lawyer was unsuccessful on a client's behalf, he should give the poor man all his money again and let him seek better workmen or do the work himself.

In the *Instruction to Judges and Lawyers*, Fox wrote on behalf of the poor man. The poor man pays for all, "suffers for all, and the Lawyers goeth away with all."[76] Like John Warr, Fox believed that English legal practice disproportionately impacted society's least affluent, and he often remonstrated from the vantage point of a poor man. Friends, many of whom were relatively impoverished in the Society's early days,[77] especially in rural areas, were sometimes ordered to pay damages amounting to triple their goods' worth, and Fox thought the value was often overestimated, including even the babies' bibs. Distraint of Quakers' property could severely impact their livelihood when officials confiscated livestock or tools needed for their work. Although William Penn protested to Parliament around 1680 that such seizures caused Friends ruin, they continued nevertheless. In 1682 officials seized four oxen, five cows, one heifer, a calf, and a horse belonging to George Shaw of Yorkshire.[78] As Friends began to engage legal counsel more extensively, lawyers advised that they bring trespass actions against those levying distraints against their property.

Literalness and Truth in Legal Documents

Fox applied his literality to legal documents. He complained that a writ issued to command a person's appearance in court actually meant that an attorney's appearance was required even though the word "attorney" did not appear in the document. Fox believed it was therefore illegal because the rule for the law should also be "so say and so do," the first of the ancient principles of truth.[79] Shakespeare similarly wrote, "Crack the lawyer's voice that he may never more false title plead."[80]

Quaker truth-telling was also implicated when a client was forced to engage a lawyer to answer a writ. A typical pleading in Fox's time, and even today, contained exaggerated claims and allegations that were "not of sound words . . . having more in them . . . than what is truth."[81] In *The Second Part of the People's Ancient and Just Liberties Asserted*, Quaker lawyer Thomas Rudyard complained that attorneys often placed a small fact in the midst of a "whole sea of their . . . obnoxious terms which they call law . . . [illustrating by example] 'To do an act with force and arms, riotously, . . . tumultuously, seditiously, illegally, deceitfully, . . . fallaciously, in contempt of the King and his laws. . . . '[82] And Penn's indictment in his and Mead's 1670 trial contained such "malicious scaring phrases" as "riotously and tumultuously with force and arms," untrue facts that the prosecutor could not prove. An influential Quaker, George Whitehead, attempted to combat frequent use of such language against Friends by researching Sir Edward Coke's *Institutes of the Laws of England* and then publishing its definitions. However, during the Penn-Mead trial, the court disregarded Mead's recitation of legal elements Coke deemed essential to prove a "riot" and defended the indictment's phrase "force and arms" as merely a matter of "form."[83] In fact, juries did acquit some defendants whose indictments were not precisely framed and contained such inflammatory and inaccurate language. Quakers naturally agreed that precise wording of indictments was critical and maintained that a statute's title should indicate its nature and intent and its preamble, its reason, and its cause.[84] If preambles had been properly drafted and carefully interpreted, Quakers would not have been indicted for violating the

Conventicle Act,[85] which was reserved for *seditious* conventicles, the Five-Mile Act, which pertained to *holy orders*, or recusancy laws that concerned *Popish* dissenters. Like the court in the Penn-Mead trial, other courts did not carefully interpret laws to make certain that each element of an offense was accurately reflected by the facts presented.

Fox wrote that lawyers dressed an answer with many fine words unknown to the client, thereby giving it a new face. If a conscientious client wanted to plead honestly, the lawyer might refuse to take his case. And if the client disapproved of the attorney's answer because it was untrue, the attorney would say that was their "little lie." Fox believed a lawyer had too much latitude because he could take a man's cause, look at it how he pleased, and then fashion the answer and measure out justice as he saw fit.[86]

Neither did the English judiciary escape George Fox's scorn. He believed that judges of his time were neither reasonable nor just, especially toward Quakers, and even if they never said a word, the judges would nevertheless complain about them. Fox thought that judges overreacted to Quakers' civil disobedience and should not imprison them for "things of nought," such as refusing to swear an oath or appearing in court without an attorney. As for Friends' refusal to doff their hats, Fox asked "doth the hat destroy Magistrates, and Government, and Ministrie both? doth it all end in the hat?"[87] He challenged the legal establishment to cite a single English statute that made it contempt for a man to enter court wearing his hat.[88] Fox thought that anyone who allows a hat to blind him and make him storm cannot judge well. William Armorer, a Berkshire magistrate, indeed became so enraged about this infraction that he ordered the hats of three young Friends' who had come to his house to be filled with water and replaced on their heads. Fortunately, a kind constable nearby threw out the water and returned their emptied hats.[89] Fox returned to the Golden Rule in asking judges if they would like to be treated as they had treated Quakers. He himself answered this: "Sure you would not."[90]

There were very few formally trained Quaker lawyers in Fox's time. In fact, in a listing of occupations of all male Quakers from 1663 to 1740, not one was specifically listed as a lawyer.[91] Indeed, it was virtually impossible for Friends to matriculate at English Inns of Court because of the required oath. Other records, however, do indicate the existence of several Quaker lawyers during this period, namely Thomas Rudyard and Roland Vaughan,[92] who were the first standing counsel to Meeting for Sufferings and seemed to have had some legal training. Vaughan helped Quakers by writing exemplars to guide them through early legal pleadings and later appeals. London Yearly Meeting minutes mention Quaker lawyer Ellis Hookes who advised Friends on getting released from prison. Hookes would respond to other requests for advice by sending the requester a "resolve" as to whether he thought relief might be available.

In a 30-year period from 1660 to 1690, Friends consulted or retained some 40 lawyers.[93] In 1688 lawyers numbered about 10,000, only 0.7% of the entire English population.[94] Quakers too comprised only a small proportion of England's population: 500 in 1652; 5,000 two years later; 20,000 in 1657, and about 40,000 by 1660.[95]

Quakers' Increased Use of the
Legal System as a Response to Persecution

One of Fox's many imprisonments occurred in late 1673 at Worcester when he was charged with meeting illegally and then charged for refusing to give surety for his appearance at the next court sessions. Thomas Corbett's successful defense of Fox in 1675 may have been an important turning point in Friends' decision to confront the English legal system with its own tools. After the Worcester imprisonment and trial, they resolved to focus on a more concerted, coordinated, and organized defense against their persecutors. Of all religious groups, Quakers alone developed a sophisticated legal defense organization, which has provided rare insight into the operation of the late-seventeenth-century English legal system.[96] Their suffering became less passive as they shaped and refined their attitude toward law and its enforcers. This was a radical step for a group who generally condemned the legal profession and "going to law."

Fox's Worcester imprisonment was also the catalyst for the 1676 establishment of the Meeting for Sufferings. It promoted test cases and, if lost, appealed to higher courts. It hired ad hoc and standing counsel and maintained a Book of Cases, a four-volume series of legal opinions and precedents.

Another important outgrowth of the Meeting for Sufferings was the development of a sophisticated record-keeping system, which documented the thousands of sufferings Friends endured during the late seventeenth century in England, America, Barbados, and elsewhere. The Meeting's verification and recordation of sufferings were collected by Joseph Besse in a two-volume work that covered Quakers' beginnings in 1650 until 1689, the year of the Act of Toleration. The names and addresses of Quaker defendants in criminal trials, prosecutors, informers, and justices as well as copies of legal records, signatures of witnesses to the sufferings, valuations of Friends' goods, and amounts of fines and distraints were also documented. Written accounts, signed by the individual concerned and two witnesses were taken to the clerk of the Monthly Meeting. A copy would be kept and another would be sent to the Quarterly Meeting for Sufferings. Copies of each case would then be entered in a county Book of Sufferings, and accounts were sent to London Yearly Meeting where annual sufferings would be checked, and totals of each type of incident, money, or property seized, and number of Friends imprisoned would be entered in Yearly Meeting minutes.

Craig Horle, a scholar of the early English legal system, delineates several reasons for Friends' greater participation in the legal system at this time. They came to realize that scriptural knowledge and their concept of equity—the Golden Rule—had proven insufficient in the eyes of English judges. The argument that Quakers should not be persecuted for holding religious beliefs out of accord with the English Church was likewise ineffective. As a corollary, Friends began to understand that survival was dependent on their acquisition and utilization of legal knowledge. A further reason was that by the late seventeenth century Quaker leadership had shifted from the agriculturally oriented men of the rural north to professional Londoners who more clearly recognized the importance of organization and familiarity with complex legal procedures.[97]

Friends' Extralegal Resolution of Disputes

Given Quakers' profound distrust of the English legal system and the refusal to swear oaths in court, it is natural that they would devise an alternative means of resolving disputes. And so the Society of Friends developed a comprehensive and effective arbitration procedure for resolving disputes within the meeting that also advanced the testimonies of harmony and community. Another reason for devising an extralegal means of resolution was the scriptural instruction not to go from the order of truth to sue at law. Friends were to end their differences quickly, either by themselves or with aid of others:

> . . . if thy brother shall trespass against thee, go and tell him his fault between thee and him alone: if he shall hear thee, thou hast gained thy brother. But if he will not hear thee, then take with thee one or two more, that in the mouth of two or three witnesses every word may be established. And if he shall neglect to hear them, tell it unto the church. . . .[98]

Paul's first letter to the Corinthians also asked why, if one has a grievance against his brother, he dares go to law before the "unrighteous" rather than before the "saints."[99] In his epistle to Titus, he again advised against foolish questions and strivings about the law.[100]

In England and America, Matthew's "gospel order" came to be Friends' preferred philosophy and practice regarding the resolution of disputes both in England and America. Instead of contending at law, differences were settled according to a stepped process: first by negotiation, then, if necessary, informally with a third person such as another member, and finally, through the meeting's more formal arbitration process. This is discussed in chapter 6.

Conclusion

The tenets of the Religious Society of Friends, set in motion by George Fox in mid-seventeenth-century England, have remained remarkably consistent throughout the ensuing centuries. The testimonies are still strongly held with the possible exception of singular speech and simplicity of dress. Truth-telling, straightforwardness, and plain-speaking—"let your yea be yea and your nay, nay"—are frequently reinforced and held as a model to live by.

Friends' early interaction with the law sprang from their persistent adherence to truth-telling and peacefulness, exemplified by a refusal to swear oaths or to fight with "outward weapons." This primary reverence for and allegiance to "God's law" caused them to run afoul of numerous English laws.

In addition, Fox and other members of the Society seemed, more than those of other religious groups, to hold passionate views on lawyers, judges, and legal process and procedure and wrote many letters, tracts, and other papers on these subjects. The trial of William Penn and William Mead exposed many irregularities in English legal procedure. Penn was among the first of Friends' civil rights advocates through his demands for adherence to the principles of the Magna Carta, especially as these affected English legal process. Both he and Quaker Thomas Rudyard revealed further aspects of the trial in subsequent writings, further enlightening others not only about Friends' treatment but also on substantive and procedural irregularities in English law and courts of that period. Moreover, *Bushell's Case*, an outgrowth of the Penn-Mead trial, contributed to the development of English law by establishing the independence of juries from interference by the judiciary.

In "speaking truth to power," Friends repeatedly offered suggestions to Parliament, Charles II, the Protectorate, and James II, not only for improvement of their own condition but also for that of the poor and society as a whole. Their pleas for a law allowing them to affirm instead of swear finally bore fruit in an Affirmation Act in the last decade of the seventeenth century.

English Friends took seriously the scriptural caution against "going to law" and devised an alternative dispute resolution system within the structure of their meetings. They did this in order to abide by the scriptural command and to keep any "differences" within the confines of the Society, important for the solidarity of a persecuted group.

The opportunity to institute legal reforms urged in England presented itself in the early 1680s as Quaker William Penn began the establishment of his "holy experiment" in America. Changes to the Duke of York's laws, already in force, and new ones Penn's drafted for Pennsylvania are part of the discussions in chapter 3.

3

Penn's Holy Experiment in Pennsylvania and His Changes to Its Laws

I . . . des[ire] that I may not be unworthy of [God's] love, but do that w[hi]ch may answear his kind providence & serve his truth & people; that an example may be Sett up to the nations. there may be room there [America], tho not here [England], for such an holy experiment.[1]

On March 4, 1681, King Charles II granted William Penn land in America in response to his 1680 petition to the king.[2] It was in this colony, later known as Pennsylvania, that the well-known Friend established his "holy experiment," which he hoped its Quaker settlers would imbue "with a spirit of dedication to the will of God."[3]

Later that year, Penn sold more than 300,000 acres of land to about 300 investors, primarily Quaker merchants, craftsmen, shopkeepers, and farmers, many from Wales and the south and west of England.[4] In one of the pamphlets Penn wrote in 1681 to recruit settlers to his planned utopian community, "Some Account of the Province of Pennsilvania [*sic*] in America,"[5] he described the land and climate. He intended to attract persons of a special spiritual quality who would obey and fulfill the highest teaching of the scriptures and the beliefs of the Religious Society of Friends. Penn believed "The way, like the cross, is spiritual: that is, an inward submission of the soul to the will of God, as it is manifested by the light of Christ in the consciences of men."[6] In a 1686 epistle, though, Philadelphia Quakers expressed disappointment that because some Friends were "Drunkards, Fornicators, Adulterers, false Accusers Blasphemers," the holy experiment suffered.[7]

Penn's Ideas on Government and Laws

Penn revealed his philosophy of government in the preface to the First Frame of Government for Pennsylvania,[8] also known as Penn's Charter. Written on April 25, 1682, it stated: "Let men be good, and the government cannot be bad. The apostle taught in his epistles[9] that the law was added because of transgression; law was not made for the righteous man but for the disobedient and ungodly." Penn wished there were no need of any laws, "but since crimes prevail government is made necessarie by mans [sic] degeneration."[10] Like Fox, Penn believed that fundamental law was God's law, basic and simple like the golden rule. In a disagreement over the boundary between Maryland and Pennsylvania, Penn quoted the essence of that rule[11] in an April 10, 1681, letter to Lord Baltimore: "I only begg [sic] one thing, 'tis short, but the text of all that can be said, do to me as thou wouldst be done to."[12]

Although he believed the virtuous had no need for laws, Penn reluctantly acknowledged that they were necessary to punish evildoers who would not answer to their own internal law. For that reason, he came to view laws as necessary to complete justice. Penn preferred a small number of well-drafted, duly enforced, and impartially executed laws, and as proprietor of Pennsylvania, he was "empowered . . . to enact laws for the good government of the . . . province" provided that these were "not repugnant or contrary to . . . the laws of England."[13]

The new province had a bicameral legislature consisting of a Provincial Council, the upper house, and a General Assembly, the lower. Until 1685 the Provincial Council was the only forum for the trial of serious crimes, and it continued to exercise other judicial functions until 1701. However, under the terms of the King's charter, the right to hear and determine appeals from provincial judgments was reserved to the sovereign.[14] The General Assembly approved or rejected bills sent by the Provincial Council, and acts the Assembly passed were presented to Her Majesty's Commissioner for Trade and Plantations who then gave notice to the British sovereign. The laws agreed upon in England, dated May 5, 1682, were superseded on December 7 of that year by the "Great Law." The Duke of York's Laws of 1664–1665, already in effect in the province, remained so for matters not covered by Penn's new enactments.

Penn's Laws and Changes to the Duke of York's Laws

As he drafted new laws for the American province, Penn seized the opportunity to institute several important reforms that he, George Fox, and others had earlier urged in England. Aided by other Quakers, he drafted laws more attuned to Friends' testimonies of pacifism, community, equality, and simplicity. As we have seen, one of Fox's principal complaints about the English legal system was the incomprehensibility of legal documents written in law French or Latin. Because lawyers' services were required to decipher these, Penn sought to eliminate them as the province's legal languages. The Seventh Part of the First Frame of Government mandated that all court pleadings, processes, and records be in

English, be brief, and of ordinary and plain character so the people could clearly understand them. With these changes, Penn hoped that justice could be more speedily administered and clients would be less taken advantage of. In his May 1682 critique of Penn's laws, Quaker Benjamin Furly advocated that a "forme of a deed be agreed upon, thats [sic] short and plain, that we be not bound to the tricks of the Lawyers of England."[15] A later Pennsylvania law on forms and writs did require plainness and brevity.[16] However, as more men educated in the law emigrated from England to America, pleadings began gradually to reflect the complicated English practice.

According to the Sixteenth Fundamental,[17] persons of all persuasions could freely appear in all courts to personally plead their own cause or to have a friend appear on their behalf. This was the realization of a reform Fox and Penn long sought. This change from former English practice, reconfirmed by a later act, simplified procedures and made hiring lawyers for pleadings and other uncomplicated matters unnecessary.

Indeed, in the early years of Pennsylvania and West Jersey, a vast majority of persons did plead their own causes in court. From 1680 to 1710 in Bucks and Chester counties in Pennsylvania and Burlington and Gloucester counties in West Jersey, of the 3,582 people who used the legal system, plaintiffs had attorneys in only 7.5% of completed cases and defendants in less than 5% leaving a vast majority of plaintiffs and defendants to pursue their cases without the aid of attorneys. Plaintiffs with attorneys had a worse record of victory than plaintiffs overall,[18] a fact which would have made George Fox smile. It is noteworthy that during the early part of this 30-year period, the largely Quaker population in these counties nevertheless went "to law" before judges who were mostly Friends.

Reformers such as Fox had long railed against high legal fees, largely because of concerns about their impact on the poor. Massachusetts, in 1641, and Virginia, in 1645, had unsuccessfully attempted to prohibit attorneys from receiving fees for pleadings. If Fox knew, he would have been delighted that in 1685 and 1686 Pennsylvania's Provincial Council proposed laws against lawyers' fees; by the terms of the one of 1686, a person could not plead in any provincial court before attesting that he had neither directly nor indirectly received any reward for doing so. However the General Assembly did not pass either, although the it did pass several acts regulating fees of lawyers and court officials in the early years of the eighteenth century that Queen Anne subsequently repealed. One provided that if an attorney drew up a defective indictment, he must draw up a new one without charge or be fined five 5£. Fox had proposed such a solution in his analogy of a lawyer and a joiner.[19] Penn continued to pursue a remedy for outrageous legal fees, advocating that moderate ones for all cases should be set by the provincial legislature and posted in every court. Finally in 1722–1723, an Act for Regulating and Establishing Fees[20] provided a detailed fee schedule for pleas, declarations, and court appearances. Drafters of Pennsylvania laws and procedural rules were aware of wealth disparities and therefore included in judges' attestations the promise of equal treatment of rich and poor. Before accepting a complaint, the court required a plaintiff to declare that he believed in his conscience that the cause was just. This concept was reconfirmed in a 1700 act against barraters, which provided that any person who harassed others with unjust suits would be punished and his suits rejected.

After the English gained control of New Netherland from the Dutch in 1664, Charles II granted it to his brother, the Duke of York, later James II of England. The Duke of York's Laws were in force in Pennsylvania and West Jersey until the time of Penn's first laws, and some continued in effect thereafter. These laws prescribed capital punishment for several crimes. For example, persons convicted of a third offense of burglary or highway robbery, homosexual acts, adultery, kidnapping, or denying "the true God and his Attributes" were to be executed. As with most Quakers, Penn disapproved of capital punishment and sought to eliminate it for all crimes except willful murder and treason. In his 1682 criticism of Penn's First Frame of Government, Benjamin Furly advised against *any* use of capital punishment: "Concerning Juries Especially where life wil[l] be concerned, as in mur[d]er & Treason . . . Let God, rather th[a]n men be intrusted with that affaire in the first place. . . ."[21] Friends' concept of the inner light was a critical component of such a humanitarian approach; the light of God resided in every person, including those convicted of a capital offense.

Another rationale for Friends' opposition to capital punishment was that it afforded no possibility for offenders' rehabilitation. For example, in a case of theft, Penn reasoned that, rather than deterring further crime, the threat of capital punishment might in fact encourage a thief to murder his victim, who, if left alive, could later prosecute him; after all, punishment for murder would be no worse than for theft.[22] Instead, Penn favored restitution because it benefited both the victim, by restoring his property, and the perpetrator, by affording him an opportunity for redemption. Neither could benefit if the crime were a capital one. And so, with the assistance of Quaker lawyer Thomas Rudyard, Penn made significant changes in the new province's criminal laws by reducing punishment for these crimes.

Penn fashioned laws that required the perpetrator to make restitution to his victim; for a second offense, double satisfaction; and for a third, triple satisfaction. In 1700, an act directing Punishment of Larceny of property below the value of 5s. required the offender to be publicly whipped and to restore the victim's property or pay its value. A 1705 law required that a burglar who broke into a house with intent to commit a felony be whipped, imprisoned for six months' hard labor, and required to make fourfold satisfaction. An arsonist who set fire to stacks of corn or hay, wood, fences, or boats was also required to make fourfold satisfaction to the victim.[23]

However, in the year of Penn's death, a law[24] reinstated arson, burglary, and maiming as capital offenses, reversing the earlier elimination of these as crimes punishable by death.[25] Extension of the death penalty to these additional felonies was believed to have been part of a political compromise with Governor Keith in exchange for support for Pennsylvania's Affirmation Act. More than seven decades later, with support from Judge William Bradford, the Act of April 22, 1794, again abolished the death penalty for all crimes except murder in the first degree.[26]

Penn's new prison system continued a prison "ministry" begun by early English Quakers and a focus of concern for some Friends today. His system focused on decent living conditions as well as rehabilitation of offenders through programs of compulsory work and religious study. Penn might have remembered Fox's observation that prisoners incarcerated for long periods learned "badness" from each other. In its time, the province's penal system was considered one of the world's best in terms of humane living conditions for its inmates.

Early Pennsylvania Statutes Protective
of Quaker Beliefs and Practices

"Historically, unrestricted liberty of conscience had always been one of the highest of Quaker values. . . ."[27] The long persecution of English Quakers for worshipping contrary to the Church of England prompted Penn's law protecting liberty of conscience: "That no person now, or at any time hereafter . . . who shall confess and acknowledge one Almighty God the Father, and in Jesus Christ his only Son, and in the Holy Spirit . . . Shall in any case be molested or prejudiced for his or her Conscientious persuasion or practice, nor shall he or she at any time be compelled to Frequent or maintain any Religious Worship Place or Ministry whatever, contrary to his or her mind but shall Freely and fully enjoy his or her Christian Liberty. . . ."[28] "England had objected to an earlier liberty of conscience act passed by the General Assembly because "none can tell what conscientious practices allowed by this act may extend to."[29]

The March 2, 1685, minutes of Philadelphia Quarterly Meeting reflected that two Friends had been appointed to request county magistrates to refrain from holding court on the day of midweek meeting for worship.[30] Perhaps this request is not surprising given that many Friends had substantial influence and held positions in the provincial courts and legislature. In 1740 Friends held 25 of the 30 seats in the General Assembly.[31]

Other Quaker beliefs and practices were incorporated into Penn's new statutes. For instance, the province legally recognized marriages performed according to the manner of Friends, without a state-sanctioned officiant to administer the vows. And a 1693 act provided that "the Registry kept by any Religious Society, in their respective Meeting Book . . . of any Marriage, Birth or Burial . . . shall be held good and authentick, and shall be allowed of, upon all occasions."[32]

Friends' strong testimony of equality was no doubt instrumental in passing Pennsylvania province's 1711 ban on the importation of "Negroes,"[33] and the 1780 Act for the Gradual Abolition of Slavery,[34] decades before it was declared illegal elsewhere in the colonies.

In principle, Friends' long rejection of swearing oaths presented little difficulty in Quaker-dominated Pennsylvania. The earliest laws provided that those who could not swear because of "tender consciences" could instead declare: "I do from the very bottom of my heart hereby engage and Promise in the Presence of God and the Co[u]rt to declare the whole truth, and nothing but the truth, . . ."[35] but Queen Anne subsequently repealed these. The Quaker-dominated legislature persisted, and clearly stated the difficulty in the preamble to a 1715 Affirmation Act:

> Whereas the governor-in-chief and greatest part of the inhabitants, freeholders and first settlers of this colony being of the people commonly called Quakers, who for conscience' sake could neither take nor administer an oath, it was found necessary to provide laws suitable in that case . . . [but] being now destitute of any such provision by reason of our late gracious Queen's repeal of divers laws of this province relating thereunto, an entire failure of judicial proceedings hath happened, which if not speedily remedied . . . may prove of ill consequence to his majesty's subjects here. . . .[36]

A 1724 act allowing Quakers to affirm Fidelity and to Declare and Affirm Otherwise included an affirmation similar to one allowed Quakers by England's 1696 Affirmation Act. For giving evidence and qualifying as a juror, justice, or assemblyman, answering affirmatively to whether a person did "solemnly, sincerely and truly, declare and affirm . . ." was sufficient.[37]

Quakers' strict code of behavior was reflected in several early-eighteenth-century laws such as acts prohibiting cursing and swearing and playing tennis, dice, cards, and "bowles." A 1710–1711 law against "tennis, dicing . . . or carding."[38] was repealed later because the English official who reviewed it thought it "restrains persons from several innocent sports and healthy diversions."[39] One of Penn's law provided that "all fines shall be moderate, and saving mens contenements merchandize or wainage,"[40] no doubt drafted in reaction to the ruinous distraints officials executed against English Quakers.

A unique Quaker custom that ran counter to prevailing mores was the designation of days and months by numerals; Sunday was first day or 1; March was first month or 1, February was twelfth month. A 1682 act allowing this was later abrogated and then reinstated. An Act for the Names of Days and Months, passed in 1700,[41] made designating months and days in this way lawful, but Queen Anne repealed it in 1705–1706. Finally, a 1710–1711 act made numbering months as legally effectual as naming them.

Distrust of Lawyers

"[M]istrust of law crossed the Atlantic with the earliest settlers whose Edenic visions of New World possibilities consigned lawyers to a role only slightly above the Biblical serpent. . . ."[42] The prevailing bitterness toward lawyers in seventeenth-century England was carried to America. Gabriel Thomas, a late-seventeenth-century settler, echoed the disdain for lawyers in *A Historical Description of the Province of Pennsylvania and County of West New Jersey in America*: "Of lawyers and physicians I shall say nothing, because the country is very peaceable and healthy; long may it continue so and never have occasion for the tongue of one and the pen of the other, both equally destructive to men's estates and lives. . . ."[43] Criticism of lawyers continued unabated in journals and writings of the next century: "He that would go to law must have a good cause—a heavy purse—a skillful attorney—an able advocate—good evidence—an intelligent jury—an upright and patient judge—and having all these, unless he has very good luck, he will stand a small chance of succeeding in his suit!"[44]

Moreover, those who lambasted lawyers in America's earlier years were not confined to Quakers or Pennsylvanians. On July 25, 1776, Timothy Dwight warned of the evils of legal practice in a commencement address at Yale College: "That meanness, that infernal knavery, which multiplies needless litigations, which retards the operation of justice, which, from court to court, upon the most trifling pretenses, postpones trial to glean the last emptyings of a client's pocket, for unjust fees. . . ." Another wrote: "With regard to the Practitioners of the Law in this Commonwealth [of Massachusetts], daily experience convinces us of the horrid extortion, tyranny, and oppression, practiced among that order of men. . . ."[45] That same year, another Massachusetts observer wrote: "If no practitioners were allowed in our Courts, the important study of law, would be followed solely with a view of doing justice. . . ."[46] In the late eighteenth century, another critic of the legal profession wrote in the National Gazette:

> Much as I respect this order of men [lawyers], I would not be sorry to see such of them as are unnecessary, more honorably employed at the plough. I expect they would make skillful farmers and useful members of society then. [T]hey would have more of a common

Figure 1. *A Lawyer and His Client* by Robert Dighton, hand-colored etching published in London, May 1812. Reprinted by permission. Courtesy of the National Portrait Gallery, St. Martins Place, London.

interest therewith, for they themselves will acknowledge that in the arts of delay, the chicane, bargains etc. in use with these gentlemen and upon which much of their profits depend . . . they have not a common interest in the community. . . .[47]

Remarkably a late-twentieth-century legal scholar makes very similar observations. Stephen Presser noted, "My own limited two-year stint in large firm private practice left me with the impression that 90% of large-firm associates' time is spent in activities without any redeeming social purpose, and that there is a need for a reconception of the lawyer's role in society."[48]

Visitors to America shared the earlier eighteenth-century views of lawyers. In his *Letters from an American Farmer* (1782), Frenchman Michel-Guillaume Jean de Crevecoeur, who owned a farm in southeastern New York, described American lawyers as "plants that will grow in any soil that is cultivated by the hands of others; and when once they have taken root they will extinguish every other vegetable that grows around them. . . . The most ignorant, the most bungling member of that profession, will, if placed in the most obscure part of the country, promote litigiousness, and amass more wealth without labour, than the most opulent farmer, with all his toils."[49] These examples show that many members of the public clearly mistrusted lawyers because they seemed inclined to value profits above clients and community and to delay or disregard justice. "[A]t no time in their history have the American people shown much disposition to revere their lawyers."[50]

Quaker Lawyers and Legal Officials in the New Province

Perhaps because of their persistent perception of lawyers' chicanery and deception and Friends' refusal to swear the requisite oaths to enter the English Inns of Court, Pennsylvania's early mostly Quaker immigrants included only a very few men educated in the law. Among them was the aforementioned Quaker Thomas Rudyard who, in England, had assisted Friends under persecution and, in America, had helped Penn draft and redraft the early laws of Pennsylvania; however, he may not received formal legal training nor did he remain a Quaker all his life. In his writings, Rudyard was scathingly critical of English legal practices, particularly as shown in the Penn-Mead trial. Rudyard contributed to Penn's accounts of the trial: *The Peoples Ancient and Just Liberties Asserted in the Tryal of William Penn and William Mead* (1670) and *Truth Rescued from Imposture* (1671). Another Quaker lawyer, Francis Daniel Pastorius, came to Pennsylvania in the early 1680s, was clerk of Germantown Friends Meeting and one of the first in America to protest slavery. He most likely authored the paper circulated at Philadelphia Yearly Meeting in September 1688 denouncing the buying and keeping of slaves.

Although not formally trained in the law, a high percentage of adult males living in the Delaware Valley counties near Philadelphia from 1680 to 1710 participated in the legal establishment as justices. Of these, 38% were Quaker and almost one-third of these were also leaders in their meetings as elders, overseers, meeting clerks, or Quarterly Meeting representatives.[51] During the late seventeenth century, many Quakers occupied high positions in the legal hierarchy.

David Lloyd (1656–1731), a Welsh-born lawyer who emigrated from England to America in 1686, became a "convinced" Quaker five years later. He assisted William Penn in England, and later in America with various legal matters related to Pennsylvania. He also held several high and influential positions in Penn's government, among them Attorney General, Speaker of the Assembly, Chief Justice of the Pennsylvania Supreme Court, and member of the Provincial Council. His value to the province was enhanced by his legal background, which was a rare commodity in Quaker-dominated Pennsylvania. In fact, only he, with John More, Thomas Story, and James Logan, had formal legal preparation.[52]

Lloyd was controversial and, even when inappropriate, he exhibited a lawyer's bent for adversarial behavior.[53] Although Penn once called him an honest man and the ablest lawyer in the province, he later changed his opinion, calling Lloyd a self-interested hypocrite. Penn, as Proprietor of Pennsylvania, would naturally consider Lloyd, leader of the General Assembly's antiproprietary democratic opposition, a troublemaker. Lloyd's reputation among Friends was damaged when he sued a fellow member over property without first attempting "gospel order." Nevertheless, Lloyd worked on several causes dear to Friends—for the right of affirmation but against the slave trade and appropriation of public funds for military purposes. Quaker John Kinsey, another eminent eighteenth-century Pennsylvania lawyer, was Clerk of Philadelphia Yearly Meeting as well as Attorney General and Speaker of the General Assembly.[54]

In the late eighteenth century, two Quaker lawyers did not continue simultaneously as lawyers and members of the Society. John Dickinson (1732–1808) was raised a Quaker and attended meeting as a young boy, but after leaving home to study law at age 18, he no longer continued as a Friend. The converse was true of Nicholas Waln (1742–1813), who studied at the English Inns of Courts and was admitted to the bar at a young age. Once he won a case for a client and, in doing so, defrauded an honest man. After that experience, he relinquished the practice of law and traveled to various Quaker meetings throughout England and Ireland. He later served as Clerk of the Meeting for Sufferings.

A birthright Quaker lawyer Jean Bouvier, who emigrated from France in the early nineteenth century, is credited with having written the first dictionary of American law. Although he was appointed a judge of the Philadelphia assizes circuit, he retained an interest in editing and writing. He authored the four-volume *Institutes of American Law,* which he dedicated to Chief Justice Roger B. Taney.

In the early 1700s, the ratio of lawyers to the general population was 1:4,000.[55] As the number of Pennsylvania lawyers increased, the General Assembly passed a law in 1722 providing that courts admit a "competent number of persons of an honest disposition and learned in the law . . . to practice as attorneys there; who shall behave themselves justly and faithfully in their practice.

And if they misbehave themselves therein, they shall suffer such penalties and suspensions as attorneys . . . in Great Britain."[56] By the mid-eighteenth century, a brilliant bar had emerged in Pennsylvania, second only to South Carolina in the number of its lawyers trained at the English Inns of Court.[57]

Gospel Order in Early Pennsylvania

Earlier in England, Quakers had actively encouraged the use of alternative dispute resolution such as mediation and arbitration to resolve disputes and restore harmony, a scriptural system of gospel order that complemented Friends' testimonies. As early as 1659, Quaker Edward Burrough advised London Meeting Friends to settle their differences not by hot contests but by "love, coolness, gentleness, and dear unity."[58]

Unlike those prescribing capital punishment, Penn approved the Duke of York's laws pertaining to the arbitration of disputes. An example was a law that provided that the constable name two impartial persons of the neighborhood to arbitrate all debt and trespass actions with a value of less than 5£.[59] As early as July 1681, Penn set forth certain conditions to Pennsylvania's first settlers: "all Differences between the Planters and the Natives shall . . . be ended by . . . Six Planters and Six Natives, so that wee [sic] may Live friendly Together, and as much as in us Lyeth, Prevent all Occassions [sic] of Heart Burnings and Mischiefes[sic]."[60] The following month, an August 28, 1681 minute of Philadelphia Yearly Meeting first urged members not to go to law against one another.

Arbitration did figure prominently in Penn's system of justice and was the chief means of resolving certain civil disputes. A 1683 law provided that persons should submit their differences to arbitration by common peacemakers whose findings were as conclusive as those of any court.[61] Arbitrators would also decide land disputes if the Proprietor and land possessor had a disagreement about boundaries. Then, as now, it cost more to take a case to court than to arbitration.

The Society of Friends preferred to order human relations so as to solve disputes outside the courts. "The American pattern of dispute settlement is, and always has been, more varied and complex than our currently constricted legal perspective would suggest. . . ."[62] One such pattern was early Friends' tradition of solving disputes by mediation or arbitration within the Society of Friends and within Penn's early legal system. Quakers' reluctance to submit disputes to courts also "grew out of the social singularity which the Society felt and sought to inculcate in its brethren,"[63] together with the perfectionist bent of a self-conscious religious community. Also, Friends' arbitration process performed an important dispute resolving function due to the paucity of formally admitted attorneys in Pennsylvania and West Jersey at this time.

A Friend who directly sued another *before* he had proceeded in gospel order was thought to have departed from the principle of truth, and he might be disowned if he continued. Usually, however, Friends would approve a court action if the situation was sufficiently egregious and more "peaceful" alternatives had been exhausted. Although early Friends discouraged suits in court and encouraged the use of gospel order, they did not make the restraint against going to law absolute. The Society cautioned Quakers not to go to law without urgent necessity, leaving open the possibility that they might under certain conditions. Although Paul advised the Corinthians to be wronged rather than go to law, Friends have not unconditionally followed this advice. For instance, William Penn recognized that some, including Quakers, would take advantage of an absolute proscription against a Quaker's suit in court. Friends underscored this possibility in the 1701 Rules of Discipline by cautioning debtors not to shelter themselves by rules designed to guard against unkind treatment, and thereby unjustly escape the reach of civil authority.

Meetings held differing views on "going to law" and on enforcement of a general restraint against it. The severity with which Friends treated this infraction also varied; whereas some Friends were punished by disownment, others were not. Some might have sensed a certain tacit assent in their meetings, which emboldened them to go to court. However, in the late eighteenth century enforcement increased, and more Quakers were disciplined for going to court before they had exhausted gospel order.

From 1680 until 1710, nearly 66% of disputes brought to meetings were successfully resolved by summary proceedings, arbitration, or an offending party's self-condemnation, and some of the remaining ones were settled within four (or more) meetings.[64] Unfortunately Friends were unable to maintain this rate of success and by 1710 unsuccessful or prolonged arbitration had increased. This may have been due to Friends' greater diligence in bringing more disputes to meetings, including more intractable ones.[65] Sometimes Friends' arbitrations were delayed to avoid unpleasant judgments or to vex opponents, thereby making the meeting process vulnerable to a weakness of the legal system. For example, New Garden monthly meeting arranged an arbitration to settle a dispute over servant William Lowden's term of service to John Smith. However, several months later, the arbitrators still had not reached a judgment. By this time, Lowden had already left Smith's service, but he did later acknowledge his fault to the meeting.[66]

Gospel order notwithstanding, some Quakers went to law without approval. More than 200 intra-Quaker disputes were brought to judgment in county courts between 1680 and 1710, yet meeting records for this period indicate that only a few had permission to do so.[67] During this period, Quakers sued fellow members at approximately the same rate as the general population.[68]

From the time of Penn's charter, members of the Society had dominated Pennsylvania's legal system out of proportion to their numbers, and the Friends-controlled courts of late-seventeenth-century Pennsylvania and West Jersey no doubt had an impact on Quakers' lack of reluctance to take their disputes to court. The frequency of suits involving Friends varied from county to county. In Burlington County, two of thirteen civil suits filed in May 1689 were brought by Quaker plaintiffs, whereas two others were brought against Quaker defendants. None were intra-Quaker. On five occasions between 1700 and 1702, meetings in Chester County had to urge their members to use gospel order instead of the courts.[69]

Occasionally, cases might proceed simultaneously in court and in meeting, or members might air their differences in meeting after conclusion in court. For instance, although the plaintiff prevailed in *Empson v. Harlin and Way*, both he and the defendants acknowledged their errors to the meeting, the defendants for their initial offense and the plaintiff for subsequently suing. "The ability of the Quakers to avoid serious contention was the single most important reason why Friends were able to dominate Pennsylvania politics to such a degree . . . [and] may have been the very characteristic that initially made them successful in Quaker Pennsylvania."[70]

However by the mid-eighteenth century, Friends' control of the judicial and political systems had ceased as many Quakers had resigned from the legislature because of their witness of the peace testimony and Fox's injunction "so say and so do." They preferred resigning rather than supporting aggression against Indians, raising a militia, and raising and paying taxes for war. These resignations naturally caused Quaker influence to wane in Penn's province. Friends move away from the vanguard of his holy experiment may have dashed his hopes and expectations for the province to become an example to all nations of realizing God's will through peacemaking.

As Friends' hold over the legal system loosened, the courts steadily lost control over intra-Quaker disputes. So the pendulum swung, and Friends began to take their differences to meetings twice as often as they took them to court. This change might support an inference that they, with or without meeting approval, went to the courts as long as their brethren were dominant there.

Quaker defendants in this three-decade period were proportionately fewer than Friends' population percentage, although when they were defendants, the cases were generally more contentious, whether or not the plaintiff was a Friend. A higher degree of discord between Quaker litigants may be attributable to an initial failure of the Quaker community to solve the dispute[71] and, perhaps ironically, to the importance of truth-telling. Quaker plaintiffs might initiate a claim only when it was necessary and truly justified, and thereafter be perseveringly contentious to the end. Litigants who wanted merely to gain by threats or bullying would be more apt to treat a complaint cavalierly and thus might eventually surrender a frivolous claim.

Courts and meetings tended to handle different types of cases. In general, the court docket showed a higher percentage of disputes involving tangible economic loss than the "Quaker docket." Because Friends' goals of harmony were preeminent, dispute resolution outside the courts may have presented a risk to creditors in recovering money. However, Quaker meetings tended to better handle suits involving intangible loss such as defamation. Unlike a public complaint in court, a plaintiff proceeding in gospel order was usually able to avoid the spread of defamatory material. For instance, the meeting might immediately order a defamer to apologize or write letters to clear the plaintiff's name.[72] Another type of complaint often referred to a Quaker meeting involved land rights. An example was William Penn's successful arbitration of a large West Jersey land dispute between John Fenwicke and Edward Byllynge in 1675. The latter was later obliged to assign his land interest to a Quaker committee of trustees that included Penn. Attending to this responsibility in America apparently piqued Penn's interest in the new land and is sometimes cited as a cause for his petition to King Charles II for a grant of land as liquidation of the King's debt to Penn's father.[73]

During the 1680s, the population of Chester County (near Philadelphia) and West Jersey was virtually all Quaker. In addition to the decline in Quaker leadership, beginning at the turn of the eighteenth century the number of Friends decreased in proportion to the population at large. A decade later, the percentage of Friends had dropped to slightly more than 40%. In West Jersey, Friends comprised only about one-third of the population. By the 1720s they had dwindled to a minority even in Penn's province.[74]

Friends' Civil Disobedience and the American Revolution

Pacifist Friends once again ran afoul of law and custom at the time of the American Revolutionary War. The Constitutional Convention of 1776 passed an ordinance against pacifists, requiring them to pay a fine of 20s. per month until the next meeting of the legislature. Those older than 21 were required to pay annual assessments based on the value of their estates. Members of the first House of Representatives passed an act that levied fines against men between the ages of 18 and 53 who did not serve in the militia, although if they hired a substitute, they became exempt. James Madison attempted unsuccessfully to include this conscientious objection clause in the Bill of Rights: "No person religiously scrupulous of bearing arms shall be compelled to render military service in person."[75] From 1776 to 1779, punishment and fines grew harsher for pacifists who refused service.[76]

Colonies that did exempt Quakers from the militia were New York (1755), Massachusetts (1757), Virginia (1766), and North Carolina (1770). Some laws did exempt them from service in the militia although a few required them to secure a substitute or pay an exemption fee. Rhode Island had exempted all conscientious objectors in 1673 with no fee or substitution requirement, but that law was repealed shortly thereafter and only later reinstated.

Quakers often repudiated members who joined the Revolutionary War effort. In 1776 Friends disowned 190 men for aiding the Revolution, most for joining the militia. Altogether, 948 Pennsylvania Friends were disowned for behavior associated with the Revolution.[77] Quaker lawyer Samuel Allison defended the peace testimony in his 1780 *Reasons against War and Paying Taxes for Its Support.*

In the eighteenth and nineteenth centuries, Friends continued their pattern of civil disobedience on issues of civil rights. For instance, Friends specifically defied the Fugitive Slave Act of 1793[78] by rescuing runaway slaves, harboring or concealing them, refusing to return them to their owners, or aiding their escape through the Underground Railroad. Some individual Friends such as lawyer Francis Daniel Pastorius had opposed slavery since the seventeenth century, and as time passed, the Society too became increasingly active in its opposition. Initially engendered by their contravention of certain seventeenth-century laws, Friends' acts of civil disobedience continued into succeeding centuries. During the twentieth century and early twenty-first, Quakers have continued to witness testimonies of peace and equality by opposition to war and active concern for the civil rights of all persons.

A Brief Account of Quakers' Experience in Other American Colonies

Friends' experience in other early American colonies was predictably different from that in Pennsylvania; after all, Penn, its Quaker Proprietor, drafted laws protective of its large Quaker population. However in many other colonies, officials persecuted Quakers and even executed some. The Meeting for Sufferings kept detailed records of their hardship.

It is an irony of history that many acts of cruelty occurred in Massachusetts where Puritans had settled after fleeing their own religious persecution in Europe, yet they who had found religious freedom did not extend it to others outside their group. Quakers William Robinson and Marmaduke Stevenson spoke plainly of this in a paper addressed to the "Rulers, Chief-Priests, and Inhabitants of Boston: Oh ye Hypocrites! How can you sing, and keep such a Noise concerning Religion, when your Hands are full of Blood and your Hearts full of Iniquity?"[79]

On October 14, 1656, the General Court in Boston enacted the first law expressly against Quakers, "a cursed Sect of Hereticks lately risen up in the World." It prohibited their entry into "any Harbour, Creek, or Cove, within this Jurisdiction." If Quakers nevertheless managed to enter, they were to be immediately sent to the House of Correction and severely whipped.[80] And if they entered the jurisdiction again after such a whipping, the law called for one ear to be severed. In 1658 this law was executed on Quakers John Copeland, Christopher Holder, and John Rouse.[81] For a subsequent offense, a Friend's other ear was to be cut off.[82] For continual offenses, officials would bore through their tongues with a hot iron and send them to hard labor in the House of Correction. Friends were fined each time they professed any of their "pernicious Ways," by speaking, writing, or meeting on the Lord's Day, or at any other time to strengthen themselves, or seduce others to "their diabolical Doctrines." "With the obstinacy of the mystic, [the Quaker in colonial America] refused to admit the existence of the enemy's cudgel, even though his own or another's head be broken by it."[83]

Persons who aided Quakers were also punished. For instance, the master of a vessel who transported them was to be fined 100£ or imprisoned if he could not pay. A 1657 law extended a fine to those who even associated with them: 40s. for every hour a person concealed or entertained Friends. A person who merely defended Quaker opinions, books, or writings was also fined. Moreover in Boston, knowingly importing any Quaker books or writings concerning their "devilish opinions" was a finable offense.

Once Quaker Thomas Harris came to a Boston public meeting and, after the speaker had finished, "warned the People of the dreadful terrible Day of the Lord." For this, he was hauled away by his hair, imprisoned, and repeatedly whipped. For five days the jailer refused him food, and he would have died except for the kindness of those who surreptitiously passed food to him through a window.[84] Like Harris, two Quaker women, Sarah Gibbons and Dorothy Waugh, were also whipped for speaking after a public lecture in Boston. Once, in a town near Boston, Quakers William Brend and William Leddra conferred in a private home with a Captain Gerish who promised they could leave unimpeded and unharmed. Despite this promise, as they rose to leave, the captain detained them to make certain they would agree to leave town. When they refused, he ordered a constable to take them to a magistrate in Salem who questioned their religious beliefs. Brend and Leddra were committed to the House of Correction but later were transferred to work in Boston. When they refused, they were denied food, even after offering to pay.[85] As in England, Massachusetts officials fined Quakers who refused to obey laws requiring oaths and distrained their most needed property. One commissioner accustomed to distraining Quakers' goods, a "furious zealot," Edward Butter, also performed random acts of cruelty. When he once needed a horse for an expedition and seeing a pregnant woman traveling on horseback along the road, he took her horse by force, causing her to miscarry.[86] However, one of the most egregious instances of Quaker persecution in Massachusetts was the 1660 hanging of Mary Dyer for witnessing her faith.[87]

In the tradition of Fox and others, Friends wrote letters to those in power explaining their civil disobedience, arguing their cases, and urging reforms. For instance, Quaker Margaret Brewster, in a 1677 letter to the Governor of Boston, cited the scriptural basis for Friends' refusal to swear oaths and urged him not to enforce laws requiring oaths against them. This principle of Friends "speaking truth to power" requires that they live "in the world" and attempt to change matters for the better. However, in doing this, they have often faced the difficulty "of making the grounds of the demands of Friends' concern, and the justification they gave for the legitimacy of that . . . demand, comprehensible to . . . [those] who did not share the Quaker understanding.[88]

In Maryland, authorities distrained Friends' property for refusals to swear oaths, bear arms, or remove their hats in court. However, in 1688 Lord Baltimore, Proprietor of Maryland, enacted a law that provided "Relief of Tender Consciences, in Relation to Oaths and Swearing," for which Quakers explicitly expressed appreciation.[89]

A law of the Puritan colony of New Haven in Connecticut provided that Quakers who came into its jurisdiction should be severely whipped and sent to work in the House of Correction; for a second offense, they were to be branded on one hand and kept at work; for a third, they were to be branded on the other hand; and for a fourth offense, the tongue was to be bored through with a hot iron as in Massachusetts.

A statute of the Dutch plantation of New Netherland, later New York, provided that any person who received a Quaker into his house must forfeit 50£. Although the independence of juries had supposedly been assured by the English court's decision in *Bushell's Case*,[90] the court in Quaker Samuel Bownas's 1703 trial was so displeased by the verdict that it threatened jurors with fines and imprisonment. One juror perhaps emboldened by the ruling in that English case, defended the jury's independence and warned, "You may hang us by the heels if you please, but if you do, the matter will be carried to Westminster Hall; for juries, whether grand or petty, are not to be menaced with threats, but are to act freely."[91]

The Virginia colony required every person, including Quakers, to take oaths of allegiance and supremacy before they assumed public office as surveyors, sheriffs, registers, and the like. If they refused, they were to forfeit 1,000 pounds of tobacco.[92] In 1660 the Virginia Assembly enacted a law suppressing Quakers, "an unreasonable and turbulent sort of people," providing that a ship's master would be fined 100£ for bringing Friends into the colony. If discovered, they were to agree to leave the colony forever or be imprisoned without bail. A second offense required the Quaker's deportation, and if one was audacious enough to come into the colony a third time, he or she would be charged as a felon. Virginians who even allowed Quaker meetings in or near their houses were subject to a fine of 100£.[93]

Conclusion

Friends' interface with the law and legal system of Pennsylvania was quite different from that in England because most early settlers were Quakers recruited by William Penn, the province's Proprietor who had joined the Society in England. They had little need to practice civil disobedience because the laws that Penn crafted were more aligned with what they regarded as God's law. In this "holy experiment," Quakers generally "did good" but also "did well" financially or politically, as successful merchants with a one-price policy or as legislators and members of the judiciary in the provincial government.

Penn had the opportunity to institute some legal reforms in his province that Fox and other Friends had wanted in England. These incorporated important Quaker principles against killing. His reduction of capital crimes led to fewer executions and provided an opportunity for offenders' rehabilitation. Penn also enabled the legal system's use of arbitrators as peacemakers. It was witness of the peace testimony that caused many Quaker legislators to resign from the legislature in the mid-eighteenth century when a majority voted to raise taxes to fund preparations for the French and Indian War. The testimony of equality and concern for the poor was evidenced in laws allowing laypersons to plead their own causes. The testimony of community and harmony was manifest in the province's preference for solving disputes by peacemakers both within and without the Society of Friends. Friends continued their own communitarian system of justice in the form of gospel order, and they developed a sophisticated and comprehensive arbitration procedure to execute it. This obviated the need to settle differences in court; nevertheless, some Friends did so, especially when Quakers were dominant in the judicial system. Friends were treated more harshly in other provinces such as Massachusetts and Virginia where officials deported, imprisoned, maimed, and even killed them.

The cases discussed in chapter 4 are court actions brought or defended by Quakers. Most were litigated in the twentieth century, chosen to illustrate plaintiffs' or defendants' witness of Friends' testimonies.

Past as Prologue

The three chapters of the first part of this volume briefly examined Friends' origins, testimonies, faith, practice, and customs as well as their persecution. They explored Quakers' early views on the law and English legal system, the caution against "going to law," their own brand of dispute resolution outside the courts, and the birth of their own brand of civil disobedience.

The first part also chronicled Friends' growth and spread to the New World and the emigration of many hundreds from the British Isles to America. As Proprietor of Pennsylvania, William Penn had the opportunity to shape and reform laws more attuned with Friends' testimonies, inter alia, reduction of capital crimes, increasing rehabilitation of offenders, and creating a system of provincial arbitration.

The three chapters of the second part focus on the interface of Quakers and the law in more recent times in the United States and on the possibilities of learning from the past to help shape the future. The potency of the earlier warning against going to law lessened as years passed[94] although a reticence to do so lingers for many Friends today. Swearing an oath to become a lawyer is no longer necessary because an applicant is now able to affirm (as are witnesses in court). And indeed, from the explosion of litigation, in the last half of the twentieth century, members of society clearly did not feel restrained from suing.

In chapter 4, we see that some Quakers stepped out of traditional gospel order to go to law. As plaintiffs, and as defendants when sued, they witnessed testimonies of peace, equality, and community. Their peace testimony was evidenced by a large proportion of cases; as plaintiffs, when seeking to avoid paying the portion of taxes attributable to expenditures for war, and as defendants when refusing to register for the draft or fight in the armed forces.

In chapter 5, 100 Quaker lawyers, surveyed for this work, voice their ideas and thoughts as well as their ambivalence and trepidation about practicing law as Quakers in late-twentieth-century America. The chapter also discusses some views of legal scholars and law professors on current law practice and the legal system. These reveal a commonality of perspectives among Fox, the Quaker lawyers, and scholars.

Chapter 6 comes full circle, discussing a possible revival of early Quaker methods of settling disputes outside the courts, a practice briefly introduced in chapter 1 and explained here. Mediation and arbitration might be resurrected for intramember disputes within Quaker meetings and more fully used within the larger community.

Finally, the author suggests that Quaker lawyers take careful notice of legal scholars' and ethicists' calls for reformation of the U.S. legal system and, with others, lead an effort to begin such a process.

Part Two

4

Quakers as Plaintiffs and Defendants in Court and as "Divine Lobbyists"

Ever since Fox and Penn challenged seventeenth-century English laws and the English legal system, Friends have persistently stood for their principles by "speaking truth to power." At its best, this uniquely Quaker practice consists of inward and prayerful listening followed by courageous speech—oral, written, or silent and symbolic—directed to those in positions of authority with the capacity to effect change. In 1955 the American Friends Service Committee (AFSC) published a pamphlet entitled *Speak Truth to Power* in which it suggested a new approach to the cold war. Quaker Milton Mayer, a member of the committee assigned to write the document, had coined the term the previous year.[1] Because the phrase is "Quakerly" in concept and because Friends had long been speaking the truth to those in positions of power, many have thought it as old as the Society. Frederick B. Tolles described speaking truth to power as "laying a concern upon those who are charged with the governing of men."[2]

Friends spoke, and speak, truth to power in two important areas of the law. Although early Quakers were most often in a defensive posture in the courts, they took a more proactive stance during the late seventeenth century as they began to employ lawyers and the English legal process to help them staunch the persecution they suffered. Later American cases discussed in this chapter involve Friends' use of courts as plaintiffs despite the scriptural admonition against "going to law."

The second area is the petitioning of lawmakers, that is, the Quaker "divine lobbyist," who attempts to persuade those in legislatures to enact laws informed by the divine spirit or to change laws toward more consonance with the principles of truth and justice. One of many instances of Quakers' attempts to influence legislative and government policy occurred during the Interregnum[3] when Fox petitioned Lord Protector Oliver Cromwell at Whitehall.[4] In the United States since 1943, the Quaker communitarian manifestation of the "divine lobbyist" has taken the form of the Friends Committee on National Legislation (FCNL) in Washington, D.C.

This chapter explores Quakers in relation to the courts and legislatures: Friends in court as plaintiffs bringing actions involving peace and equality and as defendants against laws that contravene the pacifist principles of their faith and as lobbyists for laws more attuned to truth, community, equality, and peace.

Friends have been consistent in their aim of truth-telling, the societal counterpart of the power of truth on the personal and spiritual plane that Margaret Fell spoke of in 1656: "Now, Friends, deal plainly with your selves, and let the Eternal Light search you, and try you, for the good of your Souls; for this will deal plainly with you, it will rip you up, and lay you open, and make all manifest which lodgeth in you; the secret Subtilty [sic] of the Enemy of your Souls, this Eternal Searcher and Tryer will make manifest"[5] Quakers have long bared injustices through their acts of civil disobedience. This chapter examines this tradition as expressed in court actions.

Quakers as Plaintiffs and Defendants in Court

"Religious conviction and constitutional concerns are separately powerful. Joined in struggles against discrimination, they lead to acts of legal significance."[6]

Especially in matters of liberty of conscience, Quakers have defied the Society's traditional limitation on "going to law." In Quaker thought, this means being compelled or "led" to advocate for or act on special concerns of justice and peace. In the following cases, Friends have spoken truth to the power that Justice Holmes called "the public force through the instrumentality of the courts."[7]

As court plaintiffs, they have challenged sedition statutes, laws requiring loyalty oaths, and laws that abridge the civil rights of racial and economic minorities. They have also sought redress for violations of rights the First Amendment protects.[8] Friends have also defended government prosecutions for acts stemming from witness of the peace testimony—refusal to be inducted into the armed forces, to register for the draft, and to pay the part of their taxes used for waging war.

Friends' dealt with early issues of conscience centering on their refusal to take oaths or bear arms by exercising civil disobedience. However, during the wars of the twentieth century, Quakers also pursued justice in the courts. By bringing the principle of pacifism into sharper focus in the public arena, they may have contributed to a national discourse on these wars and "conflicts" in Vietnam or Korea, but also, and perhaps more important, on the larger issue of the wisdom, necessity, and efficacy of all wars.

Early Court Cases

Many of the earliest cases involving American Friends are notable primarily because they were brought despite the scriptural admonition against doing so. Unlike later ones discussed in this chapter, the early reported cases did not often involve Friends' religious scruples or matters of conscience. For example, in West Jersey, a Quaker settlement on the eastern banks of the Delaware River, many suits dealt with ordinary matters such as trespass or debt. However, the latter was not totally separate from Quaker practice because Friends recognized people as economic as well as religious beings and advised "punctuality in the payment of debts."[9]

In 1682 *French v. Leeds* resulted in a victory for plaintiff Thomas French, whose jury awarded him damages and costs. However, a later trespass action between the same parties resulted in a jury verdict and award of costs to Leeds. In 1685[10] French brought another trespass action against Quaker Richard Basnett, but he again failed to prevail.

In a 1684 debt action, *Budd v. Potts,*[11] defendant Thomas Potts acknowledged his debt to Budd. Around the same time, Griffith Jones also sued Potts for debt, and Potts again admitted the debt; the court awarded costs of suit to Jones and, in addition, ordered the sheriff to execute on Potts's real and personal property after the magistrate appointed "substantial men of the neighborhood" to appraise these. Potts must have been a laggard in paying his debts because he was sued by another Quaker that year.

The 1691 case of *Calow v. Wright*[12] involved a dispute over the sale of a wall-eyed mare. The jury awarded the plaintiff 5£ for the mare and 45s. for costs. This incident spawned Calow's defamation action against Wright; Calow again prevailed and was awarded damages and costs.

Court records indicate that a few actions did involve Friends' religious scruples. Even in the predominantly Quaker colony of West Jersey, a court in 1705 punished several Friends for refusing to take off their hats while attesting for jury service. Samuel Frettwell and John Gariot were "committed,"[13] and John Brown was fined.[14]

Later Cases Involving Marriage, Capital Punishment, and Oaths

Many cases involving Quakers illustrate their belief in the primacy of God's law over that of any human authority. An example can be found in Friends' assertion that people enter into marriage before God and pledge love and dedication directly to each other without the need for official blessing from court or clergy. Unlike laws in England, the early American legal system generally honored this

Quaker belief through exemptions from traditional marriage requirements. In an 1820 New Hampshire case, *Londonderry v. Chester*,[15] the court applied a 1791 state law, which provided that "marriages may continue to be solemnized by quakers as formerly, without incurring any penalty,"[16] *Mathewson v. Phoenix Iron Foundry*[17] construed a Rhode Island law that also legalized marriages in the Quaker tradition.

In a 1879 Massachusetts case, *Commonwealth v. Munson*,[18] the court cited a law that declared marriages "solemnized among Quakers or Friends, in the manner and form used and practiced in their societies to be good and valid in law . . ." although, for all others, "a marriage . . . not . . . solemnized before any third person, acting . . . as a magistrate or minister, [wa]s not lawful or valid for any purpose."[19] Due to the specific nature of Friends' marriage, this freedom was limited only to them. As we will see however, Quaker perseverance in other areas of the law, including civil rights, First Amendment rights, and conscientious objection redounded to the benefit of others who could invoke rights that became recognized because of these earlier actions by Friends.

The later cases reported in this chapter are more emblematic of Quaker belief and practice, both in the abstract principles asserted—liberty of conscience and freedom of speech, assembly, and religion—and in the specific substantive contexts in which the conflicts arose—the sanctity of human life through the inner light in all illustrated by challenges to capital punishment and participation in war or its preparation, issues of equality and civil rights through challenges to racial segregation and government intrusion through unfair immigration procedures.

Divine law again took precedence for Quakers in *United States v. Cornell*.[20] The court addressed Friends' opposition to capital punishment and held that two Quaker jurors should have been disqualified because they admitted being "conscientiously scrupulous of taking away life." The court observed: "To compel a Quaker to sit as a juror on [capital] cases is to compel him to decide against his conscience, or to commit a solemn perjury, [each] of [which] is equally repugnant to the principles of justice and common sense." The court reasoned that this influence on jurors would hamper rendering a true verdict according to facts and evidence and thus would corrupt the justice system; the source of this influence—interest, prejudice or religious scruples—was irrelevant.[21]

Quakers objected to requirements of swearing in court or on special occasions because their faith required them to tell the truth at *all* times. They reasoned that because they were always to speak the truth, swearing to do so at a particular time was unnecessarily redundant. The 1829 Maryland case of *King v. Fearson*[22] involved oaths and when a witness could affirm or swear. The judge had refused to permit a witness to testify except under oath because he had not yet been admitted to the "Society of Quakers" but he did permit a Friend to testify on his behalf by affirmation. Because the central issue involved conscientious scruples, Maryland's constitutional provision allowing Friends to affirm[23] was liberally construed and the affirmed testimony was allowed.

This principle was later expanded to benefit those who were not Friends. An eighteenth-century law, initially enacted to benefit Quakers, helped a twentieth-century criminal defendant who refused to swear an oath because he did not believe in God. In his case, *State v. Levine*,[24] the New Jersey Supreme Court held that the state's 1799 Act for the Relief of Persons who are Scrupulous of Taking an Oath in the Usual Form also applied to those who were not Friends.

Unlike some pacifist groups, Quakers chose not to withdraw from the world but to struggle with their religious principles within it, and they have acted on this principle wherever it has led. From their early beginnings in America, Quakers have brought court actions emblematic of their values, both in the substantive contexts in which the conflicts arose and in the abstract principles they asserted. For example, Friends have often argued for individual autonomy and have persistently pressed for freedom of religion, speech, and assembly, values springing from the core of their beliefs and practice. Similarly, the contexts in which they have advocated these reflect other substantive Quaker values. For instance, disputes that encouraged them to work to change laws or brought them to the courts have involved the sanctity of human life—in their work against capital punishment in early Pennsylvania and in their antiwar activism during later times. Both inside and outside the courts, they have worked for conscientious objection to war, equality and civil rights, racial integration, immigrants' rights, women's suffrage, and against war, slavery, and government surveillance. Such advocacy has benefitted those who were later able to invoke rights that were recognized only after Friends' agitation.

The story of Penn asking Fox if he should continue to wear his sword after becoming a Quaker and Fox answering that he should wear it as long as he could illustrates a Friends' principle: being led not by external laws in a sacred book but by the light of truth that produces action inspired from within. It engenders a certain freedom that issues from greater understanding and an increased sensitizing of one's conscience.[25]

First Amendment Rights of Speech and Assembly

Many of the following cases grew out of Friends' desire to stand against war but are more peripheral than those involving a direct refusal to be inducted into the armed forces. They involve protests against war and government surveillance and because of such protests, they also implicated First Amendment rights.

In *Sparrow v. Goodman*,[26] a Quaker and others brought a class action seeking damages and injunctive relief against federal and state officials who had excluded them from President Nixon's speech at the Charlotte, North Carolina, coliseum on October 15, 1971. That day Lawrence Reichard, a long-haired Quaker student, went to the coliseum to take photographs for his Friends Meeting First Day (Sunday) School class. A security guard alleged that his admission ticket was counterfeit and bodily evicted him although this was a public event in a public building without notice of any restriction on attendees' clothing, ideology or hair length. Several male plaintiffs wore long hair, and in fact, a security guard called one "Goldilocks" as he told them to leave the premises.[27] The court noted: "The criteria for exclusion . . . are readily inferred from a description of the persons who were in fact excluded . . . people advocating peace in Viet Nam . . . long-haired people. . . ."[28]

Defendants asked the court to assume without proof that because the President was in attendance, everything done by Secret Service agents was within the limits of what was necessary for his protection, and they should not have to answer for their actions. The court stated that, absent a valid security reason, the officials' actions constituted an egregious violation of plaintiffs' civil rights. The "authority and duty of the judiciary to inquire into deprivations of common right by government agents (even, in Lord Coke's phrase, upon authority of 'letters of the King') can not [sic] be so cavalierly dismissed."[29] Officials' refusal to admit plaintiffs had violated First Amendment rights to petition for redress of grievances and freedom of speech and assembly. Moreover, plaintiffs' unlawful arrests without a warrant for unwitnessed misdemeanors violated their Fourth Amendment rights as well. The court denied defendants' motion for summary judgment and granted injunctive relief to plaintiffs. The district judge quoted Judge Bazelon in *Quaker Action Group v. Hickel*:[30]

> [W]e cannot agree with the Government's argument that mere mention of the President's safety must be allowed to trump any First Amendment issue. While courts must listen with the utmost respect to the conclusions of those entrusted with responsibility for safeguarding the President, we must also assure ourselves that those conclusions rest upon solid facts and a realistic appraisal of the danger rather than vague fears extrapolated beyond any foreseeable threat."[31]

The defendants later filed a motion to dismiss,[32] but the Fourth Circuit not only denied it but also defendants' request for a writ of mandamus to dismiss them from the suit on grounds of immunity and mootness of the controversy.[33]

In *A Quaker Action Group v. Hickel*, the District of Columbia Court of Appeals affirmed the grant of a preliminary injunction to allow a Quaker group to demonstrate near the White House. The Quaker plaintiffs had asked the district court for declarative and injunctive relief against the Department of the Interior and the enforcement of its regulations and policy directives that impinged on their First Amendment rights to assemble peaceably and petition the President. Judge Bazelon wrote that no effort had been made "to justify the Government's argument beyond the flat words of the Secret Service director. First Amendment rights are too precious for sacrifice upon such an unsupported altar."[34]

In *Philadelphia Yearly Meeting of the Religious Society of Friends v. Tate*,[35] Philadelphia Yearly Meeting and others filed suit against the Philadelphia police department for its surveillance of public meetings of groups with political views deviating from those of the "establishment." In a June 2, 1970, nationwide television broadcast, officials publicly discussed dossiers that the police had maintained on groups such as the Friends Peace Committee. The district court dismissed the complaint and plaintiffs appealed.

The court of appeals[36] held that police surveillance and information-sharing with other law enforcement authorities did not violate plaintiffs' constitutional rights; however, it did hold that information-sharing with non-law-enforcement entities and disclosure of information about plaintiffs as subjects of surveillance stated a justiciable claim. The court reasoned that such police actions chilled plaintiffs' rights of free speech and association and could have a substantive adverse impact on their career opportunities and travel rights.

In *James v. Board of Education of Central District No. 1*,[37] Charles James, a Quaker high-school teacher, filed suit under the Reconstruction era civil rights statute, 42 U.S.C. § 1983, alleging a violation of his right to free speech by school officials who discharged him for wearing a black armband to class. Members of James's Elmira (New York) Friends Meeting had decided to observe November 14 and December 12, 1969, as Vietnam War moratorium days by wearing black armbands to express their religious aversion to war and regret over the loss of life. Testimony in district court from James and a fellow Quaker indicated that this peaceful statement of concern was a communal as well as an individual decision. The court noted that the "original roots of [Friends'] conscience were those of non-violence. This isn't the root of any other American religious group."[38] Officials suspended James for wearing the black armband to school on the first moratorium day, but then reinstated him the following day with instructions not to engage in further political activities. Nevertheless, on the next moratorium day, James again wore the black armband.

About a month later, school officials discharged him without a hearing. After James appealed the discharge, he was allowed an informal hearing but later filed suit in federal court. The district court dismissed the complaint, ruling that his claims were barred by the doctrine of res judicata because he received a decision in the informal hearing.

The court of appeals reversed,[39] holding that the Board of Education could not forbid a teacher's benign and noncoercive expression of political opinion. It held that a regulatory policy must be narrowly drawn to achieve the social interests that justify it, and school authorities must demonstrate a reasonable basis for concluding that a teacher's conduct threatens to impair a legitimate interest in regulating school issues. James's armband had neither disrupted classes nor engendered protests from students, parents, or teachers. The court quoted *Tinker v. Des Moines School District:* "an undifferentiated fear or apprehension of disturbance is not enough to trump free speech rights and added that "vigilant protection of constitutional freedoms is nowhere more vital than in the community of American schools."[40] On remand, the district court granted James's motion for summary judgment because defendants failed to show any actual disruption of schoolwork or discipline; it awarded him almost $21,000 in damages. Neither court reached the issue of freedom of religion, although the district court wrote that, on the basis of the record, it would be inclined to characterize James's acts as religious, were such a characterization necessary.[41]

Tinker v. Des Moines Independent Community School District[42] was a case that reached the Supreme Court and again involved Friends' silent witness of the peace testimony by wearing black armbands to protest the Vietnam War. The student-plaintiffs, John and Mary Beth Tinker, whose father was AFSC Peace Education Secretary, had attended Des Moines Valley Friends Meeting for years and there had often engaged in discussions of war and peace and the role of warfare in international relations.

John and Mary Beth were suspended when they wore black armbands to school on December 16–17, 1965, to protest the war and show support for a truce. Through their parents, they filed a civil rights suit under 42 U.S.C. § 1983, alleging a violation of their rights of free speech but not the right of free exercise of religion. The district court upheld the constitutionality of their suspensions as a reasonable action by school authorities to prevent a breach of school discipline. The Court of Appeals for the Eighth Circuit affirmed and the Supreme Court granted a writ of certiorari.

The Supreme Court heard oral argument on November 12, 1968. That day the Tinkers' attorney, Dan Johnston, explained that the purpose of wearing armbands was not only to mourn the Vietnam War dead but also to express support for a truce. Justice White pressed Johnston as to whether the armbands caused a disruption of the school's work. Allan Herrick, lawyer for the school district, stressed the reasonable discretion and judgment given school districts in matters of administration. Justice Marshall questioned him sharply about the school's fear of possible confrontations or violence caused by the armbands.

The Supreme Court opinion, authored by Justice Fortas, was handed down on February 24, 1969. It held that the Tinkers' conduct was protected by the First and Fourteenth Amendments. School officials had impermissibly punished them for silent and passive expressions of opinion, unaccompanied by any disorder or disturbance. They each wore a black cloth band on their sleeve to exhibit their disapproval of the Vietnam War and their advocacy of a truce.[43] The testimony of school authorities had indicated that fear of disruption did not motivate the armband prohibition but the demonstration itself. "In our system, state operated schools may not be enclaves of totalitarianism. . . . Students in school as well as out of school are 'persons' under our Constitution . . . possessed of fundamental rights which the State must respect, just as they themselves must respect their obligations to the State."[44]

The First Amendment's free exercise of religion clause, a direct protection for Friends' outspokenness against war, was not pled in *Tinker*, probably because the free speech theory was more likely to succeed. The Tinkers had a right to speak out against the Vietnam War because they believed war was wrong, a free speech theory, and as pacifist Friends, they had a right to free exercise of their religion, which holds that war is wrong. They would naturally want to pursue the legal theory with the better chance of success. The peace testimony no doubt was strongly influential on, if not the impetus for, their symbolic war protest and support for a truce, however, the free exercise one is a legal theory that has been shown to have less traction.

Tinker illustrates a powerful witness of Friends' pacifism, melding message and action—"so say and so do"—and shows that Quakers, at their best, not only negatively protest war but also support positive alternatives to it. During this long legal process threats were made against Mary Beth's life, so the Tinkers' action required courage as well as perseverance.

Quaker witness of the peace testimony in *Tinker* and similar cases bears out Edwin Bronner's characterization of Friends as those whose active witness of belief is an integral part of their religion.[45] In *Straut v. Calissi* Straut actively discouraged young men from enlisting in the armed forces fighting the Vietnam War and so ran afoul of the New Jersey sedition statute that provided that any person who publicly advocated that a person not enlist in the U.S. armed forces was guilty of a high misdemeanor and could be fined up to $2,000, imprisoned for up to seven years, or both. The issue raised in *Straut* was the constitutionality of this statute. The plaintiffs argued that the statute was vague and overbroad and had the immediate purpose and effect of intimidating them and others from exercising First Amendment rights. The federal court agreed, holding that the law's overly broad proscription of protected expression was unconstitutional.[46] It rested its decision on the statute's vagueness rather than on the abridgment of Straut's free exercise of religion.

Liberty of Conscience and Loyalty Oaths

From the time of George Fox, Quakers have believed that there are limits to the loyalty a person owes the state and have resisted its coercion toward any undue allegiances. As we have seen, Friends believe that God's law supersedes that of man's, an embodiment of the concept of liberty of conscience.

During the McCarthy era, Quaker teacher Barbara Elfbrandt[47] read and
listened to the news about Congressional investigations into "un-American
activities," and she remembered "there was something in me that just told me
that was all wrong."[48] She decided to challenge Arizona's loyalty oath, *Elfbrandt
v. Russell*,[49] because she could not in good conscience comply with the newly
enacted law's requirement that public school teachers sign such an oath. As a
peace and social justice activist, she had worked against the loyalty oath bill
before Arizona's governor signed it into law on March 30, 1961. The legislative
gloss in the act's preamble explained that a person could be prosecuted for
perjury or discharged if he or she "knowingly and willfully becomes or remains
a member of the communist party of the United States or its successors or any
of its subordinate organizations." Elfbrandt was uncertain about the meaning
of "its successors [or] . . . subordinate organizations," and she was unable to
obtain a hearing to determine the preamble's meaning. A recently hired teacher
of eighth-grade social studies, she was the only one in her school who refused
to sign the oath. Although this refusal did not cause her termination,[50] it did
cause the termination of her salary. Nevertheless, she continued to teach without
pay until the case was decided five years later. Elfbrandt believed that the social
control exemplified by such a mandatory oath was dangerous to a democratic
society, and its use, or abuse, could intimidate and inhibit others. An author
who profiled her case and those of others before the U.S. Supreme Court quotes
Blackstone's *Commentaries,* written by Sir William Blackstone, the eminent
eighteenth century jurist. The author, Peter Irons, draws a parallel between the
Arizona law and English kings who required oaths of fealty that strengthened
"the social tie by uniting it with that of religion."[51] Although the court noted
Elfbrandt's Quaker faith and its traditional objection to oath-taking, her broader
challenge, if successful, would carve out protections for more persons than
Friends. However, her recent convincement to the Society of Friends probably
did reinforce her resolve to challenge the law in spite of the inevitable financial
and emotional hardship it would cause.

On June 1, 1961, Elfbrandt filed suit in Pima County, calling into question
the constitutionality of the statute and requesting injunctive and declaratory
relief against its enforcement. When she lost in that court, she appealed directly
to the state supreme court, which also ruled against her. One justice in the
latter court noted that the oath only "minimally and incidentally conflict[ed]
with the First Amendment."[52] Coercion by the state in requiring such an oath
is powerful because a refusal can affect one's livelihood, as it did Elfbrandt's.

The U.S. Supreme Court, in an opinion written by Justice Douglas, declared
the Arizona statute unconstitutional because it subjected state employees to a
perjury prosecution and discharge from office for mere membership in a group
with no specific intent to further illegal aims. The Court noted that persons
of character and integrity might avoid becoming teachers if it involved such

risks, and it compromised intellectual political freedom. The *Elfbrandt* Court held that a law that impacts these "delicate, vulnerable, and supremely precious" First Amendment freedoms[53] must be narrowly drawn to define and punish only specific conduct constituting a clear and present danger to a substantial interest of the state. The Court's decision vindicated this Quaker's stand of conscience.

The Philadelphia Yearly Meeting aided in the Unitarian Church's challenge to loyalty oaths by filing an amicus curiae brief in *First Unitarian Church of Los Angeles v. County of Los Angeles*.[54] The church had refused to subscribe to an oath stating that it did not advocate the overthrow of the U.S. government. "A declaration of non-advocacy of the overthrow of the government by unlawful means may not appear to require narrow partisanship, but the history of the Society of Friends shows that too often the espousal of unpopular ideas is equated in the minds of many with subversion. A notable example is the reaction that was provoked by Friends' support for the abolition of slavery.[55] The Meeting's amicus brief argued for the plaintiff's liberty of conscience by quoting a fundamental tenet from *Faith and Practice*: "We affirm the supremacy of conscience. We recognize the privileges and obligations of citizenship: but we reject as false that philosophy which sets the state above the moral law and demands from the individual unquestioning obedience to every state command." The Meeting referred to the principle of liberty of conscience recurrent in Penn's Frames of Government for Pennsylvania and argued that California, by imposing this declaration of non-advocacy, required an accountability that no man owes his government.[56]

Although the Unitarian Church had argued that the mandatory oath abridged its right of free exercise of religion, the Supreme Court instead rested its ruling on a violation of due process. It held that the oath as a precondition for a tax exemption in California Constitution, Art. XX, § 19 improperly placed the burden of proof on the plaintiff-church.

Poverty, Race, and Immigration

Quaker plaintiffs who bring actions concerning poverty, race, and immigration patently witness the testimony of equality. The concern for others' difficulties stems from the belief that all persons are interconnected by God's light and by each other as members of the world community. The source of Quakers' concern for the poor derives from scripture, the testimony of equality, and Fox's own example. By facing issues of poverty, race, and immigration in the courts, Friends witness the principle of equal dignity and respect for all God's people.

This traditional concern caused Philadelphia Yearly Meeting, the Quaker Monthly Meetings of Atlantic City, Woodbury, and Shrewsbury, New Jersey Friends Council, and the Peace and Social Concerns Committee of Haddonfield

Meeting to join some seventy other community groups who sought to secure some measure of economic equality for New Jersey's needy. In *In re Petitions for Rulemaking*[57] they supported rule-making petitions to establish a standard of need for recipients of Aid to Families with Dependent Children and other New Jersey general assistance benefits. The New Jersey Department of Human Services had denied the petitions, but the lower court found that it was the Commissioner's statutory obligation to establish a needs calculation so that benefits would be sufficient to maintain a basic standard of living. The Supreme Court of New Jersey[58] agreed and held that the department must establish a level of benefits necessary to maintain public assistance recipients in a measure of dignity envisioned by the enabling law.

Lange v. United States[59] also sprang from Quakers' concern for the poor. On June 28, 1968, a group of Friends, including plaintiff Lois Lange, journeyed to Washington to join and support the Poor People's Campaign then in progress. Following Friends' tradition of asking those in power to rectify wrongs, the group had arranged to deliver to the Speaker of the House and President of the Senate a petition in support of legislation that would further the campaign's goals. The Friends held a meeting for worship on a Capitol terrace, and then, to show solidarity, moved toward a Southern Christian Leadership Conference group being arrested. Officials then also arrested Lange for unlawful assembly under a District of Columbia law[60] that prohibited crowding and obstructing free use of a public building. The district court suspended Lange's sentence and imposed a $10 fine, but Lange petitioned for allowance of appeal. When it was finally granted on May 28, 1969, nearly a year later, the court reversed the conviction. It did not address any constitutional issues, holding only that the government had failed to show sufficient proof of a violation of law.

The testimony of equality also impelled Friends to aid in suits involving civil rights for blacks. In *Hobson v. Wilson*,[61] the Washington Peace Center, affiliated with the Society, was one of several plaintiffs who alleged a violation of First Amendment free speech rights by defendants Federal Bureau of Investigation (FBI), the Metropolitan Police Department, and the District of Columbia. The plaintiffs alleged that defendants had infiltrated peace groups, destroyed equipment, and distributed leaflets intended to create dissent between plaintiffs and certain predominantly black civil rights groups. Plaintiffs alleged that the FBI had not only targeted antiwar activists who opposed the Vietnam War but also civil rights activists who criticized federal and local race relations policies. The District of Columbia Court of Appeals upheld the district court's award of damages to some plaintiffs as well as the individual and conspiratorial liability of the FBI defendants.[62]

United States v. Lansdowne Swim Club[63] is another instance of Quakers' witness of equality. A white Quaker, whose husband was black, charged that the club's rejection of several black and mixed-race families for membership was discriminatory.[64] The government then brought an action on their behalf to enforce Title II of the Civil Rights Act of 1964.[65] The district court held that the swim club, as a place of public accommodation, had violated the Civil Rights Act by engaging in a pattern and practice of discrimination against blacks. The Third Circuit affirmed and ordered that the swim club pay the costs of suit.[66]

Hirabayashi v. United States also involved racial discrimination, in this case, the treatment of Americans of Japanese ancestry during World War II. It was one of a series of cases involving Quaker Gordon Kiyoshi Hirabayashi; although these all involved the same set of facts, he was initially a defendant and, years later, a plaintiff. He was tried for violating a law[67] that made it a misdemeanor to knowingly disregard an army commander's restrictions on persons in a "military area." The commander had discretion to exclude any and all persons from such an area and to determine conditions under which certain ones might remain. Hirabayashi had disobeyed a curfew order on Japanese Americans in Seattle, and for this the court convicted and sentenced him to three months in prison. He appealed to the Ninth Circuit Court of Appeals, which heard argument on March 27, 1943, and then certified the case to the U.S. Supreme Court.

The Supreme Court[68] emphasized that 1942 was a time of crisis and war, and the statute's intent was to protect against sabotage of war materiel and utilities in an area thought to be vulnerable to Japanese air attack. The Court upheld Hirabayashi's conviction, but sidestepped a ruling on the law's constitutionality. It held, more narrowly, that the curfew order, as applied at the time, had a reasonable basis and was within bounds of congressional war powers. Nevertheless, Justice Murphy's concurring opinion rightly noted that "the war power, like the other great substantive powers of government, is subject to the limitations of the Constitution."[69] Several decades later, in 1983, Hirabayashi, with similarly convicted Japanese Americans Fred Korematsu and Minoru Yasui, filed a writ of error coram nobis under 28 U.S.C. § 1651(a) to vacate their 1942 convictions. The bases for the writ were government agencies' numerous acts of misconduct during and after the trial. Intelligence reports, available to the government at the time of trial, indicated that any security problems posed by Japanese Americans living on the West Coast did not warrant the issuance of military curfew and evacuation orders. Hirabayashi alleged that the government wrongly suppressed these reports and other exculpatory evidence that would have enabled the defendants to rebut government arguments.

As a Friend, Hirabayashi believed that each person should follow God's will according to his own conscience, but he had difficulty reconciling God's will with the curfew order, which discriminated against American citizens of Japanese ancestry. In his book on these Japanese curfew cases, Peter Irons writes that Hirabayashi expressed through his resistance "the separate commandments of the Christian and constitutional decalogues" and was an example of the challenger moralist.[70]

On February 10, 1986, the U.S. district court concluded that the War Department's withholding of the report was a fundamental error, which had caused Hirabayashi serious prejudice. Despite this, it refused to reverse the convictions because the curfew was merely a mild burden. On April 28, 1986, the court reconsidered, but again refused to reverse. On appeal, the Ninth Circuit finally did so, stating that a "United States citizen who is convicted of a crime on account of race is lastingly aggrieved."[71] A Quaker lawyer, Arthur Barnett, was on the Gordon Hirabayashi Defense Committee and worked on the later *Hirabayashi* cases that ended with a vindication of the Japanese-Americans' rights—a victory of justice.

Another civil rights case played out during most of the 1950s. In 1950, David Scull, a white Quaker, sued a restaurant for refusing to serve his black companions. Four years later, the Committee on Law Reform and Racial Activities of the Virginia General Assembly subpoenaed Scull to testify on his membership in interracial organizations. This committee, chaired by James Thomson, was established a few months after the Assembly adopted a resolution concerning the Supreme Court decision in *Brown v. Board of Education*, pledging to take all lawful measures to resist public school desegregation in Virginia. When Scull refused to answer the committee's questions, he was convicted of contempt, fined, and sentenced to jail. He appealed, but the Arlington County court ordered him to answer. Scull persisted in his refusal and was again convicted of contempt.

Scull then appealed to the U.S. Supreme Court. The Court in *Scull v. Virginia*[72] held that the purposes of the legislative inquiry were so unclear and conflicting that Scull could not understand the bases for the committee's questions or its justification for seeking his answers. In unanimously reversing Scull's conviction, the Court reasoned that if it were sustained, Scull would have been punished for a crime he could not with reasonable certainty know he was committing.[73]

Quaker tradition was evident in a suit filed by the American Civil Liberties Union, the AFSC, and five other civil rights and social justice groups as intervenors in *Seattle School District No. 1 of King County, Washington and ACLU v. State of Washington*.[74] By joining the plaintiff as an intervenor, the AFSC looked to fulfill one of its basic goals, described in the court's opinion as "the protection and promotion of the civil rights and liberties of all persons."[75] The suit challenged a section of Initiative 350 passed in response to the King County school system's attempt to achieve racial balance in its schools. To help ensure racial integration, the plaintiff school district and intervenors sought to strike down the part of the initiative that prohibited every major technique for achieving it.

The federal court held that the racially disproportionate impact of Initiative 350, its relevant historical background, the sequence of events leading to its adoption, and its departure from the norm of allowing autonomy to local schools all led to the legal conclusion that the initiative had a racially discriminatory intent or purpose. The court awarded a permanent injunction against the initiative's enforcement. On appeal, the Ninth Circuit[76] agreed and ruled that the initiative created legislative classifications impermissibly based on racial criteria, was unsupported by a compelling state interest and thus contravened the equal protection clause of the Fourteenth Amendment. The court also reversed the denial of attorneys' fees, ruling that plaintiffs were entitled to them as prevailing parties under 42 U.S.C. § 1988; it remanded to the district court for the computation of attorneys' fees under that statute. The Supreme Court in *Washington v. Seattle School District No. 1*[77] affirmed the unconstitutionality of the initiative in a 5–4 decision.

The Pendle Hill Consultation on the 1986 Immigration Reform and Control Act

In the fall of 1990, about 20 Friends gathered at Pendle Hill to discuss and consult for several days on the decision of the AFSC Board of Directors to refuse to comply with the part of the Immigration Reform and Control Act of 1986 (IRCA), which required employers to document the legal status of their employees. The AFSC Community Relations staff had initially suggested the IRCA consultation, a Quaker process of communal discernment, not unlike the clearness committee. The group gathered in a spirit of worship to search for divine guidance on its concern about IRCA compliance with the law. Such a process usually includes thrashing out, silent reflection, and consensus-building. Here it was intended to provide clarity on the issue by reexamining and clarifying AFSC's reasons for its initial refusal and by reaching consensus about its next step. In preparation for the consultation, participants and staff had carefully gathered documents for discussion during the sessions and had reserved time for "seasoning" and reflection afterward.

The AFSC also wanted to consider its response if a religious objection were not recognized and it had to match belief and action in another way. In its search for an effective method to persuade the government that IRCA was an inappropriate means to stop illegal immigration, Friends looked to the Society's history to learn how George Fox and other Quakers might have approached similar ethical dilemmas. As in Fox's time, Friends believe that the testing of certain laws is respectful of law and government.

The consultation brought into focus Friends' age-old conundrum: whether or how to disobey a law they felt in their religious consciences to be unequal and therefore unjust. The AFSC challenge emanated from its understanding that God calls us to love our neighbor *and* the stranger who live among us, and the covenant with God requires that we have only one law for both.[78] Friends have been consistent in their demands for the right to freedom of religion by trying to maintain the integrity of the social testimonies, that is, equality in the IRCA consultation and AFSC's subsequent suit.

Those participating in the Pendle Hill consultation were reminded of two differing, but equally beneficial, Quaker approaches to civil authority. One, the "prophet," holds a vision of the ideal and feels called to adhere to an absolute standard by witnessing against society's shortcomings. The other, the reconciler, is less of an absolutist who feels called to bring adversaries together. "[T]he social testimonies of Friends probably can never make an impact in the larger society without the complementary working out of those two. . . ."[79] These are not contradictory and might even be simultaneous; the overarching consideration of service is common to both, and both call for a certain courage. "It is risk-taking to 'reach to the witness' in the human spirit . . . which testifies for justice," and, in the immigration matter, speaks for those who, as refugees, not only suffer dislocation but also the injustice of denial of the fundamental right to employment."[80] To serve God in human society means to serve especially God's children who have the greatest need and the least power.[81] The consultation resulted in a clarification of the participants' thoughts and goals and a general confirmation that AFSC should continue its stand of conscience.[82] Although it acknowledged that Friends do not take adversarial actions such as lawsuits lightly, the AFSC Board decided that it could not comply with IRCA and would initiate a lawsuit to seek an exemption from its requirements on the basis of its right to free exercise of religion. Quakers met together to communally discern whether to file suit to witness equality of treatment for its employees. This is an example of Friends being led to bring court actions, thereby temporarily suspending harmony in order to witness other testimonies, in this case, equality. AFSC was "called to confront . . . injustice by forthright, public, principled refusal to comply with the law."[83]

The AFSC, and seven individual plaintiffs, did file an action against U.S. Attorney General Thornburgh.[84] In *American Friends Service Committee v. Thornburgh*,[85] the AFSC alleged that certain requirements of the IRCA[86] violated its First Amendment right of free exercise of religion by criminalizing the lack of verification of employees' immigration status and the knowing employment of aliens.[87] It sought injunctive and declarative relief that certain IRCA requirements were in violation of their sincerely held and profound religious beliefs, that is, that all persons are equally children of God with an obligation to care for each other as members of the human community. The AFSC argued that compliance with certain sections of the law required its active participation in document examining, verifying, and attesting. This indirect immigration control resulted in excluding undocumented immigrants from employment and thereby inflicting hunger and other deprivations on them. The AFSC argued that IRCA improperly deputized it and other employers as border guards.[88] Although it acknowledged a society's right to regulate immigration and secure its borders, AFSC feared that employers could exploit and oppress undocumented workers by low wages and unsafe and unhealthy working conditions. It rejected the government's implication that undocumented immigrants were a threat to national security or to the jobs of U.S. citizens. Racial or ethnic exclusion by its nature produces inequality and the label of illegality given undocumented workers legitimizes their marginalization. Finally, the AFSC argued that while it did not support undocumented immigration, it did not believe that employer sanctions under IRCA would cause it to cease.

The AFSC argued that the denial of employment to a class of immigrants would go against the committee's fundamental religious principles and practices. Stephen G. Cary, then-chairman of its board, stated that the IRCA provisions contravened the very life dynamic of AFSC, its commitment to the dignity of life, and equality of all before God. These principles were the source for AFSC work for Mexican workers' rights in Texas, against the exclusion of Asians in the 1920s, and against the exclusionary treatment and forced evacuation of Japanese Americans in the 1940s.

The government defendants in *Thornburgh* countered that judicial review of immigration matters was restricted and such statutes could be overturned only if they were wholly irrational. The court concurred and dismissed the case, holding as a matter of law that plaintiffs' free exercise rights, even if substantially impacted, could not overcome the even stronger governmental interest in controlling immigration. As in all summary proceedings, this case was not thoroughly examined. And indeed, the AFSC reply brief argued this, that there should be a trial on the merits so that all issues could be carefully aired. For instance, the court's summary ruling foreclosed AFSC's presentation of factual evidence in support of its claim that employment sanctions were not vital to border control. However, the court stated that the government's overriding interest in immigration control did not require the development of a factual record on employer sanctions, and on August 2, 1991, the Ninth Circuit upheld dismissal of the case.[89]

The AFSC persevered in a petition for rehearing, requesting the court to reexamine *Employment Division v. Smith*[90] to distinguish between the free exercise rights of individuals and those of religious institutions such as AFSC. Neither did *Smith* answer whether an institution was absolutely subject to general laws *requiring affirmative acts* that violated central religious tenets. The Ninth Circuit denied AFSC's petition on the basis of its previous interpretation of *Smith*. The AFSC chose not to petition the Supreme Court for a writ of certiorari, but did support enactment of the Religious Freedom Restoration Act of 1993 (RFRA). Once more, the right to free exercise of religion was trumped by government regulation. But Friends continue undaunted as they have for centuries.

Could the AFSC have prevailed in its suit had it been brought *after* RFRA's enactment? Had the district court not made a summary ruling and had instead allowed a full airing of the facts, it might have concluded that employer sanctions under IRCA ran afoul of RFRA for two reasons. One, the more case-specific factor, is the section of the act that punishes employers who do not comply with the examination, verification, and attestation requirements. Two, IRCA required the AFSC to perform *affirmative acts* that directly contravened its religious beliefs. As the AFSC stated in a 1989 motion, sanctions were punitive actions taken against an employer for refusing to discriminate against its employees on the basis of legal status, anathema to a Friends institution. The Congress found that neutral laws may burden religious exercise as surely as those *intended* to interfere with it. RFRA was intended to restore religious freedom through the compelling interest test of *Sherbert v. Verner*,[91] and *Wisconsin v. Yoder*,[92] guarantee the applicability of RFRA to all federal laws, statutory or otherwise, whether adopted before or after its 1993 enactment, and provide a claim or defense to those whose religious exercise is burdened. Under the act, plaintiffs must prove by a preponderance of the evidence that their free exercise has been substantially burdened. If they do this, the government must then show that such burden on the plaintiff is in furtherance of a compelling government interest *and* is the *least restrictive* means to further it.

A Digression on Summary Judgment Sparked by *Thornburgh*

The *Thornburgh* case is but one example of the proliferation of decisions reached over the last several decades through truncated court proceedings such as summary judgments. This kind of court judgment cannot reach the "whole truth" because there is no testimony of witnesses and therefore no opportunity for the fact-finder to assess the demeanor and veracity of those with knowledge of the facts and circumstances surrounding the dispute. When the disposition of a case hinges on determinations of fact, credibility of witnesses, motive, state of mind, or intent, anything less than a full hearing impairs the search for truth and thereby undermines justice. A witness is to swear or affirm that he or she will tell the "whole truth." Should parties and the public expect less from court proceedings? Except in rare circumstances, *all* relevant facts should be before the judge or jury for careful and thoughtful consideration and disposition. For instance, before making its ruling in *Thornburgh*, the court should have allowed a thorough examination of RFRA's legislative history and any alternative proposals for a "least restrictive means" of furthering the government's interest.

Judge Patricia Wald added her voice to the few judges and legal scholars who complain of the overuse of summary proceedings. In a Federal Practice and Procedure Symposium honoring Professor Charles Alan Wright,[93] she declared that although the original purpose of Rule 56[94] was only to weed out frivolous and sham claims, *federal civil jurisprudence is now largely the product of summary judgments* (emphasis added).[95] This federal rule of civil procedure specifies that summary judgment is to be used only when there are no genuine issues of material fact in dispute that would make a trial the proper vehicle for decision of those issues. These judgments have assumed an increasingly larger role in the disposition of cases than the rule's plain language allows, and Judge Wald says that this state of affairs has crept up on us. She strongly believes that Rule 56 should be used with great caution, as it was originally, and not as a stealth weapon for clearing court dockets. She cites approvingly Charles Alan Wright's considered opinion that Rule 56 jurisprudence has undermined the rule itself. Justice Robert Jackson believed that summary judgments were treacherous for deciding issues of far-flung import because they lack the thoroughness that ought to precede judgments; indeed it is the purpose of the judicial process to provide such judgments.[96] Judge Wald holds the legal realist's view that "the law should percolate upwards from the terra firma of actual events, rather than dropping down like gentle rain from the hornbook and precedents of appellate courts."[97] Instead of cryptic and unprobed affidavits, decisions should be based on the maximum available knowledge of relevant real-world facts because without this completeness, courts may leave critical issues unaddressed and unexplored. Moreover, summary judgments do not invariably save court resources because they are often appealed. This is often because judges give such judgments short shrift. Fact-specific issues are best seen within the totality of the particular circumstances and should be given a full trial. The measured and proper application of Rule 56 is vital because otherwise the outcome of the case could be determined prematurely, incompletely, or incorrectly. Although some courts have urged sparing use of Rule 56, many continue to routinely overdispose of cases by summary judgment, thereby depriving parties of their "day in court."

Although section (c) of Rule 56 is clearly ameliorative in that it requires all facts and inferences in submitted documents to be viewed in the light most favorable to the party opposing the motion, all judges do not diligently follow this requirement. More than one jurist has slipped into fact-finding mode during the pretrial phase of a case despite the cautionary words of the Supreme Court: "the judge's function *is not himself to weigh the evidence* and determine the truth of the matter but only to determine whether there is a genuine issue for trial"[98] (emphasis added).

If the real aim of our judicial system is justice through the search for truth, as it purports to be, then the facts and surrounding circumstances of the case must be completely examined. Margaret Fell's reference to the Light to "lay . . . open . . . naked and bare" is also necessary to reach the "truth" in court proceedings, but this takes judges' time and effort. The judiciary should closely adhere to the intent of Rule 56 by treating it as the exception it was originally meant to be. Courts are more likely to reach the truth through a thorough examination of all germane facts and legal theories and therefore are more apt to reach justice.

Refusal to Be Inducted into the Armed Forces

Friends have steadfastly held to the testimony of peace since they first declared 350 years ago that they were against all wars and "fightings," and numerous Advices have often reminded them of this. A 1948 Friends Advice on Conscription and War stated the Quaker philosophy on service in the armed forces: Friends were advised to adhere faithfully to the testimony against all wars and fighting, and, specifically, not to unite in any way with warlike measures such as the Selective Training and Service Act of 1940 or Universal Military Training and Service Act, the name given the 1948 amended version of the Selective Service Act. It also confirmed civil disobedience under "Divine Compulsion" as an honorable testimony in keeping with Friends' history and practice. This Advice against war comes as close as the Society does in prescribing or proscribing conduct to its members. Friends' pacifism stems not only from the commandment not to kill, but also from Friends' belief that there is that of God in every human being so to kill is to kill the divine spirit or inner light that resides in every person.

This pacifism, one of the Society's most salient attributes, is steadfastly practiced by virtually all its members even in the face of punishment by the state. During the early Nuremburg trials in 1946, Sir Hartley Shawcross observed that there comes a point when a man must refuse to answer to his leader if he is also to answer to his conscience. Quakers, who have often refused leaders' commands to bear arms, have understood this for centuries. If they must choose between leaders, they choose God, not any human authority.

Friends' peace testimony has overridden the early prohibition and traditional disapproval of going to law. As the following cases demonstrate, Friends have been willing to forego harmony to witness the peace testimony in a larger, more global, sense—to publicly testify that war is wrong by suing, or defending, in the courts.

In a series of six early-twentieth-century cases known as the *Selective Draft Law Cases*,[99] the Supreme Court construed the Act of May 18, 1917,[100] legislation intended to raise an army by a selective draft of all male citizens between ages 21 and 30. The law did exempt from combatant service "a member of any well-recognized religious sect or organization at present organized and existing and whose existing creeds or principles forbid its members to participate in war in any form and whose religious convictions are against war or participation therein, . . ." but did not exempt him from noncombatant service in the military.

Friends' Testimony on Conscientious Objection
in Congressional Hearings

Friends pressed for an exemption from noncombatant service in the military before the United States entered World War II. On January 10, 1940, representatives of the traditional "peace churches"—the Religious Society of Friends, Church of the Brethren, and Mennonite Church—wrote President Roosevelt to express their hope that the United States would cooperate with other neutral nations in offering mediation and other peace-promoting techniques for the earliest possible establishment of peace. Signed by Rufus Jones and Walter Woodward on behalf of Friends, the letter also urged that, in lieu of noncombatant service in the military, conscientious objectors be given an opportunity to perform constructive civilian humanitarian service in the United States or abroad such as the relief and service work Friends had recently performed in Spain, China, Paraguay, Brazil, and hoped to perform soon in Poland. In the letter, the peace churches asked for an opportunity to recommend concrete proposals and procedures for handling conscientious objectors in order to avoid a repetition of the confusion, distress, and delay that attended the pacifism issue in World War I. This suggestion must have had an impact because the groups were invited to propose ideas for improvements to the conscientious objector provisions of the Selective Training and Service Act of 1940. Friends testified before the House and Senate Committees on Military Affairs.

In July 1940 Harold Evans of Philadelphia testified before the Senate committee[101] by explaining Friends' conscientious objection to war. He stated that Quakers have maintained their testimony against war and for freedom of conscience and religious liberty because they believe that no lasting good can be accomplished by war and violence but only by service and an appeal to the divine spark in every person. In asking that Friends' rights of conscience be preserved, Evans repeated the story of Fox, Penn, and Penn's sword.

Evans suggested that the true defense of America's cherished principles might be found in new avenues of constructive public service in the United States and abroad, and to that end, specifically proposed that the law provide for a civilian rather than a military authority for handling conscientious objectors. He also suggested the creation of a special register for them, a complete exemption for those with sincere conscientious scruples against all forms of compulsory service—combatant and noncombatant—and equal treatment for conscientious objectors of all denominations whether or not they were Friends or members of peace churches.

Evans completed his testimony by sharing portions of Friends' Richmond (Indiana) Resolution of July 4, 1940, drafted within days of the Senate Hearing: ". . . we are opposed to conscription in war and compulsory military training in time of peace . . . as a radical departure from American principles of freedom and democracy, as an unwarranted infringement of individual liberty, and as an unnecessary and dangerous step toward the regimentation of a free people." The resolution, which accurately reflected all American Friends' thoughts on war, showed concern not only for Friends' testimonies but also for the nation's good.

At the Senate hearing, another Quaker, Paul Comley French, read a minute adopted by the Friends General Conference shortly after the Richmond meeting.

French summarized Friends' views on war for Senator Minton by stating that Quakers were not unwilling to die for America, but they would not kill for any reason.

Witness of the Peace Testimony

The Vietnam War provided fertile ground for testing Quakers' peace testimony. Although *United States v. Flower*[102] was a case that involved a Quaker defendant, it sprang from John Flower's witness of the peace testimony in his distribution of pamphlets about a town meeting to discuss the war. The court's opinion enables the reader to draw a thought-provoking parallel between military and civilian life in U.S. society and strikingly shows the distinctions between different mind-sets inherent in the conduct of war and peace.

John Thomas Flower, AFSC Peace Education Secretary for Texas, Oklahoma, and Arkansas, had gone inside one of the entrances to the Fort Sam Houston military base in San Antonio to distribute leaflets announcing a town meeting on the Vietnam War at Trinity University in that city. The district court rejected as immaterial Flower's offers of proof regarding public access to Fort Sam Houston. However, Judge Simpson's later dissent noted that the discussion of the military's right to control was academic and uninstructive when such control had been abandoned. Fort Sam Houston was a completely open post with 31 gates through which the public could enter, and because it was a public street, Judge Simpson thought there should be no prior restraint on Flower's exercise of his right to distribute leaflets.[103]

For his action, Flowers was arrested, tried, and convicted of unauthorized entry upon a military reservation. He appealed the conviction, but the appellate court affirmed, holding that a commanding officer's exclusion of civilians did not violate due process because a military base is not dedicated to general use by the public at large. It reasoned that the military, with its own set of discrete rules and powers, occupies a different sphere from civilian society. Upon entering a military reservation, individual citizens must necessarily surrender certain rights so that military discipline and security can remain inviolate. The court stated that by its very nature, function, and purpose, a military reservation is distinguishable from a normal public community and its adjuncts.

To this, many Quakers might say "Indeed!" Friends' refusal to participate in war actively or passively encompasses the unspoken recognition that the military is a part of society beyond the normality of our lives. Because the military is not part of the "normal public community and its adjuncts," it has its own special rules and regulations, and, therefore, those who enter its domain must relinquish certain rights and privileges enjoyed elsewhere in society.

Quakers might argue that this very dichotomy between the military and the normal public community elucidates the futility and wrongness of war and the military operations that fuel and support it. Friends believe that each person who has the light of God within has the capacity to deal with conflict in ways other than by violence and war. Most also realize that the military's training, mentality, and environment hamper and deter any consideration of the possibilities and promise of peacemaking. The military requires of its member-soldiers a focused demonization of the enemy accompanied by action designed to accomplish its elimination. That focus would seem to thrive best isolated from the normal public community. When considered in isolation, a demonized adversary becomes an easier target for elimination because the soldier can be persuaded that, in killing the enemy, he is eliminating evil. In the normal community, there is exposure to other points of view, commonalities, and connections, which can ameliorate differences and produce alternative solutions.

Cases involving Quaker antiwar activism also tested and advanced First Amendment freedom of speech, albeit in a civilian setting. In *Green v. F.C.C.*,[104] petitioner Green, Peace Committee Chair of Baltimore Yearly Meeting, sought appellate review of a Federal Communications Commission (FCC) ruling that refused him air time to broadcast messages opposing military service after the airing of military recruiting announcements.

The FCC ruled that the "fairness doctrine" requiring broadcast licensees to afford reasonable opportunity to present opposing viewpoints on controversial issues of public importance was not triggered because military recruiting was neither controversial nor an issue of public importance, and therefore airing a message against it was not required. Of course, Quakers believe that military recruiting should be controversial and is indeed an issue of public importance.

In upholding the FCC decision, the court of appeals ruled that, whereas the goal of the fairness doctrine was to promote informed public decision-making, it did not require identical treatment of opposing views. Moreover, the court thought that a ruling to the contrary would be overly burdensome for broadcast media. The "mechanics of achieving fairness . . . is within the discretion of each licensee, acting in good faith. . . ."[105]

Friends' witness of the peace testimony may take a more positive form than the refusal to bear arms; it can also involve helping those caught in the midst of war's horrors. The Quaker plaintiff in *Welch v. Shultz*,[106] filed suit for declaratory and injunctive relief against the Treasury Department's Office of Foreign Assets Control for denying his application to send $2,000 to the Canadian Friends Service Committee for medical supplies to benefit civilians in North and South Vietnam. The department's interpretation of Trading with the Enemy Act[106] prohibited the distribution of money or commodities to a nation in conflict with the United States when there was no assurance that it would be used for nonmilitary purposes. However, on advice of the State Department, it had allowed 10 such donations in 1966. Shortly thereafter, however, the department reinstated the total prohibition policy, in effect at the time of *Welch*. After the district court granted summary judgment against Welch, he appealed. The signing of the January 27, 1973, Vietnam peace agreement occurred before the *Welch* appeal was heard, so the controversy became moot. Although the appellate court reserved its jurisdiction over the case, it remanded it to the court below for any necessary determination.

The arrest of Quakers for participating in a peaceful prayer vigil near the White House was the subject of a 1977 appeal in *Tatum v. Morton*.[107] The plaintiffs sought damages of almost $1 million against police, federal officials, and the District of Columbia. The purpose of the vigil, sponsored by Albany (New York) Friends Meeting, was to hold President Nixon in the light with the hope that he might see fit to change U.S. policy in Vietnam. It was also meant to show Friends' strong heritage of pacifism and to correct any misimpression that Nixon's war policy was somehow related to his Quaker background. The district court awarded damages to Friends, but limited the amount because the demonstration was voluntary and many had, on principle, chosen to be jailed rather than post bond. The Quakers appealed.

The Court of Appeals for the District of Columbia disagreed that damages should be limited simply because Friends had demonstrated voluntarily. It emphasized that vindication of the right to demonstrate—a significant strand of First Amendment freedoms—was important, and taking a reasonably spacious approach to a fair compensatory award for its curtailment was in the public interest.[109] The demonstrators' willingness to endure further confinement for the sake of principle did not negate the substantiality of the injuries already suffered.

One might reasonably question the Quakers' persistence in demanding such a large damage award, but the appellate court answered this by reasoning that the Quakers' vindication of First Amendment rights deserved more than token acknowledgment. A significant damage award might also deter further governmental interference with the right and cause others to notice. The Quakers wanted the publicity of the arrest to "lay . . . open . . . naked and bare" the injustice and destruction of war. The divine law against killing[110] may indeed transcend various religious boundaries. However, killing done by a member of an armed force at the behest of the state has been interpreted to fall outside this proscription, perhaps because the justifications for war are as legion as the citizenry's reasons for accepting them. Capital punishment, anathema to Friends, is another example of killing legitimized by the state. "A [state] that usurps God's office as judge vitiates its own authority. . . . Human beings cannot play judge . . . without suffering profound corruption in their identities as human beings."[111]

Philadelphia Yearly Meeting was among many—including Lord Jenkins of Putney of the British House of Lords—who filed amici curiae briefs in support of plaintiffs in *Greenham Women against Cruise Missiles v. Reagan*,[112] a federal action involving another war-related issue. Plaintiffs, including two U.S. Congressmen, challenged the decision of the President and the Secretaries of Defense, Air Force and Army to deploy cruise missiles. The court dismissed the complaint, holding that it could not grant relief in a case involving a nonjusticiable political question.

Quakers' refusal to participate even in preparatory actions for war was an issue presented in *Dickinson v. Bell*.[113] Quaker Katherine Dickinson and two other women students challenged regulations authorized by Title IV of the Higher Education Act of 1965[114] and §1113 of the Department of Defense Authorization Act of 1983.[115] These provided that any student, required to do so, and who failed to register with the Selective Service, would be ineligible for federal financial aid for college. Katherine and coplaintiffs were denied financial aid after they refused to sign the college's statement of registration compliance. The women argued that forcing them to sign the statement certifying that they had either registered with the Selective Service or that they were not required to do so improperly required their cooperation in the enforcement of laws they believed were morally wrong. The suit alleged violations of the rights of free speech and equal protection, but not a violation of the right to free exercise of religion.

Judge Gerhard Gesell noted that Friends' deeply felt opposition to war in any form was well established and that Katherine had decided not to comply only after consulting other members of her faith.[116] The court reluctantly dismissed the complaint, holding that plaintiffs' First Amendment rights had not been violated because the form's language did not explicitly require them to endorse war or Selective Service registration, and in fact they were free to express their views in the form's margin. The plaintiffs who had not violated any law and were not required to register would have been entitled to federal financial aid except for their failure to complete the requisite form. The judge chided both the Secretary and the colleges:

> While the Secretary's [of Education] position in this dispute can be legally justified, the rigidity with which the Secretary and the educational institutions involved have applied the regulations does not reflect favorably upon them. . . . [T]he Secretary has demonstrated no willingness to offer . . . any alternative for establishing the obvious fact that [plaintiffs] are women and thus not subject to Selective Service registration requirements. Nor have the educational institutions in which plaintiffs are enrolled apparently interceded

on their behalf to seek a common-sense solution to the conflict
between the government's bureaucratic requirements and plaintiffs'
reasoned beliefs.[117]

Mediation could likely have achieved that common sense solution. The fact that
the students were women and thus not subject to Selective Service registration
should have made it relatively easy to craft a common-sense solution, but the
stringency common to government bureaucrats and bureaucracies may have
made this virtually impossible.

Refusal to Be Inducted into the Armed Forces and *United States v. Seeger*

The congressional testimony of Evans and French apparently influenced Congress
to broaden the exemption from military service in the Selective Training and
Service Act of 1940 to extend to "any person who, by reason of religious
training and belief was conscientiously opposed to participation in war in any
form, . . ."[118] not just those eligible by virtue of their membership in a historic
peace church. In *United States v. Seeger*, the Supreme Court construed the
language of this later amended law.

   In 1948 the 1940 law was amended to define "religious training and belief"
as "an individual's belief in a relation to a Supreme Being involving duties
superior to those arising from any human relation," § 6 (j) of the Universal
Military Training and Service Act. The Supreme Court in *United States v.
Seeger*[119] examined this provision to decide whether "Supreme Being" meant
the orthodox, or a somewhat broader, concept of God. In each of the cases
consolidated for argument and decision in *Seeger*, the defendants, including
Seeger who was raised a Catholic, had argued that their rights under the First
Amendment's establishment and free exercise clauses had been violated by the
act, but the court nevertheless convicted them for refusing induction into the
armed forces.

   When Daniel Seeger first registered for the draft in 1953, he was an
undergraduate at New York's Queens College in a traditional liberal arts course
of study. He read the primary works of Gandhi, Thoreau, Tolstoy, and through
them, came to understand and appreciate the philosophical underpinnings of
pacifism. In addition to academics, he was active as head of the student court
and editor of the college newspaper.

   Seeger's first draft classification was 1A, then 2S, the latter a student
exemption he retained until 1957. During these years, his status was reconfirmed
quarterly. Each time he heard from the draft board, his thoughts on war and the
draft were stimulated, and his views gradually became clarified and crystallized.

In 1957 he was ordered to report for a preinduction physical exam. Seeger did so but wrote a letter to the draft board outlining his conscientious scruples against going to war. The army sent him a form for conscientious objectors that included a question about his belief in a "Supreme Being." Seeger had not previously considered that a refusal to kill was inextricably connected to a belief in God or a Supreme Being, and he was slightly surprised to discover that it was considered in that light. He returned the form with an essay explaining that because of his religious belief, he was conscientiously opposed to participation in war in any form. He straightforwardly acknowledged that he could not definitively answer whether he believed in a Supreme Being because such existence could be neither proved nor disproved, however he professed a devotion to goodness and virtue. He concluded that from a practical standpoint, war was futile and self-defeating and from the more important moral view, it was unethical. Resorting to the immoral means of war did not preserve or vindicate moral values but instead became collaborative in destroying moral life among people.

The draft board then reclassified him 1A and ordered him to appear for a second physical. Although Seeger's views on war did not initially derive from Friends, both were attuned to one another. After he received his new classification, a friend advised him to contact the Quakers. He did so, and thus began a long spiritual and professional association. First, Seeger went to the AFSC New York office for draft counseling where executive secretary Robert Gilmore realized that his case might be an appropriate vehicle through which to challenge the Selective Service Act.

In 1960 and 1961, the AFSC began to set the stage for Seeger's legal defense by forming a committee to manage the case through the Army's administrative appeals process. The Rights of Conscience Fund, administered by the AFSC, contributed money for the suit, as did many individuals; however, the primary sponsor and organizer was the Central Committee for Conscientious Objectors in Philadelphia. Although lawyers contributed many pro bono hours in preparing and prosecuting the case, funds were nevertheless necessary to pay other trial-related costs.

The lapse of time from Seeger's first draft board hearing to the Supreme Court decision was approximately eight years. During that period, he worked as AFSC College Secretary in New York and began to attend Morningside Heights Friends Meeting where he felt uplifted by the meeting's support.

During his administrative appeal, a hearing officer decided that Seeger should not be drafted. However, that decision was overturned by General Hershey and President Kennedy, who did not consider him a bona fide conscientious objector. Soon thereafter, he received an induction notice. At the site, he announced his intention not to formalize induction by stepping forward and raising his right hand. Two years passed without a hint of government prosecution. Despite the uncertainty of his situation, he had absolute confidence in his draft counselors and his attorney Kenneth Greenawalt whom he described as a warm, yet "formal and majestic" man.[120]

At last, the federal trial began. U.S. Attorney Robert Morgenthau prosecuted the case for the government, and Greenawalt, of the New York firm Davies, Hardy, and Schenk, defended Seeger. The court convicted and sentenced him to a year and a day in prison; he then appealed to the Court of Appeals for the Second Circuit. On January 20, 1964, the Second Circuit reversed Seeger's conviction, stating that the district court had denied his claim for an exemption solely because it was not based on belief in a Supreme Being. The court reasoned that the Supreme Being requirement, which distinguished between internally-derived and externally-compelled beliefs, was an impermissible classification under the Fifth Amendment's due process clause. "We here respect the right of Daniel Seeger to believe what he will, largely because of the connection that every individual is a child of God; and that man created in the image of his Maker is surrounded for that reason with human dignity."[121] The decision was front-page news in the next morning's *New York Times*, and Seeger subsequently became something of a celebrity.

The government appealed the Second Circuit's reversal of his conviction to the Supreme Court. Dressed in the traditional regalia of the U.S. Solicitor-General, Archibald Cox, the father-in-law of Seeger's AFSC colleague, argued the case for the United States. Several groups, including the Unitarian and Methodist churches and Ethics Society, filed amicus curiae briefs supporting Seeger. He and his parents attended the oral argument and observed the Court's rigorous questioning of counsel.

In its opinion, authored by Justice Clark, the Court traced the history of exemptions for conscientious objectors. Until the American Civil War, conscription was largely a matter regulated by the states, which often recognized the moral dilemma posed for persons of religious faiths who conscientiously objected to a call to arms.[122] However, after the Federal Conscription Act of 1863, the federal government entirely occupied the field. The Draft Act of 1864[123] exempted conscientious objectors who were members of groups religiously opposed to bearing arms, and the Confederacy, too, exempted members of certain pacifist religious groups. The Draft Act of 1917[124] required the induction of conscientious objectors but allowed them to perform noncombatant service within the military. Friends and others had contributed suggestions for further broadening the conscientious objector exemption during House and Senate hearings on the bill that became the Selective Training and Service Act of 1940. The 1948 version of the act's conscientious objector provision excluded a personal moral code or political, sociological, or philosophical grounds from eligibility for the exemption.

After its analysis of legislative history, the Court's task was to construe the meaning of "Supreme Being," whether it meant the orthodox God or a "power, being, or faith to which all else is subordinate or upon which all is ultimately dependent." The Court chose the latter and devised a new standard of eligibility: a "sincere and meaningful belief which occupies in the life of its possessor a place parallel to that filled by the God of those admittedly qualifying for the exemption. . . ."[125] Seeger, whose religious training and belief did not *specifically* oppose participation in war, nevertheless, could qualify for an exemption under this definition. The Court noted that had Seeger's draft board applied such a test, it would have granted an exemption because it was clear that "the beliefs which prompted his objection [to military service] occupy the same place in his life as the belief in a traditional deity holds in the lives of his friends, the Quakers."[126] After the case ended, Seeger joined the Religious Society of Friends and became like "his friends, the Quakers. Justice Douglas's comparison of Seeger's beliefs to those of Buddhists actually ignited his active interest in Buddhist philosophy.

Seeger was elated at the outcome of the case and later was especially gratified to know that the precedent it set helped other young men during the Vietnam War era. Seeger was not ordered to perform alternative service, perhaps because by the time of the decision, he was no longer of draft age. Friends' interest in *Seeger* was primarily as a vehicle for witness of the peace testimony. The AFSC no doubt knew that a victory in the case would widen the circle of conscientious objectors who could legally exercise their rights of conscientious refusal to fight and kill.

Three years after *Seeger*, the Ninth Circuit Court of Appeals in *Briggs v. United States*,[127] reversed Briggs's conviction and three-year prison sentence for refusal to be inducted by taking the symbolic forward step, although its reasoning seems a bit strained. The court held that the military's denial of a physical examination of Briggs at the induction site was prejudicial because, had there been such an examination, he might have been rejected or reclassified, thus obviating his need to refuse. Briggs had noted on his conscientious objector form that Friends had been a powerful influence on his thought.

In the same year, the Second Circuit Court of Appeals heard *Purvis v. United States*[128] and decided similarly. Jeffrey Purvis's father, a Quaker, had strongly influenced his son's religious thinking. Purvis attended Quaker meeting and considered himself to be a conscientious objector. Although the FBI reported that his conscientious objection was sincerely held, Purvis was classified 1-A-O, exempting him from combatant, but not noncombatant, service.

The issues in *Purvis* were whether his Department of Justice hearing had been fair and whether there was sufficient basis in fact for his classification.[129] The court reversed Purvis's conviction, citing as precedents *United States v. Nugent*[130] and *Gonzalez v. United States*.[131] *Nugent* and *Gonzales* stood for the proposition that the conscientious objector's right to file a statement before an appeal board meant a meaningful statement based on all facts in the file and with opportunity to have notice of others' recommendations and arguments so that he would have a fair chance to counter them. However, Purvis had not been notified that he had been quoted incorrectly on crucial points, and so had no opportunity to correct the misinformation. In addition, because Purvis's conscientious objection was considered sincere, his file should have included a statement that the peace testimony was critical to his Quaker faith.

The defendant in *United States v. Peebles*, whose Quaker roots were several generations old, had refused induction; nevertheless, the district court convicted Peebles and sentenced him to three years in prison. The president of Earlham College and the clerk of Western Yearly Meeting had written on Peebles's behalf to the draft board and to General Hershey, the national director of the Selective Service System, who then requested an adjustment of Peebles's classification. The Court of Appeals for the Seventh Circuit reversed his conviction[132] because the biased attitude of draft board members shown by their written comments had probably prejudiced and influenced the Appeal Board's adverse decision, thereby denying Peebles's right of procedural due process.[133]

Refusal to Register for the Draft

Although refusal to be inducted into the armed forces, to fight, and refusal to register for the draft, to take a step in preparation for war, both stem from Friends' peace testimony, the courts have generally treated the failure to register more strictly than an unwillingness to fight because of conscientious scruples against war. The Quakers in the following cases believed that no step should be taken toward war, not even that of registering as a conscientious objector.

Arle Brooks, an AFSC staff member, refused to register and was tried in federal district court in Philadelphia in January 1941. Brooks's counsel, Walter C. Longstreth, and the presiding judge were both Quakers. As a Friend, the judge must have understood, and perhaps empathized with, Brooks's pacifist stand of conscience. Nevertheless, the judge explained, "I have got to obey the law. . . . you, having defied the law, are subject to penalty. . . . If you were my son, I could not feel differently about it."[134]

United States v. Henderson[135] was a consolidation of four appeals from convictions for refusal to register. Three of the four defendants were Quakers, and each appealed his conviction, 90-day sentence, and $100 fine. They had explained to the draft boards their belief that war was never justified and that registration in aid of war was wrong; nevertheless, they expressed a willingness to accept the consequences of disobedience. In a letter to President Truman, defendant Frantz explained his membership in the Society of Friends and his opposition to war and to any step taken in anticipation of war. He wrote that to register would implicitly recognize the government's right to conscript for war, which was wrong because war was wrong.[136] The court affirmed the defendants' conviction despite their contention that the Selective Service Act was unconstitutional as applied to pacifists.

Vail Palmer was convicted after he had refused to complete Selective Service forms and had instead written letters explaining his refusal to register. In affirming Palmer's conviction in *United States v. Palmer*,[137] the Third Circuit reasoned that, at some point, a sympathetic society can say that a man who wants recognition for his religious belief must take the required steps to accomplish that.[138] The dissent suggested that the majority's decision exalted form over substance because the regulations provided that all written information in a conscientious objector's file must be considered whereas Palmer's letters had been ignored.

In *United States v. Baechler*,[139] the Fourth Circuit Court of Appeals affirmed, per curiam, the conviction of Quaker Bruce Baechler for refusal to register. Because a conscientious objector classification would not be considered until after he had registered, he argued that the free exercise of his Quaker peace testimony had already been violated.

Another district court had revoked a Friend's probation because of his continued refusal to register. On appeal, the Eighth Circuit in *United States v. Crocker*[140] decided for Crocker without reaching his First Amendment free exercise of religion claim. On the basis of Supreme Court precedent, it held that failure to register was not a continuing offense but was complete upon failure to register within a certain time.[141] The revocation of Crocker's probation was improper because the judge had not initially made registration a condition of probation; moreover, assigning conditions of probation was a nondelegable judicial function.[142]

Refusal to Pay Taxes for War and the
Religious Freedom Restoration Act of 1993

Friends' pacifist beliefs have caused them to challenge laws that require their monetary support for war, although for a long period in Friends' history, these mutually contradictory ideas coexisted: Friends' condemnation of fighting because war is wrong and their simultaneous, if inadvertent, support for war through payment of taxes to the government. In the mid-eighteenth century, a delegation of about 20 Friends spoke before the Pennsylvania General Assembly in opposition to funding the king's prosecution of the French and Indian War. However, the fundraising measure did pass, and soon thereafter, many Quaker lawmakers resigned. In *An Epistle of Tender Love and Caution to Friends in Pennsylvania*, some explained their reasons and encouraged others to follow their stand of conscience: "And being painfully apprehensive that the large sum granted by the late Act of Assembly for the King's use is principally intended for purposes inconsistent with our peaceable testimony, we therefore think that as we cannot be concerned in wars and fightings, so neither ought we to contribute thereto by paying the tax directed by the said Act, though suffering be the consequence of our refusal. . . ."[143]

In the twentieth century, some Friends' persistent refusal to pay taxes for purposes of war made them defendants in enforcement suits brought by the government or plaintiffs such as the AFSC in *American Friends Service Committee v. United States.*[144] Two employees had asked the committee to stop deducting from 51.6% of their wages, at that time the estimated percentage of the military-related portion of the federal budget. Plaintiffs claimed enforcement of this amount subject to withholding under the Internal Revenue Code[145] deprived them of the right to free exercise of their religious beliefs opposing war. The AFSC obliged but paid the government the full amount of the employees' taxes owed, and then sued for a partial refund. The issue before the court was whether the AFSC could lawfully cease withholding this proportionate allocation of employees' taxes used for military spending.

A prominent Quaker historian, Edwin Bronner, testified as an expert: "it has been true throughout the[ir] history . . . that most Quakers have considered it an integral part of their faith to bear witness to the beliefs which they hold . . . that simple preaching . . . is not sufficient, and that one's actions must accord with and give expression to one's belief."[146] The district court referred to AFSC's candor in dealing with the Internal Revenue Service (IRS) and ruled in its favor:

> Because of its nature and goals, and because of the character of the men and women who are drawn to work for it, the AFSC as a body is almost unique in its corporate concern with matters of war and peace and with matters affecting the conscience of its employees. . . . [T]he withholding method of collecting their taxes directly forecloses their ability to freely express their opposition to the participation in war in any form which opposition is a vital and fundamental part of their religious practice as Quakers.[147]

Nevertheless, the U.S. Supreme Court in *United States v. American Friends Service Committee*[148] reversed, holding that the AFSC suit was barred by the Anti-Injunction Act.[149] This federal law prohibits suits for the purpose of restraining the assessment or collection of any tax unless it is clear that the government could not prevail. The AFSC had conceded with characteristic Quaker frankness that the government could prevail. The Court did not reach the right of free exercise claim because under the terms of the act the constitutional nature of a taxpayer's claim is of no consequence.[150]

In a lengthy dissent, Justice Douglas wrote that the forced withholding of conscientious objectors' wages was unconstitutional because it directly abridged their right to their cherished religious belief, which opposed participation in war in any form. "Under the opinion of this Court, they are deprived of bearing witness to their opposition to war. . . . Quakers with true religious scruples against participating in war may no more be barred from protesting the payment of taxes to support war than they can be forcibly inducted into the Armed Forces and required to carry a gun. . . ."[151] Justice Douglas stated that the First Amendment's free exercise clause permits no exceptions. "No law" means no law, including the Anti-Injunction Act, and he objected to the majority's judicial revision of the Amendment's plain command. Here Justice Douglas correctly interpreted the First Amendment as Fox might have.

Friends' rebellion against the payment of taxes for purposes of war caused them to use the First Amendment free exercise of religion clause in their defense. The government brought an action against a Yearly Meeting in *United States v. Philadelphia Yearly Meeting of Religious Society of Friends*[152] to enforce two IRS levies and a 50% penalty for failure to honor the levies without reasonable cause. The IRS had demanded the Meeting levy on the salary of two employees who refused to pay the portion of their taxes that funded the military. The Meeting had resisted and explained its policy, adopted in 1975 and reaffirmed in 1983 and 1988, of not coercing or violating its employees' consciences nor acting as agents for those who would.

Citing *Employment Division v. Smith*,[153] the court noted that the statute at issue was a neutral generally applicable regulatory law designed to facilitate the collection of delinquent taxes, which, under *Smith*, did not violate defendant's right to the free exercise of religion. Even after *Smith*, religious beliefs do not excuse noncompliance with otherwise valid federal tax laws. However, the court refused to impose the statutory penalty against the Meeting because its constitutional defense was neither unreasonable nor frivolous. The district judge was distressed by the *Smith* precedent he was obliged to follow:

> It is ironic that here in Pennsylvania, the woods to which Penn led the Religious Society of Friends to enjoy the blessings of religious liberty, neither the Constitution nor its Bill of Rights protects the policy of that Society not to coerce or violate the consciences of its employees and members with respect to their religious principles, or to act as an agent for our government in doing so . . . But "unless we wish anarchy to prevail within the federal judicial system, a precedent of the [Supreme] Court must be followed by lower federal courts no matter how misguided the judges of those courts think it to be."[154]

In *United States v. Haworth*,[155] the defendant was found liable for more than $4,000 in taxes. He had argued that, as a member of the Religious Society of Friends, he opposed war, and forced payment of taxes for war denied his right of free exercise. Furthermore, income tax revenues from 1966 to 1969 had been spent in active prosecution of an illegal war in Vietnam, illegal because Congress had never declared war pursuant to Article I, Section 8, Clause 11, of the Constitution. In a memorandum opinion, the district court held that Haworth's right to the free exercise of his Quaker faith had not been violated, and his defense on that basis was insufficient as a matter of law. It quoted *Autenrieth v. Cullen* stating,[156] "nothing in the Constitution prohibits the Congress from levying a tax upon all persons, regardless of religion, . . ." and dismissed Haworth's second argument on the basis of *Orlando v. Laird,*[157] there was sufficient evidence of Congressional concurrence in U.S. military involvement in Vietnam to render it a legally authorized war.

In *United States v. Harper,*[158] Robin Harper, like Haworth, argued that payment of taxes for war purposes during 1962 to 1967 violated his right to free exercise of religion and involved him unwillingly in the collection of war revenue. He had made "equivalent tax" payments to organizations such as the Philadelphia Yearly Meeting and the AFSC. Harper also contended that enforcement of an IRS summons to identify his assets for purposes of levy violated his Fifth Amendment right against self-incrimination for any subsequent criminal prosecution the government might bring against him.

Although the court noted the origins of Friends' peace testimony: "since the beginnings . . . in the seventeenth century, Quakers have taken the position that they could not engage in war or violence of any kind and could not take the life of another human being,"[159] it nevertheless denied Harper's claim because the government's compelling interest in forcing him to produce the requested information outweighed his religious interest.[160] However, the court did uphold Harper's Fifth Amendment claim against self-incrimination. The courts rejected Friends' free exercise of religion defense of right to the free exercise of religion once again.

In *United States v. Snider,*[161] Quaker defendants Lyle and Sue Snider were convicted for supplying false and fraudulent information on federal tax withholding certificates.[162] They had claimed 3 billion dependents, then the approximate number of the world's people to whom they felt some responsibility. At one point, the jury was deadlocked, but it ultimately found the Sniders guilty, and Lyle was sentenced to eight months in prison. The Sniders were "convinced" Quakers. Sue had attended Quaker meeting since high school and Lyle had done so since the two were students at Swarthmore College. Members of Durham (North Carolina) Friends Meeting, they had taught in Quaker schools, most recently at Carolina Friends School. Like most Quakers, they were concerned about the consonance of their beliefs and actions, particularly with regard to pacifism. The Sniders' May 30, 1972, letter to the IRS explained:

We also refuse to pay our taxes willingly to the U.S. Government on the ground[s] that we are conscientiously opposed to any and all wars. We have a strong Christian faith which is the basis of our opposition to war and violence among men. We are conscientiously opposed to the use of violence to settle conflicts and we are committed to removing the causes of violent conflict. . . . As one of the most powerful military nations on earth, we [U.S.] must start leading the world toward peace. . . . We will pay our share of money and resources to life-affirming, positive programs such as medical care, welfare, psychological care and counseling, and education. . . . We are called by God to affirm life and love with our resources and to resist and eliminate war and violence. . . .[163]

The trial itself had been the source of another perceived offense related to Quakers' testimony of equality. When the judge had entered the courtroom, Lyle and Susan had not stood as the marshal commanded, "All rise." The court found the Sniders in contempt of court for this and sentenced them to jail—Lyle for 30 days and Sue for 10. The district court judge had treated the Sniders' apparent disregard for his high position with only slightly more equanimity than his English counterpart had treated Penn during his 1670 trial in London. He had refused Lyle's request to avoid continuing citations by entering after the judge was seated and exiting before he left; instead, the judge cited him 16 times.[164]

In a lengthy opinion, the Fourth Circuit Court of Appeals reversed the Sniders' convictions because the prosecution had failed to prove an essential element of the offense—that the withholding information had been supplied with an intent to deceive, was false in the sense of deceptive, or could reasonably have affected the withholding of taxes to the government's detriment. The appellate court also reversed the Sniders' convictions for contempt, holding that a "mere failure to rise on command of the marshal in a United States courtroom is not 'misbehavior' within the meaning of the [federal contempt statute]."[165] The court specifically noted the continuity of Friends' witness of equality from the seventeenth century to the present. A footnote in the court's decision referred to the 1670 prosecution of Penn and Mead,[166] comparing the Sniders' conscientious refusal to stand in deference to the court to Penn's and Mead's refusal to doff their hats. The *Snider* court also mentioned Penn's argument that his and Mead's contempt citations violated their rights under the Magna Carta.[167] The Sniders had similarly argued that the contempt citations had abridged their rights under the First Amendment.

United States v. Wilhelm[168] was a consolidated case that also involved convictions for false statements on withholding exemption certificates, similar to *Snider*, but here the focus is on Friends' historic preference for pro se representation. The *Wilhelm* defendants argued that the court had denied their Sixth Amendment right to effective assistance of counsel by refusing to allow a lay friend to represent them. Section 35 of the Judiciary Act of 1789 provides: "In all courts of the United States the parties may plead and conduct their own cases personally or by counsel. . . ."[169] In construing the statute, the court recognized that in predominantly Quaker colonies, the right to representation by a friend was permitted, but it found no intent evidenced in the ratifying debates to preserve the practice. Accordingly, it affirmed defendants' convictions and three-month prison sentences.[170]

The *AFSC*, *Philadelphia Yearly Meeting*, *Haworth*, *Harper*, and *Snider* cases have shown that Quakers' arguments based on the right to the free exercise of religion were largely unsuccessful, either because the right was trumped by a compelling interest of the state or because the courts bypassed that First Amendment theory to rest the decisions on statutory or other constitutional grounds. The decision in *Elfbrandt v. Russell* was based on freedom of association, and in *James v. Board of Education* on the right of symbolic free speech. The right to free exercise of religion came squarely before the Supreme Court in *Employment Division v. Smith*.[171]

Although this case did not involve Quakers, its repercussions and the legislation, the Religious Freedom Restoration Act of 1993 (RFRA), that was enacted in response to it had the potential to affect subsequent actions based on a right to free exercise of religion. At least in actions involving Friends, the new RFRA seems to have done little to strengthen the right to free exercise; these cases were not decided differently from ones decided before its passage. This may have been partially due to the recurring use of summary judgment, which is especially inappropriate in cases involving complex tests such as that prescribed by RFRA.

Smith involved Native Americans' ceremonial use of peyote, a substance prohibited under Oregon criminal law. The Supreme Court held that the right to free exercise of religion could be violated by a general social regulation *only if* that regulation was specifically directed at religious practice or if it attempted to regulate religious beliefs or their communication, or the raising of one's children according to them. "Conscientious scruples have not, in the course of the long struggle for religious toleration, relieved the individual from obedience to a general law not aimed at the promotion or restriction of religious beliefs. The mere possession of religious convictions which contradict the relevant concerns of a political society does not relieve the citizen from the discharge of political responsibilities."[172] The free exercise of religion defense failed once again, and moreover, *Smith* had narrowed its scope. In direct response, the first session of the 103rd Congress passed RFRA.[173] Congress found that a neutral law, like the one in *Smith*, can burden free exercise as surely as one that intentionally interferes. The new law's purpose was to protect the right by applying to all federal and state laws and their implementation and to restore the compelling interest test enunciated in *Sherbert v. Verner*[174] and *Wisconsin v. Yoder.*[175] The government cannot burden free exercise unless it is in furtherance of a compelling governmental interest and is the least restrictive means of doing so.

The RFRA was not effective as a basis for Quakers' challenge to payment of taxes used for war expenditures. Priscilla Adams, Philadelphia Yearly Meeting Quaker Peace Secretary, claimed that RFRA required the government to accommodate her belief that war was morally wrong by using her tax payments for nonmilitary spending. Adams acknowledged the government's compelling interest in collecting taxes but contended that it had not met its RFRA burden of showing its method to be the least restrictive. She had convened meeting clearness committees to help her test this concern, and it seemed to be a result of God's leading. She offered to consider any accommodation the government might suggest. The appellate court ruled against her in *Adams v. Commissioner of Internal Revenue,*[176] disagreeing that the IRS was required to produce evidence under RFRA's "least restrictive means" prong. It viewed the law's requirements through the lens of pre-*Smith* case law, specifically *United States v. Lee:*[177] "If . . . a religious adherent believes war is a sin and if a certain percentage of the federal budget can be identified as devoted to war-related activities, such individuals would have a similarly valid claim to be exempt from paying that percentage of the income tax. The tax system could not function if denominations were allowed to challenge the tax system because tax payments were spent in a manner that violates their religious belief."[178] The court also affirmed Adams's liability for penalties despite her "appealing but unconvincing" argument that she was compelled by conscience to refuse payment and therefore should be exempt on grounds of reasonable cause.

Browne v. United States,[179] involved Quakers Gordon and Edith Browne who withheld 28% of their income tax payments from 1993 through 1995 because of their conscientious objection to support of the military. The court granted the government's motion for judgment on the pleadings, rejecting the Brownes' free exercise claim on the basis of *Smith,* and their RFRA claim because voluntary compliance is the least restrictive means by which the IRS can ensure uniform participation in the government's income tax system. The Court of Appeals for the Second Circuit affirmed.[180]

On December 7, 1997, New York Yearly Meeting endorsed a minute supporting member and longtime tax protestor Rosa Packard's effort to seek legal recognition for the reasonableness of her tax witness under the First Amendment's free exercise clause.[181] Some six months later, the Meeting approved the submission of an amicus curiae brief on her behalf in *Packard v. United States*[182] to explain Friends' testimony of peace that underpinned her refusal to pay taxes for war.

The district court rejected Rosa's free exercise claim,[183] stating that she was not compelled by religious conscience to withhold tax payments because she would not incur sanctions from her Quaker meeting if she did not. The court apparently did not understand that a Quaker's conscience is inwardly, not outwardly, controlled. In its brief, the Meeting attempted to explain this individualistic religious concept—a Friend's conduct is dictated by religious conscience if it flows from the Inner Light.[184] In an unreported opinion, the Second Circuit nevertheless affirmed[185] on the basis of *Browne v. United States*[186] and *Adams v. Commissioner*[187] that voluntary compliance was the least restrictive means of furthering the state's compelling interest in collecting taxes. In this case it is doubtful that the court rigorously applied the two-pronged requirement the RFRA prescribed—the government must demonstrate, through burdens of production and persuasion both a compelling interest of the state and its compliance method was the least restrictive way to further that interest. The courts seem to apply the *Browne* and *Adams* precedents pro forma without any exploration of alternatives. For instance, Quaker tax resisters might place their proportionate amount of taxes used for military expenditures into nonmilitary-related funds that benefit the government or local communities or they might perform some community service of equal benefit.

The more recent case of Daniel Jenkins also concerned a Quaker's refusal to pay taxes to fund the military. Jenkins was supported in his leading by a clearness committee of his Saranac Lake (New York) Meeting. As it had done for Rosa Packard, the New York Yearly Meeting filed an amicus curiae brief in support of plaintiff in *Jenkins v. Commissioner of Internal Revenue*.[188] The Yearly Meeting also submitted one to support Jenkins's petition for a writ of certiorari from the U.S. Supreme Court, which was denied.

In 2005 the U.S. Tax Court granted summary judgment against Jenkins and imposed a $5,000 penalty for filing a "frivolous" claim. Jenkins, who appeared pro se, had requested that the IRS accommodate his Quaker-based conscientious objection to war by allocating his income tax payment for nonmilitary purposes on the basis of the Constitution's First and Ninth Amendments and RFRA.[189]

In his appeal to the Second Circuit, Jenkins argued that the right not to be compelled to participate in war could be discerned in the First Amendment's free exercise clause, as elucidated by the Ninth Amendment's rule of construction: "The enumeration in the Constitution, of certain rights, shall not be construed to deny or disparage others retained by the people." He also argued that the requirements of RFRA be given measured consideration. Indeed, a law expressly passed by Congress in direct refutation of a Supreme Court ruling should be carefully followed and its prescribed tests rigorously applied. Furthermore, Jenkins showed that the right of liberty of conscience had been explicitly recognized even before the creation of the Bill of Rights. Article 40 of the 1777 New York State Constitution expressly protected persons with conscientious scruples from forced military service: "That all such of the inhabitants of this State being of the people called Quakers as, from scruples of conscience may be averse to the bearing of arms, be therefrom excused by the legislature, and do pay to the State such sums of money, in lieu of their personal service, as the same, may, in the judgment of the legislature, be worth." Moreover, Jenkins argued that subsequent New York statutes and constitutional provisions preserved these exemptions, thereby showing a history of governmental accommodation of Friends pacifist beliefs.

The amicus brief of the New York Yearly Meeting quoted its minute of April 1, 2006, explaining that paying for war violates Friends' religious convictions, adding that Friends' peace testimony is living a commitment to peace. A Quaker's belief is expressed in action and action is grounded in belief.

As is clear from these cases, U.S. courts recognize the state's compelling interest in the collection of taxes including those used for war. The state refuses to consider "least restrictive means" nor do courts seems to require it to consider, for example, redirecting Friends' tax payment funds toward nonmilitary uses such as peace-making projects that would have lasting impact over time. If good minds were put to the task of finding an accommodation, it could occur. Many, not only Friends, might look and work toward a time when avoidance of war would be a primary compelling interest of the state. However, these efforts will take courage and perseverance from those who engage in them." In his speech accepting the 1947 Nobel Peace Prize for the AFSC, Henry J. Cadbury reminded us that even ordinary men and women can promote a more peaceful world:

> You are saying . . . here today . . . that common folk—not statesmen nor generals, nor great men of affairs—but just simple plain men and women like the few thousand Quakers and their friends . . . can do something to build a better peaceful world. . . . To this idea, . . . persons everywhere may contribute.[190]

Until we learn to live in a way that takes away the occasion for all wars and we have a "better peaceful world," Friends' free exercise of religion will most likely be superseded by the government's compelling interest in raising armies and collecting taxes to sustain them. However, the concept of a compelling state interest in this context is, to a large extent, a contrivance or legal fiction to overcome the First Amendment's plain language: "Congress shall make no law . . . prohibiting the free exercise thereof. . . ." Quakers' witness of the peace testimony and their use of the First Amendment's free exercise clause in so doing, has inadvertently exposed a certain intellectual dishonesty in the judiciary's interpretation of the First Amendment, a point that Justice Douglas tellingly exposed in his dissent in *United States v. American Friends Service Committee*. Preventing erosions of constitutional rights like this one takes the vigilance of an alert and aware citizenry.

The universe of thought has always included the notion of wars and fighting, and it has become "second nature" to think of wars as an inevitable part of the human experience. Women's voices are becoming increasingly salient and bear within them the idea that the inevitability of war is not a given and is not to be considered so. Legal scholars such as Roberto Unger and Michael Perry have begun to recognize and encourage within the law a feminizing kind of lawyering as a legitimate alternative. There may eventually be a parallel in issues of war and peace.

A Lawyer's Stand of Conscience

Although lawyer Clyde Wilson Summers was a Methodist, not a Quaker, *In re Summers*[191] is an important case for inclusion in this book because it illustrates the dilemma lawyers face when their religious beliefs, their philosophical beliefs, or both clash with the expectations and demands of their profession.

During World War II, the Illinois State Bar Committee on Character and Fitness refused to certify Summers for admission to its bar because of his stated unwillingness to bear arms. At that time, Article XII of the Illinois Constitution required all able-bodied men between ages 18 and 45 to serve in the state militia in wartime, although those with conscientious scruples against war could be exempted only in peacetime. Summers had been classified a conscientious objector under the 1940 Selective Service Act, but the Illinois constitution did not provide a similar exemption. Summers argued that the bar's denial of admission deprived him of his constitutional rights to due process and equal protection. He petitioned the Supreme Court for a writ of certiorari to review the Illinois decision. The petition stated. "Instead of merely reading or preaching the Sermon on the Mount, [Summers] tries to practice it. . . . We respectfully submit that under our Constitutional guarantees even good Christians who have met all the requirements for the admission to the bar may be admitted to practice law."[192] (One hopes that this ironic statement was not lost on the law clerks who read it!)

Because the outcome of the case had serious ramifications for conscientious objectors, the AFSC filed an amicus curiae brief, stressing the importance that Quakers attach to the peace testimony and to freedom of conscience. The AFSC expressed Friends' belief that emphasizing connections and unity among people and working toward social and economic justice can obviate the necessity for war. It also expressed concern that if Summers's exclusion from the bar were allowed to stand, the rights of conscientious objectors—both inside and outside of the Society of Friends—would be seriously compromised. Moreover, as long as that section of the Illinois constitution remained unchanged, conscientious scruples against killing would be considered sufficient proof of bad character.[193]

The AFSC questioned any reasonable connection between an unwillingness to be a soldier and unfitness to do the work of a lawyer.[194] Summers's attorney had also argued that freedom of conscience was not incompatible with the practice of law: "The worst one can say against him is that he may be a bit too conscientious for the wear and tear of ordinary life, but the bar can well afford to have a few members with that fault."[195] However, the secretary of the Bar Committee on Character and Fitness wrote to Summers stating, "I do not argue against your religious beliefs or your philosophy of non-violence. My point is merely that your position seems inconsistent with the obligation of an attorney at law."

The Supreme Court held, 5–4, that the bar's denial of admission was not discriminatory and therefore did not violate Summers's rights under the Fourteenth Amendment; the court stated that Illinois had responsibility for choosing members of its bar. In dissent, Justice Black emphasized the AFSC statement that, under the test Illinois applied to Summers, no Quakers, true to the tenets of their faith, could qualify for its bar. Referring to the Society of Friends as a religious group with a long and honorable place in the growth of the nation, he wrote:

> I cannot believe that a state statute would be consistent with our constitutional guarantee of freedom of religion if it specifically denied the right to practice law to all members of one of our great religious groups . . . if Illinois can bar this petitioner from the practice of law it can bar every person from every public occupation solely because he believes in non-resistance rather than in force. . . . [A] lawyer is no more subject to call for military duty than a plumber, a highway worker, a Secretary of State, or a prison chaplain. Under our Constitution men are punished for what they do or fail to do and not for what they think and believe.[196]

Justice Black quoted Summers's own philosophy on practicing law:

> I think in law if I did not do anything else, I might get a few more people to settle things without going to court. . . . When people start suing each other in court, they are mad at each other and do not understand each other and have not made an honest attempt to get together and I think . . . I have something to offer . . . because I believe in settling it peacefully and . . . on terms of friendship and understanding rather than going through court. If there is no other way to obtain justice, then that is what the courts are for but it seems to me that the lawyers' main job . . . is to try to get people to work things out peacefully. . . . Lawsuits do not bring love and brotherliness—they just create antagonism.[197]

The general tenor of Summers's thoughts on practicing law and his specific reference to the antagonism lawsuits engender are both Quaker and Gandhian. Like Gandhi,[198] Summers advocated a more peaceful and friendly way of resolving conflict. This approach to settling discord is part of the whole fabric of peaceableness that has at its heart a refusal to bear arms and kill for one's government or for any person, group, or institution. Advocacy of the peaceful resolution of individual conflict, refusal to bear arms, and active peacemaking are all of one piece.

In a letter dated March 23, 1943, Summers wrote that the whole episode with the Illinois State Bar had forced him to examine the relationship between his beliefs and the practice of law, a relationship this book also studies. He discussed his convictions in connection with the then-current situation in Nazi Germany:

> If in the practice of law I should find myself expected to act in a way inconsistent with my inner convictions, then I should immediately withdraw. I am sure that if I were in Germany, I would have no part in helping enforce the anti-Jewish laws. If it happened in this country I do not believe I should be bound to help in such un-Christian law enforcement. Every man with any moral integrity will draw the line at some point. The man who will not draw a line is not fit to practice law.

It may be that men and women such as Summers draw the line more carefully than those for whom the lawyer's role is more distant from the dictates of his or her conscience. On a continuum where a lawyer in his role as Lawyer is at one end and a lawyer who heeds his conscience is at the other, Summers's position would be closer to "personhood" than to "lawyerhood," as would most Quaker lawyer respondents to the survey reported in chapter 5.

S = Summers; QL = Quaker lawyers; ROL = Role of Lawyer

Lawyerhood _____ S/QL _____ Personhood (encompassing one's conscience)

Lawyerhood _____ ROL _____ Personhood (encompassing one's conscience)

Summers's place on a continuum between his part in enforcing Nazi genocide laws and laws designed for the societal good would be further apart from the place of lawyers who consciously, or unconsciously, see their actions as lawyers and persons more disparately and are more conditioned to maintain the status quo and carry out their duty. This is not to say that most, or even many, lawyers, regardless of their faith, would embrace the enforcement of genocide laws in Summers's example, certainly not hypothetically. It simply illustrates that on a continuum of various ethical or moral dilemmas, Summers's place would most likely be further from the point of the Nazi laws than some other lawyers for whom the rule of law is paramount. It is unfortunately rare that contemporary lawyers have, or take, the opportunity to consider how they might act in situations that pose such ethical dilemmas.

Nazi genocide laws _____ ROL _____ S/QL _____ laws promoting social good

Summers chafed at criticism that a logical extension of his ideas would be to eliminate all force. He explained that his approval of police forces was not inconsistent with the idea of peacefulness. Those who criticized his being a conscientious objector could not reasonably extrapolate this stand to dissimilar situations, but he admitted that the distinction was difficult to articulate logically. He believed armies were different from police forces because the former killed and the latter restrained, and nonviolence did not necessarily include nonresistance. Gandhi and Friends knew this difference well. Another similarity between Summers's and Quakers' view of law and lawyers in society is that law can help ensure a certain equality among people. Like Fox, Summers believed that law courts are where people should be able to go to get justice without paying too much.

Friends Committee on National Legislation

"The Friends Committee on National Legislation is, in a sense, an institutionalization of the age-old [Quaker] practice . . . of the divine lobbyist."[199]

From their beginnings Quakers have spoken forthrightly to kings and lawmakers in an attempt to persuade them to enact laws informed by a concern for peace and justice, and they have continued this tradition in the FCNL. Formerly the Friends War Problems Committee, the FCNL came into being in the summer of 1943 at Quaker Hill in Richmond, Indiana. A small pacifist organization registered with Congress as a non–tax-exempt lobby, it attempts to further effect peace, social justice, and equality by "friendly persuasion" of Capitol Hill lawmakers. The FCNL is connected with Friends and their beliefs in both the process and substance of its work.

In its process of discernment and decision-making, FCNL adheres to the procedural principles Friends use to reach consensus and unity. In applying these principles, the committee considers Friends' leadings by seeking input on legislative priorities from more than 1,000 Friends Meetings throughout the country on what the Quaker witness in Washington should be. It then reviews the meetings' responses and distributes a second series of questions to refine the emerging areas of legislative concern initially identified. The FCNL also keeps Friends informed about their activities through regular newsletters.

Representatives of 26 Yearly Meetings meet in Washington biennially,[200] first to discuss and then write priority statements defining the most critical issues to receive attention during the upcoming congressional session. A wide divergence of views on public policy issues can emerge during this process, but despite this, the Quaker process of seeking divine guidance and discerning the best understanding of God's truth eventually and almost invariably results in consensus. Friends who initially held quite different opinions seem to discover a sense of unity, first, through listening to each other with openness and care, and second, through inward listening in communal silence. In the view of an FCNL staffperson who has witnessed this, it is an example of Quaker process at its very best.[201]

In addition to process, Friends' testimonies are evident in FCNL's substantive work and in its approach to the legislators it attempts to influence; much of its work and many of its statements exhibit deep Quaker influence. For example, an FCNL witness testified before the House Ways and Means Committee on March 7, 1958, that, in the last analysis, government policies can be satisfactory only if they coincide with fundamental moral and spiritual convictions. And most of the world's people subscribe to a spiritual or religious code that emphasizes human brotherhood as a truth that should inspire and direct them. Quakers show this through a witness of community that stresses the commonality of all persons sharing the Inner Light.

In its earliest years, the FCNL concentrated its efforts on antimilitarism, postwar relief, and support for international organizations. Due to its strong dedication to Friends' peace testimony, its emphasis on antimilitarism continues unabated. Its other constants are its support from most American Friends, the persistency of its witness, and discernment on policies and priorities through worship and waiting on the Spirit. Those who have worked with FCNL indeed attribute its ability to persist on core issues as the fruit of this waiting on the Spirit.[202]

Another attribute of FCNL—and British Quaker Peace and Service[203]—is its neutrality. For example, during the 1999 war in Kosovo, FCNL did not favor either side but instead concentrated its efforts on the plight of the people, whether Kosovars or Serbs. It prefers to look at situations absent political ideology and to search for nonviolent solutions to end conflict. It attempts to acknowledge good and bad where it lies, but refuses to demonize any one faction, recognizing that each side in that conflict had acted in a condemnable way. It believes that demonization is dangerous because it tends to blind people to the truth of a situation and thus can become a justification for violence. In Kosovo, FCNL worked toward a cease-fire, accountability of those who committed war crimes, and involvement by the United Nations (UN) and the Organization for Security and Cooperation in Europe (OSCE) to provide nonmilitary security and help in rebuilding the society. The Committee also wrote to President Clinton on March 23, 1999, asking that the United States not initiate a bombing attack but instead take specific diplomatic and peacebuilding steps in concert with the UN Security Council and the OSCE. "Better to take years of political talking and spend millions of dollars on this kind of war prevention than to spend billions for a militarily imposed 'peace' that will require decades of occupation forces to maintain." Given later U.S. involvement in Iraq and Afghanistan, this was a prescient and important suggestion.

In lobbying Congress, FCNL attempts to look at the totality of circumstances, seek that of God in all parties, respond to the truth they see, and candidly speak it. Before approaching a legislator, staff members prepare by trying to discern what the divine spirit asks and then respond to that of God in each legislator by listening respectfully to his or her views, framing issues, and persuading by appealing to his or her sense of reason and moral sensibility. The committee tries to keep its vision clear and take small practical steps to move its work along but refuses to compromise its values or deal in political trade-offs.

When the immediacy of war diminishes, FCNL priorities shift. In peacetime, its lobbying thrust turns toward reconciliation, development of human resources, environmental protection, and other efforts toward the realization of a more just and equal society. For instance, during the postwar McCarthy era, FCNL testified in Congressional hearings against wiretapping and for protection of the privilege against self-incrimination, and during the Kennedy years, it lobbied for establishment of the Peace Corps and the Arms Control and Disarmament Agency.[204]

Although FCNL represents the views of many Friends, it is careful to point out that it does not speak "officially" for all. It stated in its testimony before the Internal Security Subcommittee of the Senate Judiciary Committee on May 1, 1959: "This committee of the Religious Society of Friends seeks to represent many of the concerns of Friends, but does not claim to speak for the whole Society, whose democratic organization does not lend itself to official spokespersons and whose members reserve to themselves the right to speak on issues of importance. . . ." Friends are often individualistic in their worship as well as in their thoughts on public policy issues, but if "there is any distinctive posture vis-à-vis politics, it is . . . the role of the divine lobbyist."[205] Over the centuries, Friends have held varying views regarding the wisdom and appropriateness of Friends' involvement in public service as well as in individual paths of service to others.

A Quaker historian has described two kinds of Quakers who have coexisted over the years: the absolutist, like George Fox, and the relativist, like William Penn.[206] Both can work complementarily and make valuable contributions to society. The relativist needs the absolutist to keep alive and clear the vision of the City of God while he or she struggles to realize it in some measure in the City of Earth. But the absolutist also needs the relativist to translate the vision in the possession of a few into a degree of reality for the greater world.[207] FCNL combines both prophetic vision and practical action. It acts as an absolutist in its unwavering persistence of goals such as disarmament, a state far from the imaginings of persons both within government and outside it. However, in its congressional lobbying efforts, FCNL is a relativist working in the real City of Earth toward some realization of spiritual values in the City of God.

As an absolutist, the Committee issued a 1956 statement on disarmament, only slightly changed since: "We favor . . . immediate and complete disarmament by the United States together with constructive and far reaching revision of its foreign policy . . . the present policy disregards the sacredness of human life, and is contrary to God's will." FCNL rejects the view that violence is necessary to overcome evil or that evil must be met in kind.

In addition to disarmament, the Committee tries to be faithful to other Friends' concerns such as conscientious objection, abolition of the death penalty, and rights of minorities. An example of the latter involved its work on redress for Japanese Americans interned during World War II, addressed in the *Hirabayashi* cases discussed earlier in this chapter. Since its beginnings, the FCNL has worked to abolish the death penalty because Friends have held that punishment by death violates the sacredness of human life, is irreversible, and forever forecloses the possibility of spiritual growth, rehabilitation, and redemption. The committee testified against the death penalty before congressional committees in the 1960s, 1970s, and 1980s and has aided in several efforts to abolish it.

FCNL began serious work on civil rights issues in the mid-1950s, around the time of the Supreme Court's decision in *Brown v. Board of Education*. Through David Scull's congressional testimony, it urged the creation of a Civil Rights Commission. Scull, who had been active in attempts at racial integration,[208] quoted extensively from the writings of Quaker abolitionist John Woolman. By the early summer of 1964, the FCNL office had become a central locus of activity to urge passage of the Civil Rights Act, enacted later that year. On this and other peace and social justice issues, FCNL has often worked in coalition with other groups who share its concerns.

Quakers' respect and concern for Native Americans is deeply rooted in Friends' history, beginning with William Penn's arrival in America in 1680. By 1795, the Yearly Meetings had begun to appoint standing committees on Indian affairs.[209] Since the 1970s, issues important to Native Americans have been an integral part of the FCNL legislative agenda including those of tribal justice and the provision of housing and health care for all Indians. In the mid-1970s, FCNL created the Native American Advocacy Project, supported by Friends and other religious groups, and helped create the permanent Senate Select Committee on Indian Affairs. From the time of the creation of that project until the mid-1990s, the FCNL was alone among the non-Indian religious community in Washington with a full-time staff person solely dedicated to Native American affairs.[210] A Quaker lawyer has successfully worked, on his own, to secure treaty fishing rights for the Muckleshoot Indians of Washington state.

However, one Indian rights issue did conflict with Quaker values: the development of gaming casinos to increase Indian job growth and revenues. Friends have traditionally been opposed to gambling because people's chance of gain is disproportionate to their contribution. In addition, when gambling becomes a habit for those who can least afford it, families and communities suffer. Despite its discomfort, FCNL respected and supported the Native Americans' right to make that choice and supported and urged conflict resolution processes between tribes and their surrounding communities regarding this and other issues.

Prison reform is another area of traditional Quaker concern on which FCNL has expended time and effort. Like Elizabeth Fry in England and William Penn in America, the committee has worked toward legislation that would make prisons places of rehabilitation. Committee staff has testified for incarceration alternatives and against the continuous building of new prisons. Like Penn, the FCNL has advocated against making the criminal code more punitive and, in addition to inmates' rehabilitation, has urged preventive solutions such as better education and increased job opportunities.

The Quaker testimonies of community and peace are sources for FCNL's work on international cooperation. In its early years, FCNL proposed amendments to the UN charter, which if approved would have given the UN real authority to control armaments and make laws enforceable against individual citizens.

In addition to the UN and its agencies, the Committee supports other multilateral organizations and has advocated ratification of several international treaties including the UN treaty on Law of the Sea. This treaty was an example of the applicability of international law to all nations and was important for at least two reasons: (1) the treaty prescribed all nations' duty of stewardship of the seas and their precious resources; and (2) the treaty aimed to promote peacefulness and preempt conflict by establishing a system of cooperation among nations on sea-related issues.

FCNL believes that although law can provide a framework for justice, it can become harsh and sterile without a spirit of love and reconciliation. Its legislative priorities have included bringing spiritual values to bear on public policy and promoting values of mutual respect, integrity, and a cooperative spirit vital to many Friends. During the 106th congressional sessions, the committee specifically worked toward passage of a Senate bill that would lift restrictions on the sale or donation of food, medicine, and medical supplies to Cuba in the belief that coercive withholding of food and medicine should never be used as an instrument of U.S. foreign policy.

Over many years, FCNL has worked steadily on promoting peace in the Middle East and has for the past several years advocated talks with Iran. In early 2007, Quakers visited Iran as part of a delegation of faith groups. In encouraging talks with Iran, FCNL has urged that different national experiences be considered in articulating a new relationship between the two nations in the hope that the people of each nation might help prevent war by mobilizing to construct bridges to peace.[211] As the possibility of conflict loomed larger, the Committee focused on work to prevent preemptive strikes or invasion of the Islamic Republic. At the same time, it continues to build support in Congress for an energy policy that would reduce danger of future wars for oil. In keeping with Friends' Janus-like peace testimony, it tries to balance antiwar negatives with peacemaking positives; in 2007, FCNL supported passage of a House bill authorizing a "civilian peace-builder corps . . . to help secure delicate peace agreements."[212]

The Quaker United Nations Offices in New York and Geneva

Friends had a presence at the League of Nations, and now continue important endeavors with the League's successor, the UN. Consistent with their commitment to world peace, Friends now maintain a presence at UN headquarters in New York and Geneva. Both Quaker United Nations Offices (QUNOs) have general consultative status at the UN through their relationship with Friends World Committee for Consultation (FWCC) and through the UN Economic and Social Council, enabling them to make oral and written statements at the UN. The FWCC and the AFSC work with QUNO–NY as stewards of Friends testimonies of truth, peace, and social and economic justice at the UN and its New York-based agencies. The primary areas of work in both New York and Geneva revolve around issues of peacebuilding, disarmament, human rights, refugees, and economic and criminal justice. Over the decades, the QUNOs have done both facilitative and prescriptive work.

QUNO–NY, located near the UN Secretariat, is overseen by the FWCC and the AFSC, and employs six part- and full-time staff. Since 1953, QUNO–NY has facilitated dialogue among UN diplomats, staff, and representatives of nongovernmental organizations (NGOs) by offering Quaker House for informal off-the-record conversations on difficult issues before the UN. Over the decades, its primary task has been to prevent and de-escalate conflict.

Some of the QUNO–NY work has included various civil society initiatives of the UN, peace in the Middle East, the Earth Summit, World Conference on Women, the Law of the Sea Treaty, North and South Korea relations, and issues pertaining to small arms and light weapons. Quaker House also hosts small seminars and conferences and once served as the residence of the QUNO–NY director and family.

Not far from the Palais des Nations, the Quaker UN office in Geneva is located in historic La Maison des Quakers, also home of Geneva Friends Meeting. QUNO Geneva concentrates on issues of criminal justice, human rights, and peacebuilding. In its postconflict work, it attempts to look at a given country and its needs in a holistic way.

One recent endeavor is support for the UN Peacebuilding Commission (PBC), created in 2005 to aid postconflict countries as they move toward sustainable peace. The PBC, a body of thirty-one member states, has devised peacebuilding strategies for Burundi, Central African Republic, Sierra Leone, and Guinea-Bissau. The PBC is a forum for the government of the target country, the World Bank, the International Monetary Fund, and other civil society organizations to coordinate efforts and renew their commitment to peace. QUNOs link their own peacebuilding efforts to those of the UN and the PBC. QUNO–NY has held several informal dialogues on important issues before the PBC such as restorative justice and reconciliation through dialogue, attended by representatives of UN member states, UN agencies, and NGOs. The office in New York coordinates its work with PBC with QUNO–Geneva; for example, in the summer of 2009, a daylong evaluative session on the PBC was held in Geneva. Both offices will continue their support of this new UN commission's important and innovative work.

In the area of disarmament, the QUNOs have made their central focus the relationship between armed violence and development. In addition to the proliferation and use of small arms, the offices also engage in the study and understanding of the economic and social roots of conflict. For 30 years, QUNO–Geneva has studied and worked in the related area of the causes and consequences of the use of child soldiers. It researched the subject for the UN Study on the Impact of Armed Conflict on Children and published the results.[213] It has also worked to develop international standards to prohibit military recruitment and use of children in combat in any armed groups or forces.

A related area is conscientious objection to military service, because as long as there are weapons, there will be war, and as long as there is war, some, like Quakers, will conscientiously object to participating in it. Quakers at QUNO–Geneva have worked for more than 50 years to ensure that conscientious objection to military service would be recognized as a legitimate exercise of the right to freedom of conscience and religion. In its many statements to the Human Rights Council and its predecessor over the decades, QUNO–Geneva has insisted that this human right be protected. Now it is, under Article 18 of the International Covenant on Civil and Political Rights. A state violates this article if it punishes or harasses conscientious objectors or fails to accommodate their refusal to serve in the armed forces.

The QUNOs share a characteristic with other Friends' groups—pioneering new efforts in the area of peace and social justice, and then as these become established, passing them on to partner groups that carry on the work to strengthen and sustain them. The centuries-old strength of Friends' peace testimony, through their peacemaking and peacebuilding efforts, have earned them a certain respect within the international community, not only for their truthfulness and integrity but also for the depth and breath of this commitment to peace. This reputation aids QUNO–NY to work more productively on its three primary areas of current concern: peacebuilding, preemptive diplomacy, and "the responsibility to protect." The responsibility to protect is a new concept intended to engage the international community in responding preventatively and collectively to help nations avoid societal conflict, ethnic or otherwise, but if conflict nevertheless occurs, to take actions to avoid genocides such as those of Rwanda and Kosovo. This peacebuilding effort at the United Nations is intelligent, important, and worthy work.

Conclusion

Friends, at their best, bear active witness to peace, equality, community, simplicity, and truthfulness, which often manifests itself through voicing a protest or taking an action and occasionally through bringing or defending actions in courts of law. Through its discussion of Quaker witness in the courts, this chapter has revisited the incongruity of overriding the Society's traditional disapproval of going to law. Usually after individual and communal discernment, Friends' testimonies have compelled them on occasion to bring actions in court. Quakers have long been attuned to resolving disputes by gentle and direct talk, yet, for issues of broad public significance, rare in the universe of disputes, public courts of law are the appropriate forum.

At first blush, this may seem paradoxical, but both are opportunities for Friends' witness. As we will see in the final chapter, the methods of dispute resolution Friends historically favored, that is, mediation and arbitration, are best suited for disputes that need privacy and involve contenders who want or need to preserve an ongoing relationship. These extralegal alternatives occur in a less threatening and less formal environment, and many, many disputes could be more gently and efficiently settled by these means.

For purposes of illustration, we might analyze *Tinker* in terms of a choice between mediation or litigation for resolution of the dispute. For instance, if

Mary Beth Tinker had a dispute only with a single classmate who taunted or harassed her for wearing a black armband to protest the Vietnam War and support a truce, she and her classmate would have benefitted from using "gospel order." It would be counterproductive and damaging for Mary Beth to sue the classmate, assuming she could or would do so. Instead, she might talk directly and privately about her feelings surrounding the taunts and harassment and share the significance of wearing the armband to her. The classmate could also share with Mary Beth her reasons and feelings behind the taunts. An understanding might then emerge in such an atmosphere of sharing and privacy.

On the other hand, issues of public significance such as the Tinker students' freedom to witness against war by silent, symbolic speech are better suited to a public forum where important issues of civil rights and public policy can be aired according to evidentiary and procedural rules in the more formal environment of a court. In this setting issues can be explored and clarified through the presentation of evidence, and outcomes can be broadcast and enforced by the power of the judiciary. For example, the Tinkers' wearing of black armbands and their decision to challenge the prohibition against it set several actions in motion. These ultimately resulted in a Supreme Court decision that secured the same rights of free speech for students as their elders. Neither mediation nor arbitration could have achieved such a uniform and precedent-setting decision.

Friends raised issues in cases such as *Elfbrandt, Hirabayashi, Seeger,* and *Tinker* that have resulted in precedents that have benefitted, and will continue to benefit, litigants in the sphere of constitutional rights. Moreover, because some degree of publicity attended these suits, dialogues may have been stimulated. Indeed, civil discourse in a democratic society is beneficial, even essential to the thorough understanding of issues and ideas.

In addition, Quaker meetings and groups, frequently the New York and Philadelphia Yearly Meetings and AFSC, have participated in several court actions as amici curiae or intervenors to explain Friends' distinctive beliefs and history to the court when it is germane to the suit. They also support those who are not Friends, as Philadelphia Yearly Meeting did in First Unitarian Church's First Amendment free exercise claim against Los Angeles County. This testimony of community causes Friends to bring those within the broader community within the arc of their care and concern.

The FCNL has been, and continues to be, an important, albeit relatively recent, component of Friends long tradition of "speaking truth to power." By all accounts, it has gained the trust and respect of most legislators on Capitol Hill through its careful attempts at friendly persuasion. Its deep adherence to Friends' process of seeking the light in silent waiting enables it to be a calm but persevering voice for peace and social justice. Like Quakers who are ever-reminded of the obligation to truthfulness, FCNL tries to remind legislators that there are alternatives to war. In the international arena, the QUNOs do likewise.

If Clyde Summers's stand of pacifism would disqualify him and most Friends from becoming lawyers under the Illinois Constitution of the 1940s, does Quakers' adherence to the testimonies of truth-telling, peace, equality, and community also make them ill-suited for the legal profession? These and other questions are explored in chapter 5.

5

Quaker Lawyers and Lawyer Ethics

"A lawyer does not have to be an etymologist or Kantian philosopher to know what honesty, good faith, and fairness mean in the everyday practice of law."[1]

Several queries from *Faith and Practice* of Baltimore Yearly Meeting go directly to the heart of the issue explored in this chapter—whether there is a tension between being a Quaker and being a lawyer: "Do you seek employment consistent with your beliefs and in service to society? Do you strive to be truthful at all times, avoiding judicial oaths? Do you live in accordance with your spiritual convictions?" Can one be a Quaker and a lawyer and assiduously respond to these queries in the affirmative? Some might say no. Some might further contend that "Quaker lawyer" is an oxymoron.

A law professor believes that teachers and practitioners of American legal ethics have ignored religious thinking, "almost rigorously so since the Civil War, . . ."[2] even though theology is a useful discipline in moral science of which law is a part. "We old-fashioned, pre-positivist natural lawyers would say, with Blackstone and most nineteenth century Americans, that *all* law school discussion depends on the first principle of ethics: Do good and avoid evil."[3] In the matter of legal ethics, he believes that the views of Jesus are as relevant as those of law professors or Supreme Court justices.

This chapter explores the connection between Friends' testimonies and ethical lawyering because, in essence, a concern with ethics in law practice derives from a kind of religious concern at least in its broadest sense. One could even argue that both spring from the same source. This chapter reviews some current thinking on legal ethics, the "role" of the lawyer, conscience, and "personhood." It also explores the relationship between lawyers' identity as Quakers and their daily practice of law to determine if, or how, Quaker beliefs create conflict or tensions in these lawyers.

As the 1991–1992 Henry J. Cadbury Scholar at Pendle Hill, the author devised a survey of 30 substantive questions, factual and open-ended, intended to elicit Quaker lawyers' views on the law and legal system in the contemporary

United States, particularly as it relates to their Quaker faith. The survey was pretested with the help of Pendle Hill staff and a sociology professor at Swarthmore College, and is reproduced in Appendix 1. The questionnaires were distributed to men and women who were, or had been, practicing lawyers or judges and members or attenders of Quaker meetings. Factual questions, in addition to gender and age, included the type(s) of law they practice, involvement in pro bono public work and alternative forms of dispute resolution, and whether being Quaker affects their law practice. The open-ended questions were designed to solicit respondents' views on whether fundamental changes should occur in the way law functions in society or in contemporary law practice, how being Quaker affects their law practice—if it does—and how they would prefer to practice law absent any constraints. Their narrative answers are discussed throughout this chapter as these subjects are examined. Some key answers are cross-referenced and presented descriptively herein.

Quaker Lawyer Respondents: The Profile

In order to gauge the views of Quaker lawyers on the interplay between practicing as a Quaker and a lawyer and to test some propositions of legal ethicists concerning possible conflicts, the author sent the survey to 206 Quaker lawyers in the United States; 108 responses were returned and of those, a few replied that, although lawyers, they had never practiced law. The total sample of U.S. Quaker lawyers who were practicing, or had once practiced, law and were Quaker members or attenders of Friends meetings then became 100,[4] 65 men and 35 women, a few of whom were interviewed in person. Certain variables, such as gender and age, are considered significant to some responses and are discussed separately.

Length of Time as Quakers and Lawyers

Sixty-two percent of the Quaker lawyers had been members or attenders of the Society of Friends for more than 20 years. About one-fourth (26%) had been Friends between 1 and 20 years (17% for 11–15 years, and 9% for 16–20 years) and 12% had been Quakers for 10 years or less (4% for 1–5 years and 8%, for 6–10 years).

Almost two-thirds (64%) of the lawyers were "convinced" Quakers, converts in the parlance of other religions. Less than one-fourth (21%) were birthright Quakers, and 14% were attenders, that is, they usually attend meeting but have not formally become members of the Society. An overwhelming majority (86%) were members or attenders of unprogrammed meetings, the kind on which this book focuses.

Forty-one percent had practiced law for more than 20 years. Almost as many, 37%, had practiced between 11 and 20 years. The remaining 22% had practiced 10 years or less.

The women had practiced less time than the men. Fifteen of the 35 women respondents had practiced less than 10 years, whereas only 7 of the 65 men respondents had practiced that short period of time. Eighty percent of the men had practiced law at least 16 years while only 23% of the women had practiced that long.

Thirty-eight percent, including only two women, attended law school immediately upon graduation from college. Sixty-two percent did not attend law school immediately after college graduation; of these, 13 attended law school more than 10 years later. The time lapse between college and law school was greater for women. Of the 33 women who did not attend law school immediately after college graduation, 19 (58%) attended law school more than 5 years after receiving their baccalaureate degrees.

Why Respondents Wanted to Become Lawyers

Question 7 asked why respondents wanted to become lawyers. They could choose more than one reason from: "prestige," "money," "altruism," "family pressure" (a family member urged them to go into law), "family connection" (respondent had a parent or other relative in law), "intellectual interest," or "other." Perhaps

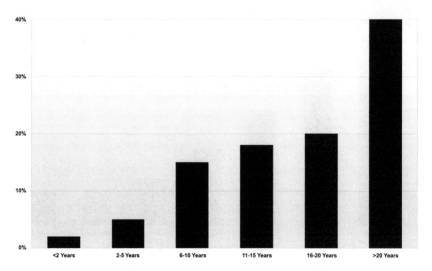

Figure 2. Length of Time Practicing Law

it is not surprising that the most frequent response was "altruism" (one wrote "of course"), followed by "prestige," and then "intellectual interest." They cited "money," "family pressure," and "family connection" considerably less often.

Half a dozen respondents explained similarly altruistic reasons for wanting to become a lawyer: to change or save the world; to work for or help others; or "to be of service." Men and women chose altruism at similar rates.

One was convinced from a young age that law was the avenue for him "both to put some talent to use and for [the] best contribution to society." A woman wanted "to help, especially battered women and other women frustrated with the legal system." Another chose law as a "form of social activism"; one, to have a satisfying career that would both generate income and contribute to society. Another saw it as an opportunity "to work with the poor." One wrote wistfully, "I wanted to change the world for the better. I thought lawyers did that."

One followed a "leading" toward law because it matched her skills and interests. Another, believing the services of a lawyer were necessary for the family business, decided to enter law, and, in addition, its income would allow him be involved in Quaker and community affairs. One wanted "an opportunity to work in a field where [he] could make the world a better place . . . and . . . [be] provided reasonable financial security."

One respondent became a lawyer, in part, because he had been impressed with the intellectual vigor of two 80-year-old attorneys in a firm where he had

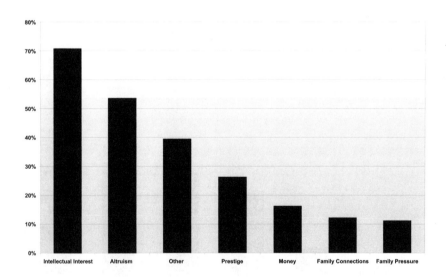

Figure 3. Reasons for Becoming a Lawyer

worked one summer. A woman wanted "the tools to try to change the world while using my mind"; however, intellectual interest as a reason was chosen by half as many women (9%) as men (18%).

Several respondents, all men, mentioned independence as an attractive aspect of practicing law. One liked the opportunity for one-on-one service. Another responded that he "didn't want to work for anyone else." A third chose law for its "self-sufficiency and independence" and because it was "interesting, useful, practical, versatile, [and] helpful."

A respondent wrote that he had been "influenced by the model of Thomas Jefferson whose profession was law but whose life's work was public service. I have used a legal career as a foundation from which to be very active in community affairs. . . ." One, attracted by altruism, chose law so he could be politically involved as did another with an interest in politics. One wanted to become a lawyer because she liked a "certain quality" about the lawyers she knew. Another, previously a paralegal, wanted to expand the areas in which she could help clients.

Another respondent wrote that emulation of her lawyer-father must have been subconscious because he did not want her to become a lawyer. As a single mother in a rural area, she felt she needed the best possible set of skills because, as a small entrepreneur, she "would have somewhat less credibility" than a man. Another single parent wanted to become a lawyer because she had "[n]o marketable skills. I'm good with words." One wrote that results of aptitude and interest tests pointed her toward law. Another felt channeled into law because while growing up people always remarked that she would be a "perfect lawyer." However, at the time of their responses, neither woman was practicing.

A few respondents felt that becoming a lawyer ensured job security and kept them from being at the mercy of others. One, who dreamed of becoming a constitutional law professor, had intended to earn a law degree and a doctorate in public law. However, during the McCarthy era, his Ph.D. study was aborted when he refused to sign a loyalty oath his university required. After that experience, he wanted a law degree to ensure employment "not dependent upon acceptability to an employer." A respondent became a lawyer partly because, as a plaintiff in a controversial court case, she had become unacceptable in her former field. Gaining skills as a lawyer allowed her independence as well as a degree of social and political usefulness.

Women responded from their special perspective as women, and their explanations are enlightening. For instance, proportionately more women (37%) than men (20%) chose "prestige" as their reason for choosing law. One "wanted to be self-supporting and found that difficult as a female in our society." Another needed work where she could be "in control." One "wanted to feel important," and another wanted "power to do." One wanted to have the "power to promote equality." A woman, who chose almost all reasons for becoming a lawyer, explained they coalesced to fill a need "to build [her] own sense of self-worth and take responsibility for taking care of [her]self and the family [she] wanted. . . ." Another wrote that "women needed extra 'credentials' to command attention to their concerns and to the struggle to preserve the planet and promote social justice." One who chose prestige wrote that, for her, "prestige" meant dignity and respect. "As a female in 1970 when I started law school, I was partly motivated to be treated with respect instead of like a thing that types. Indeed since I obtained my J.D. nobody has asked 'How fast do you type?' "

A man reflected: "[i]n retrospect I think I also had a need for a 'protective cloak' of authority, prestige, power. . . ." Another wanted "to aid, hopefully as a judge, in [the] dispensation of 'justice,' which I now define as fairness at a given time and place, realizing that genes and experience will color what is fairness more than one's religion or philosophy." One was interested in how human affairs worked and how one could help the system to evolve. Another wanted to further his liberal arts education and initially had no intention of becoming a lawyer: "I went on with law because law school tends to mold you to [do] just (and perhaps only) that." One man, a Friend and lawyer for more than 20 years, answered with a large question mark. Another wrote, "'It beats clerking' as they said marching off to Manassas in '61."[5]

One candidly answered that although she experiences serious tensions, it would be difficult to forgo law:

> I do like having people call on me for my expertise, the status of arguing before the state supreme court so often I'm about on a first-name basis with the judges, seeing my name in the published cases, etc. So I continue to live with the compromises and tensions, but I don't feel good about my reasons for doing so. . . . I have always assumed that at some point I would give up/grow beyond practicing law. Right now I've bought into the need to save for our children's college education, retirement, etc. and that means bringing in a certain level of income.

Respondents' Mode of Practice

Most respondents (61%) practiced either as solo practitioners (34%) or with small firms of fewer than fifteen lawyers (27%). Men and women were in solo practices about equally, but almost three times more men worked in small firms. Only 13% were employed in firms of more than 15 lawyers, and none were women. Thirteen percent were also employed in government service, the number of men and women about equal. Of the latter, some were judges and public defenders. Thirteen percent worked outside the stated categories: one worked in a family business, one in the Quaker United Nations Office in New York, one as corporation counsel, one in a public interest nonprofit organization, two as executive directors of state legal services, and three in legal services organizations. There was one of counsel, a municipal solicitor, a director of an alternative dispute resolution office within a state court system, and a nonprofit public defense firm lawyer. Eight lawyers who had practiced law in the past did no longer.

Quaker Influence on Respondents' Practice of Law

Respondents strongly identified with Quaker beliefs and testimonies according to their answers to question 4 (How strongly do you identify yourself as a Quaker and with Quaker beliefs and testimonies?). An overwhelming 91% chose either "very strongly" (49%) or "strongly" (42%). None answered "not much" or "not at all."

More than one-half (51%) answered "a lot" to question 14 (Does your being Quaker influence the way you practice law—a lot, somewhat, a little, or not at all?) Not surprisingly, because Friends try to live the testimonies, a majority stated that their beliefs influenced the way they practiced law.

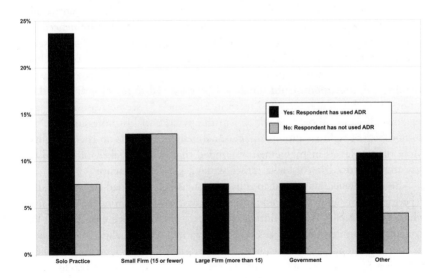

Figure 4. Size/Kind of Practice with Use of Alternative Dispute Resolution (ADR)

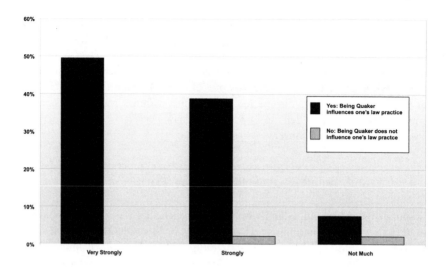

Figure 5. Strength of Identification as Quaker with Influence on Practice

Twenty-five of the 29 women (86%) who answered this question wrote that being Quaker influenced the way they practiced law "a lot." Four women (14%) answered "somewhat," but no woman answered "a little" or "not at all."

Of the men who answered, 42% wrote that being Quaker influenced the way they practiced "a lot," whereas 31% answered "somewhat." Twenty-seven percent wrote they were influenced "a little" (21%) or "not at all" (6%). Those who answered "not at all" explained, "You can't let it. My Quaker precepts are not useful in the courtroom. Unfortunately, I have learned to my chagrin that there is not a little bit of goodness and truth in everyone"; "I see no reason why one's religious affiliation should be relevant to the practice of his profession . . ."; "I do not feel the right to impress my personal 'religious' beliefs on clients' rights." More than twice as many women responded that being Quaker influenced the way they practiced law a lot, a rather striking gender difference.

Because one's morality is shaped by religion as well as myriad factors including a person's upbringing and unique life experiences, determining with certainty which factors predominate is difficult. The recognition of such enmeshment was evident in some respondents' answers. One wrote: "Has Quaker influence been its thorough good self on me thru and thru [sic]? Or did I become a Quaker because a number . . . of these influences were already present? Perhaps it's a combination." Another answered, "I can't separate 'being Quaker' from who I am as a whole. How would I be a different person (let alone a different lawyer) if I had never come in contact with Friends? After 25 years, it's one of those global identity questions that you can never really answer." One respondent who was somewhat influenced wrote: "It's hard to know which is the chicken and which is the egg. I practice as a gentle reconciler whenever possible; it is hard to know if that is because of my personal traits or my religious beliefs."

In keeping with Friends' belief in the inner light in every person, one respondent wrote how her Quaker influence manifested itself in her practice: "I try to respect each client and to find 'that of God' in each one." Several mentioned Quaker influence in the context of the cases they chose. One would not accept *any* case; another wrote that, as a Friend, he was "more careful about representations than many lawyers. The careful, deliberate representations I see in older Quakers build a lawyer's reputation for integrity, which is a valuable asset. . . ." Being Quaker influences the way another practices "a lot" because her "primary objective is to make the world a better place."

Several respondents attributed the ability to listen to Quaker influence. Careful listening is a salient characteristic of Friends' faith—listening to the inner spirit in meetings for worship, meetings for business, clearness committees, and mediations and arbitrations. One wrote: "I . . . am willing to listen to what the other party in a dispute says and to attempt to make sure my client listens to the other party's position." Listening is also critical to the work of the Friends Committee on National Legislation (FCNL) and may be a reason why it is respected among Washington lawmakers.

A man wrote that being Quaker influenced his practice a lot, explaining that he tries to help parties "find a solution that fits both, rather than trying to ensure that my client gets his way." This concern for a client's adversary is relatively uncommon in lawyers and most likely would be discredited by those who see zealous advocacy as the be-all and end-all of law practice. Gandhi, however, would have understood this Quaker's response.

Another wrote that being Quaker influenced him to try always to be honest, courteous, and fair; this man was a Quaker for more than 20 years before he became a lawyer. Another who was a Friend before becoming a lawyer wrote that being Quaker somewhat influences his "sense of fairness, respect for other positions, willingness to encourage compromise that results in longer lasting benefit to [the] client. . . ." and his "desire to do the honorable—ethical thing." One thought that because he was a Friend, he counseled clients not to be "part of the problem," and he tried to be considerate of opposing counsel. Another wrote that being Quaker influenced him to be honest with clients, partners, adversaries, and the court; to provide some free legal services; and to advocate only what he believed in.

One respondent wrote: "Ethics is a problem/concern in any law firm. I am known in my law firm as 'the Quaker' for my insistence on not overbilling (or as my partners put it, 'low billing')." One wrote that practicing law "requires a Gandhian approach." Two respondents wrote that being Quaker influenced them to "settle litigation short of trial" and "try harder to resolve conflict rather than 'win' the case."

Question 16 asked if being Quaker "*should* influence the way you practice law." A resounding 89% of those who answered wrote yes, and only 4% said no. A large majority of men who answered thought that being Quaker should influence the way one practices while every woman who answered thought so. One wrote, "It means I don't practice"; and another answered that being Quaker "influenced [her] leaving the active practice of law."

The Type of Law Respondents Practice

Question 10 asked what type(s) of law respondents practiced, that is, the substantive area such as wills and estates, personal injury, or civil rights as distinguished from the way one practices (Question 14) the general mind-set or outlook regarding the law and lawyers' resulting actions.

The practice areas most often cited were corporate law, where men outnumbered women six to one, and real estate law (landlord-tenant and "Quaker real estate"). An expectation that Friends who were influenced by their faith would tend to practice civil rights and public interest law was borne out to some extent. The next highest number of lawyers practiced in the fields of civil rights, including employment discrimination, and domestic relations, both more or less equally divided between men and women. Eight percent practiced probate law and 7%, criminal law. Three men practiced personal injury, and three, tax. Eight percent were litigators. One or more practiced in environmental, administrative, health (including medical malpractice), bankruptcy, consumer, elder, zoning, and alternative dispute resolution. Respondents were underrepresented in the areas of immigration, labor, patent, and copyright.

Several were judges. One answered that he felt tensions and conflicts: "I must interpret the law; I must seek my faith and understanding; if faith conflicts, I must recuse. So far I have not had to. . . ."

A lawyer practicing workers' compensation law expressed discomfort that a quantitative value was placed on clients' body parts: "I try to be a human being mediating between this system and the people . . . caught up in it." One chose immigration law because of his Quaker beliefs: "I wanted to work in an area where I could in some small way work to make this a better world [and where] . . . I could serve people who needed help."

Question 12 asked whether "being Quaker influences the *type* of law you practice?" Two-thirds (67%) answered affirmatively. Twenty-eight percent said it did not, and several did not answer. There were more affirmative answers from younger lawyers. Ninety-three percent of those between ages 31 and 40 stated

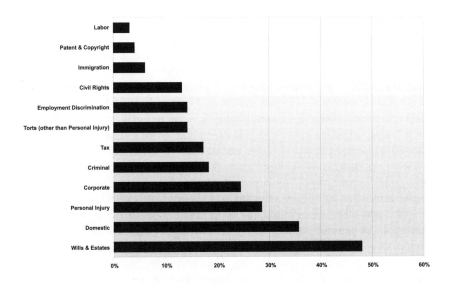

Figure 6. Type of Law Practice

that being Quaker influenced the type of law they practiced, while being a Friend influenced less than half in the group older than age 50. The responses revealed that being Quaker influenced more women (85%) than men (63%) in the type of law they chose to practice.

The Effect of Gender

In all, 35 of the 100 respondents were women. 8 were between age 31 and 40 years; 16 were between age 41 and 50; 9 were between ages 51 and 60, and two were older than 60. One wrote that gender is "a strong factor in how people feel about their work [and] place in the legal profession."

A pair of legal ethicists sees Sophocles's Antigone as the archetypal woman who revered principle over pragmatism and who saw familial ties as a natural law that superseded—and was superior to—the law of the king.[6] Rand and Dana Crowley Jack have studied and written about the moral distance between the personal and professional morality of lawyers. The Jacks see Antigone's strength not in the law but in her opposition to the law. She speaks to Creon, "Your edict, King, was strong. But all your strength is weakness itself against the immortal unrecorded laws of God. They are not merely now: they were, and shall be, operative forever, beyond man utterly."

The Jacks have called responsiveness, avoidance of harm, care, and relationship interdependency a "feminine" view of morality and have considered the effect of the influx of women into the legal system in this light. They believe that women carry a disproportionate share of care orientation into their lawyering and, therefore, in the present state of law practice will probably experience the most tension between their professional and personal moralities. In fact, they believe the stark dilemma for some women is either to forsake the law or forsake "self." Several Quaker lawyers in this survey did, in fact, leave the practice of law. "Because [this] choice is unfair and destructive to individuals, and because society risks losing an enrichment it can ill afford to do without, the legal system must push beyond the dilemma to find what new structures and attitudes will invite integration of fairness of rights and responsiveness of care."[7]

Women often see relationships as interlinking so that a particular good becomes a communal good. Two survey respondents affirmed this. One wrote that casting family law in an adversarial mode does not produce the greatest good. Another tries to avoid viewing an adversary in "zero/sum, black/white terms" but instead in relation to the "larger needs of society, community. . . . [W]inning a criminal case may be right for the client but not always the best for overall reconciliation." A woman lawyer may also see an individual "evil" more broadly—as one suffered by others beyond her client.

The women respondents clearly favored a less aggressive style of lawyering, as many were bothered by the fighting born of the "win-lose" mentality. One wrote, "my mind, when presented with a problem, seeks a resolution rather than a conquest and therefore the competitive 'dance' that underlies the practice of adversarial law is distressing to me." The women appeared quite uncomfortable with a perceived need for lawyers to be ruthless, particularly in trial and pretrial settings. One complained, "The name of the game is to beat up on the enemy, [t]o perform as a hired gun."

A greater tendency of women respondents to see interdependencies was reflected in a desire for a more cooperative stance. One emphasized the importance of finding a common solution. Another considered mediation to be more compatible with Quaker values; the adversarial process "felt like fighting rather than cooperating." Another stressed interconnectedness by suggesting a shift toward a realization that what happens to one often has a reverberating effect on another. The Jacks suggest the adversary structure of legal discourse precludes voices of cooperation and interdependence, and those with such voices risk alienation.[8] Several of the Quaker women respondents in the survey did feel such alienation.

Some legal scholars have begun to examine traits of "feminine" thinking and lawyering because of a growing recognition of gender-differentiated styles of practice. A willingness to encourage a traditional "feminine" style would accept a greater emphasis on discerning patterns of interconnectedness and recognizing that the once-feared "feminine" and less aggressive style of lawyering properly stresses accommodation over confrontation.[9] Women's greater sense of interconnectedness and Friends' testimonies of harmony and community may be synergistic; Quaker lawyers would most likely welcome a greater acceptance of this style, which some already practice and many admire. A few respondents rightly suggested the difficulty of separating some Quaker and feminine elements.

Women lawyers will probably bring a further humanizing influence to the practice of law as their ranks in the legal profession swell, but the prevailing legal culture might instead change them. A woman respondent articulated this possibility: "It [law practice] needs to become more humane. I sense that this is happening (slowly!) as women enter the profession. My fear—with some justification—is that women won't change the profession, but that it will change them."

In 1971, 5% of admittees to the bar were women; by 1987 this figure had increased more than sevenfold to 36%. Nevertheless, only one year later, women comprised only 16% of the U.S. lawyer population.[10] Although in many law schools, women students now equal or outnumber men, women have yet to take their proportionate place in the population of practicing lawyers. Clearly substantial attrition occurs between law school matriculation and actual law practice. One respondent provided an insight; she wants "to live a sane life, and law requires too many hours and too much investment of emotional energy." Women's work as child-bearers, nurturers, and caregivers makes a law career problematical for many young women lawyers.

Although women are well represented in government, education, private associations, and legal aid and public defender offices, they have not yet penetrated the judiciary or law firm partnerships to a similar degree. This may be partly due to women's shorter tenure in the profession. In the early 1990s, the median age of retired or inactive women lawyers was 39 years compared to 71 years for men.[11]

Any significant change in law practice for which women may be responsible will most likely occur further in the future. Before women lawyers dare to be different and assert their own particular strengths, they have needed, or felt they needed, to be "one of the boys." One respondent wryly noted: "Law practice is like high school. You gotta be one of the boys." "American women entering the law were made to prove that [they] . . . were basically no different from men lawyers, that a woman could do all of the legal jobs a man could do, and in precisely the same way."[12] If there is a fresh look at the strengths women can bring to the practice of law, there may come a day when such proof is no longer necessary.

Although there are signs of change, some women may still not be confident and secure enough to mentor young women lawyers. One respondent recounted her experience in a small firm where she hoped to be mentored by an older woman lawyer. However, instead of encouraging her, the older lawyer harshly criticized the respondent. This experience caused her to think that women had "bought into the system and . . . undercut other women lawyers." Another woman articulated her feelings vis-à-vis male colleagues: "I work in a very conservative environment where an old boys' network operates to discriminate against women at both a conscious and unconscious level (largely the latter). There is a great deal of socializing (somewhat like a fraternity) and drinking. I sometimes feel a tension about how to manage . . . because I am an outsider and different, and am concerned how I can advance as such."

The Effect of Age

Of the 100 respondents, none were younger than 30 years of age; 14 were between ages 31 and 40; 42, the largest group, were between ages 41 and 50; 23 were between ages 51 and 60; and the remaining 21 were older than 60.

Lawyers who come to the profession after other life experiences have naturally been "out of role" longer and therefore, do not have the Lawyer's predisposition to compartmentalize life. If an older lawyer is a woman, this effect is augmented. The larger number of younger men may be related to men's long dominance of the legal profession, when a person trained for the law, or both. The time lapse between college and law school was greater for the women respondents. More than half of them—19—began their legal education more than five years after receiving baccalaureate degrees. The women's law practices may have been affected by the longer time they had before law school to experience and be influenced by other aspects of life. Those without such life experience are more easily molded into the mind-set of the Lawyer. Because an older woman has been a lawyer less time, she is less inclined to differentiate decisions as a lawyer from those springing from her "personhood." And, according to the Jacks' theory, her care orientation will cause a greater inclination toward compassion, cooperation, and accommodation, "feminine" traits more actively encouraged in girls raised in earlier eras. The older woman lawyer would seem then to be among the least fit for the role of Lawyer and would be particularly vulnerable to feeling conflict between her professional and personal/spiritual "selves." In addition, the doubled effect of latent age and gender discrimination may have practical effects on an older woman's "success" in the profession.

Another way age affected respondents relates to societal changes over the past several decades. One respondent wrote, "I'm from the era that your word was your bond and [I] always looked for a way to bring about settlement. . . ." Another said that "older lawyers in my age category try to quickly solve clients' problems, in contrast to many young lawyers who are more litigious" and more likely to delay resolution. Aside from these two respondents, the men older than 60 did not experience tensions between their "Quakerhood" and their law practice nearly as much as the younger male lawyers. They have practiced law for several decades and so may have incrementally become accustomed to the gradual and insidious aggressiveness, incivility, and deceptiveness of present-day practice. They may take unquestioningly for granted what is bothersome to lawyers newer to the profession.

Respondents' Pro Bono Work

Question 13a asked if respondents performed pro bono work, and if so, how often. Of those who answered, more than three-fourths (77%) did; 18 did not. Those who answered affirmatively were asked whether being Quaker influenced their performing pro bono work, and if so, how? Of those who answered, 10% performed more than 20 hours per month and 8% performed between 16 and 20 hours. Of the respondents who performed pro bono work and answered the subquestion, 74% wrote that being Quaker influenced the work, and 26% said it did not.

The Quaker lawyers considered pro bono work worthy of lawyers' time. One suggested that it should be made mandatory; one thought lawyers should do more, and another who contributes many hours, agreed. He also thought that lawyers should care more about clients as people. Those whose Quaker faith influenced them to do pro bono work explained their reasons: the concern for equal access to the law arises from the belief of God in every person; Quaker testimony of equality; a sense of community responsibility confirmed by Quaker experience; loving kindness for people confronted by legal problems they would otherwise find insoluble; promotion of the Quaker-based Alternatives to Violence Project; the urge to fight for those who otherwise would be voiceless; desire and need to help people, whether or not they can afford to pay, perhaps especially when they cannot; help whenever there is injustice regarding a nurse or patient; help Friends schools; counsel tax resisters; and a way to do God's will.

Others did pro bono work in connection with human rights, civil liberties for the underrepresented, and the pursuit of social justice in daily life. "'Inasmuch as ye have done it unto one of the least of these my brethren, ye have done it unto me'[13] . . . what doth the Lord require of thee, but to do justly, and to love mercy, and to walk humbly with thy God?' pro bono work allows this."[14]

Others performed pro bono legal work because: as a Quaker she felt an internal drive to provide social service; Quakerism meant being an idealist and activist; deliberate decision to witness with the skills most powerful to this Quaker lawyer; mediation work "as part of the peace witness; . . ."[15] "it gives a setting and opportunity to rethink one's life and recommit to doing God's will by helping others." One answered simply, "I do pro bono because it is part of being good."

Those who answered that being Quaker did not influence their performing pro bono work did it out of a "sense of professional responsibility"; enjoyment of serving others, especially "nonprofit organizations on the cutting edge of social change"; "being poor should not deprive one of legal help."

Respondents' Experience as Quaker Lawyers

Question 17 asked if respondents felt any tensions or conflict between Quaker testimonies and the practice of law. If they answered affirmatively, they were asked to elaborate. Of the 95 respondents who answered this question, almost two-thirds (62%) said they experienced tensions or conflicts; one answered "yes and no." The comments show that they have thought about the distinction between their preferred behavior in witness of Friends' testimonies and the behavior expected of a Lawyer. The responses show that virtually any compulsion to follow the latter produces tension.

Only a slightly higher percentage of women (67%) than men (61%) experienced tensions. The relatively high number of men is somewhat surprising given that they do not have to contend with the additional challenges women face. Nor are men presumed to possess a strong "care" orientation that makes aggressive legal battling especially distasteful to women. Still, Quaker lawyers who are men may be more oriented toward care and compassion than other lawyers because of Friends' reiteration of the principles of harmony and community. This may be considered peculiar in legal practice and surely distinguishes them from some members of the bar. The relatively high degree of tension the men experience is most likely due to their "Quakerness," especially for those who identified "very strongly" or "strongly" with Friends.

From early childhood, most persons are encouraged to tell the truth, but this admonishment tends to become more diluted as one travels along life's way. This dilution may occur less frequently in Friends because of the Society's constant reinforcement of this commitment. According to one respondent the crux of Friends' belief is to "speak truthfully and plainly." Moreover, this emphasis on truth-telling makes role-playing morally objectionable, including the professional "role of the Lawyer." When speech, thought, and action are contradictory or skewed, the resulting dissonance can be deafening. Active witness of Quaker testimonies—so say and so do—creates a sharpened sense of personal morality.

The age distribution of responses to the question of tensions or conflicts produced interesting findings. Most tensions were experienced by those in their 40s, followed next by lawyers in their 50s. In all age groups except the oldest— those older than 60—respondents who experienced tensions outnumbered those

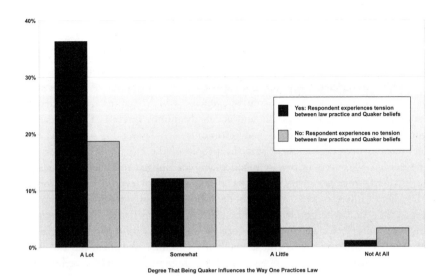

Figure 7. Quaker Influence on Practice with Experience of Tension

who did not. Lessened tension in those older than 60 is probably due to at least two factors. After practicing 30 or 40 years, older lawyers may have become comfortable with the way law is practiced and have come to accept it without challenge. Second, lawyers older than 60 were trained and began practice in an era of fewer lawyers, more civility, and less tendency to break, or bend, court rules. However, one respondent older than 60 remarked: "Of recent date there has been a win-at-any-price atmosphere prevailing with some practitioners, so that all possible means towards victory should be used. This means disregarding common courtesy toward other lawyers and making the whole business one where a careful practitioner must have everything agreed to in writing." In spite of his clear disapproval, he did not articulate it as a tension.

Other older male respondents wrote: "I do not expect everyone to agree with my way of doing business (but I do not encourage people with whom I do not feel comfortable to become/remain clients)"; "Quaker beliefs and testimonies, without being sanctimonious, permit such independence of or from 'special interests,' religious, economic, political"; "I believe that there is a demand for honest, straightforward lawyers living by Quaker principles. Those who want any other kind of service can go elsewhere"; and "I believe every lawyer should try to act ethically." These preferential observations did not rise to tensions or conflicts for these men.

Some respondents who were 51 to 60 years old who did not experience tensions explained there was "always an ongoing tension between who you are and what your clients want you to be for them, whether one is a Quaker lawyer or not," and "I am not generally an adherent of specific testimonies which would bring me in conflict with the law." Another wrote that he had not experienced tensions or conflicts for awhile because he had already worked out what he would and would not do in light of his Quaker beliefs.

Other respondents who did not experience tensions practiced in areas such as public interest law: "administrative agencies, which I counsel, are generally established to protect the public and act in the public interest. This is usually consistent with Quaker beliefs and testimonies." A lawyer for a city did not feel tension because her client was the people of the city so she did not feel the burden of lawyers in private practice who are obliged to zealously represent their client's interests "which may be a 'mixed bag' or even a negative one." Her client's interests were, almost by definition, what she considered the most beneficial. Another respondent noted that she did not experience conflicts because she took only "cases which I believe can be processed within my belief system. My clients know my beliefs and when there's a conflict, the client has the right and my blessings to go . . . elsewhere." One thought that lawyers' actions did not really conflict with Quaker values that much.

Affirmative responses to the question of tensions fell into several categories, although a respondent's answer could embrace more than one. The most frequently cited tension was the general lack of truth-telling. Next was aggressiveness and ruthlessness. Others were disturbed by a lack of equality, a few by "hat honor," a few by the death penalty, and one by the lack of simplicity.

Several respondents mentioned negotiation as a source of discomfort, which is somewhat surprising because it is a temperate area of practice involving an active search for agreement. They disliked the deception they believed intrinsic to the process. One noted that in negotiations, lawyers are most successful if they state they have less authority than they actually have; doing this enables them to yield later without exceeding a predetermined fair and favorable figure. Yet to do it best and most effectively, the respondent wrote, lawyers probably have to lie. This troubled the respondent because lying is anathema to Quakers. One respondent was uneasy in the offer-counteroffer process in personal injury negotiations. Another wrote: "I 'fib' during settlement negotiations, should I? It's expected and it's the only method that works."

Richard Burke has also noted that duplicity is common, even expected, among lawyers in negotiations. In discussing the 1983 Model Rules of Professional Conduct, he observes that rule 4.1 only prohibits affirmative misrepresentations, and comment to this rule further qualifies it: "Under generally accepted conventions in negotiations, certain types of statements ordinarily are not taken as statements of material fact."[16] In Burke's view, the rule excuses deceit in negotiations by saying, in essence, that "lying is only in the ears of the listener, and therefore, if the listener believes that lawyers lie, then there can be no lie." He calls this reasoning "casuistry, if not pure nonsense," arguing

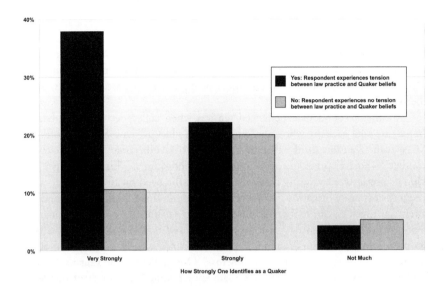

Figure 8. Strength of Identification as Quaker with Experience of Tension

that it excuses a wrong action because it has come to be expected and thus is common and customary.[17] Still another respondent was uncomfortable in settlement negotiations because of the lack of truth-telling: "If I speak truth, I cannot open negotiations with anything but my bottom line."

One respondent felt tension when she was "pressured to fudge on truth-telling" in depositions. Another tended to avoid litigation because of this, thereby earning less than she otherwise might. She has considered leaving law to return to the nursing profession. A respondent stated that her tensions centered on justification for fees and on clients who hated their adversaries. One wrote that she felt "conflict in the entire structure of the system. I . . . am distressed and . . . lose sleep over court cases that seem to escalate and not move toward resolution." A man noted that clients, colleagues, and adversaries often do not share respect for others or their points of view but rather tend to see an opponent as the embodiment of evil rather than as a person with a different perspective. He touched on an important point also mentioned by others: confrontation is urged because attempts at nonconfrontational solutions appear weak.

One respondent wrote bluntly: "I must bury my true Quaker beliefs to function." Asked how he tried to resolve the tensions, he replied, "What's to resolve? They are irreconcilable."

Another who was a "heavy duty dude" before he became a Friend, found Quaker testimonies and law practice to be virtually incompatible: "In large scale litigation, I found that I got carried away and would find opponents' weak spot and go for it with intensity, irreconcilable with Quaker thought. I could do this while being Catholic [but] being a Quaker has unstrung me for the practice of law."

Another respondent experienced tension when colleagues pressured her to "refuse to take a client who can't afford it." A Harvard Law School professor, Mary Ann Glendon thinks that today's lawyers have become "connoisseurs of conflict" who feel pressure to bill more and more hours. This discourages the kind of preventive lawyering that might obviate the need for time-, money- and energy-consuming litigation.[18] A respondent agreed: "I would like more head-on attention given to preventing disputes than to settling them (by running up fees) once they've occurred." Another also believed that law should be focused on prevention because it "functions expensively, inefficiently and acrimoniously when it is a system for solving problems." One believes that litigation often "polarizes rather than reconciles." A male lawyer said, ". . . much of our legal system promotes conflict [and] I seek to find ways to avoid [it]." Another lawyer, a woman, noted that, in child custody litigation, spouses reactivate long-forgotten mistakes and weaknesses to use as weapons against each other.

One respondent saw the relationship between the frequency of litigation and its cost in an interesting way. He thought that the high cost of litigation may prove to be an effective brake on "those who want to nail their adversaries to the wall," but who do not want to pay the fees involved in doing that; conversely, he wrote, if lawyers will work pro bono, litigation can go on forever.

Several legal ethics scholars and respondents alike believe that aggressive lawyering can have a constitutive effect on one's character, making lawyers become what they do. One respondent wrote that she was not yet as evil-minded and cutthroat as some opposing counsel and hoped that she would not acquire those traits. Note this respondent's use of "yet." The Jacks, who have discussed the personal and professional morality of lawyers, state: "Repeatedly turning off the personal alarm has an erosive effect on the claims of personal morality. Over time, what is subjugated grows accustomed to its secondary status and becomes less insistent in its claims."[19]

The Lawyer's role and one's own sense of personhood diverge when lawyers play a role that does not ring true. The result is subtle, but over time this can result in a diminution of integrity, both in the conventional sense and in a dis-integration of the lawyer's personality. Richard Wasserstrom has written about the role differentiated behavior of lawyers: It is especially hard because of the nature of the profession—lengthy educational preparation, prestige and financial reward, and the concomitant enhancement of sense of self—for one's professional way of thinking not to dominate one's entire life, making it difficult to shed one's professional role even when that role is unnecessary and inappropriate. The Jacks and other scholars discussed here believe that often lawyers allow, or feel they must allow, the professional aspects of their lives to dominate their gestalt so they *become* that role.

Another respondent experienced "pressure to prevail at all costs, pressure solely to pursue money for self and client, sometimes, pressure to be unethical." A woman wrote, "the adversarial system promotes aggressiveness, dishonesty and places emphasis on money awards as the solution to all social problems and conflicts. The materialism and 'trial by combat' nature of the law stands in direct conflict with Quaker spiritual values. . . ."

According to Wasserstrom, the role-differentiated amorality of a lawyer in today's legal environment promotes aggressiveness over accommodation, competitiveness over cooperation, ruthlessness over compassion, and pragmatism over principle, character traits also fostered by the capitalistic ethic.[20] Some respondents echoed this. One pithily observed that being a lawyer allowed him to remain in "competitive sports." Another experienced tension when "clients expected him to be their surrogate warrior in a zealous assertion of their 'rights' . . . the idea of win-win is foreign. . . ." He explained that it is stressful not to be the kind of lawyer many clients want because he likes to please others and be successful. Another wrote that he feels tension when "a client—or a situation—suggests that advantage can be gained by sharp practice, by being less than honest."

A respondent was uneasy when she felt compelled to be cutthroat and ruthless with opposing counsel because she thinks it is detrimental to clients' emotional well-being. One feels a tension between finding a peaceful resolution of conflict and feeling the need to stand up and "fight." Probably referring to Friends' "gospel order," a man replied with a question: "Should people sue at all? Should they sue to get money for injuries? Morally, biblically, the answer may be no." This respondent knew the origins of Friends' gospel order and no doubt had thought about and witnessed the ramifications of suing in court. A respondent, appointed by the court to defend a person charged with heinous crimes, described the tension she experienced when the defendant's prior criminal record disclosed a pattern of similar convictions and "in whom it was often very hard to discover any good, spirit, or light."

Some aspects of law practice that bothered respondents were more Friends-specific. For instance, a respondent's supervising prosecutor's directive to seek the death penalty in a first-degree murder case caused her considerable tension because, like most Friends, she does not think the death penalty should be imposed on any person. Another wrote that imposition of the death penalty directly conflicted with his Quaker beliefs. One respondent was once asked to leave a firm because certain of his pro bono representations advocated positions contrary to those held by some of his firm's important clients. Another contributing factor was his refusal to accept representations of companies in the nuclear industry or ones marketing military goods because these conflicted with his peace testimony. One respondent wrote that his imprisonment for draft resistance would "sometimes" scare away clients. Another used a Quaker term in describing a tension between his inclination to be kind and the perception of him as Lawyer; as an attorney, he may be "too *tender* with people." One Quaker lawyer refused to use "your honor" when addressing a judge and instead used "judge" or "the court." Another also spoke of her opposition to hat honor toward judges but recognized that giving it full expression might jeopardize her clients' welfare. Perhaps due to the same lawyer's witness of equality, she opposes capital-gains special treatment even though it might benefit some of her clients. One respondent touched on the lack of simplicity in law practice: "Personally and spiritually I move towards simplicity, living lightly on the earth, spending more time grounded in prayer and in community. . . . In my office I am weighted down by books, periodicals, . . . a copier machine, and computer. . . ."

One respondent wrote "there is tension in any work you do in this society where it is impossible to escape entanglement with government in its dark forms—war, defense, [and] lack of environmental awareness." Another identified a dilemma germane to Quakers and others alike: the inherent "tension between doing what is good for your firm (in terms of . . . income) and doing what is good for the client." Differences involving income generation are more apt to surface in partnership or firm settings because in solo practices, lawyers answer only to themselves. A lawyer who discourages a lawsuit by advising a client to forgive and forget a de minimus wrong might be doing well for the client but not for the firm's income. However, this dilemma is not unique to law practice but can present itself in other businesses and professions. Taking more time is financially better for those who are paid by the hour or day, but taking less time is better for clients or customers; the expectation of a reasonable profit should be balanced with a sense of fairness.

One respondent articulated another tension: "At times I find myself buried in work to the point where I lose some of my concern for individuals, but then I try to focus more on helping and I am normally able to get things back in order. I do feel there is a conflict in that my work . . . does not address much of the real suffering in the world." A respondent, not now practicing, described the "top down" pressure to achieve a particular result he experienced as corporate counsel and his realization that bottling the tension this pressure caused was unproductive. Another mused about her probate practice: "do you inventory the furniture, etc., which is legally required, when the result is having to pay a confiscatory . . . tax? Or do you say to the client, 'here's what the law tells you to do. If you're doing something else, just don't tell me about it'?" One respondent, "painfully aware of the [daily] tension," said that she would quit if she could let go of a "need to earn $x a year and the status and prestige, and all that." Another felt a tension of trying to balance a rewarding legal practice with a fulfilling personal and spiritual life.

How Respondents Try to Resolve Tensions

Question 18 asked respondents who experienced tensions in their practice how they tried to resolve them: talking with Quaker colleagues, talking with non-Quaker colleagues, Friends meeting, a Meeting Clearness Committee, or other ways.

About 30% worked through their conflicts by talking with Quaker colleagues. About 20% discussed them with non-Quaker colleagues. A few had gone to their meetings, and a few had convened meeting clearness committees.[21] Others focused on prayer, the inner light, spirituality, meditation, self-reflection, meeting for worship, or talking with a Quaker spouse. Several relied on group support: one organized a consultation group on legal and ethical problems, and another met with a group that discusses legal dilemmas in relation to basic human values. One met with a spirituality group, and another met with other attorneys who look for alternative approaches to the system. A woman sought to resolve the tensions by trying harder to put her "Quaker convictions into practice." Another wrote, "I rationalize and vow to work to change the law."

One dealt with the tensions by leaving the field because she did not want to experience them so frequently. Several others had either left the practice of law or had changed jobs within the legal field. One moved to a job where she "could feel good" about her work, and another explored alternative options. However, a man admitted, "By and large, the tensions are unresolved." The Jacks believe that this tension is inevitable when the requirements of a professional role are incompatible with the dictates of one's individual morality.[22]

The conflicts articulated by respondents raise further queries germane to Quaker lawyers. Will the institutions of law simply remold them into current ways of valuing and thinking? Will the tension persist at the expense of those who experience it? Could changes in the law result in a system that would exact less of a price from its lawyers? One respondent worried that practicing law "may be a series of acts which validate the institutions involved, instead of changing them. . . ."

One study, sponsored by the Maryland State Bar Association, found a high degree of dissatisfaction among members of the state's bar. In fact, more than one-third of the lawyers surveyed at the time had either decided to abandon the legal profession or were unsure they would remain in it.[23] The study indicated the existence of a persistent malaise within the profession. A 2006 study of 800 lawyers, sponsored by the American Bar Association, found that slightly more than 50% were satisfied with their legal careers while only 40%

of those who had practiced less than 10 years were satisfied. Only 40% would recommend the profession to others, but despite this, more than 75% expected to be practicing in five years. Lawyers practicing in the public sector were the most satisfied, however this group was the most concerned about politicization of the law and judicial independence.[24]

Another important question is whether a change in the legal system would better serve the public. A 1998 American Bar Association study polled 1,000 people on their views of lawyers and the U.S. justice system. The respondents believed that there should be fewer lawyers and that the discipline of lawyers was too lax. Three-fourths thought the legal system was too costly and involved too much delay. A very large percentage believed that treatment was unequal and that corporations and the wealthy had a clear advantage over others. More than one-half believed that the justice system needed a complete overhaul.

Can Quaker lawyers and other lawyers who recognize a need for legal reform spur modifications to the system with a concerted effort? This may depend on whether a small and diffuse band of Quaker lawyers have the will and organizational ability to influence and rally like-minded colleagues of the bar to launch this endeavor. Friends' strength for such a challenge lies in a unique perspective born of several centuries of individual and communal observations and involvement with law and legal systems. A respondent wrote, "Like many things, the practice of law is a reflection of a society and its values. I am not sure change can be made other than in an organic way by the persons who make up the profession." Quaker lawyers might discuss their own observations and tensions concerning current practice with colleagues; like many Friends, some might also yearn for more fulfilling legal work that allows for more integration of "Lawyer" and "self" and more compatibility with personal or spiritual morality. Quaker lawyers might engage these colleagues in discourse that, in turn, might rally further support for important, beneficial change. Historically, the influence of Friends has been disproportionately great relative to their small numbers, and therefore it is reasonable to think that Quaker lawyers might indeed be a powerful vanguard of a thrust toward legal reform. This reform would also be of significant benefit to the public.

Advantages of Being a Quaker Lawyer

Question 20 asked if respondents perceived any advantages to being a Quaker lawyer; if so, they were asked to explain in what respects: getting new clients, settlement negotiations, at trial, counseling or advising, relationships with peers, or other ways.

Three-fourths of the respondents answered that being a Quaker lawyer did have some advantages. One-third saw an advantage in settlement negotiations, followed by counseling and advising and getting new clients. Least cited was "at trial." One respondent thought all were advantages "except they are not from being 'Quaker' but from exhibiting Quaker values in dealing with others. The legal profession cherishes . . . honesty, truthfulness and integrity, and over time those values (although not uniquely Quaker) are recognized in your practice." She thinks that many lawyers possess and exhibit many "Quaker" traits. But if the legal profession cherishes "honesty, truthfulness, and integrity," then it must find better ways to communicate this to its practitioners. If lawyers are to practice these traits—and they do not, then the profession must be prepared to discipline them.

A man described an advantage as a "persistence, even to the point of exasperating judges who are accustomed to dominating lawyers; patience, even when disagreeing with judges and adversaries; and a reputation for being careful to never mislead [the] court [on the] facts or law." Another wrote, "Because of my honesty and reliability in performance, people feel they can trust me. This is a psychological reward more [important] than $." One answered, "I mean what I say and say what I mean. My ability may be questioned, but I don't think my integrity is." Another respondent believed that Quakers "may have a little more credibility with judges and other lawyers." Many mentioned trustworthiness, listening, and caring as advantages of being a Quaker lawyer. Nevertheless, one respondent wrote, "Quaker integrity and ethics get more recognition probably than they deserve!"

One respondent who does not think that "one should wear one's religion on his sleeve" rarely mentions that he is a Friend, and he is "embarrassed when Quaker business and legal acquaintances do so." Another noted that there was no advantage in being *known* as a Quaker lawyer but there was an advantage in *practicing* as one. One wrote that his colleagues and others assume that "because I am a Quaker, if I say something, it is true." Another said that the "conscientious 'stereotype' [of Friends] has never hurt and has sometimes helped." A respondent wrote that the "Quaker search for truth and honesty and tendency to under-statement allows a vantage point that can permit significant insights" and can be very helpful in settlement negotiations and intrafirm relations. Another noted that an advantage was the reputation for being fair, reasonable, and moderate, although this might be a "double-edged sword" because people may think that such lawyers are not "hard-nosed enough [or] tough enough" or "willing to go all the way for the client." Numerous respondents echoed this thought.

Several mentioned patience as an advantage of being a Quaker lawyer: one because of his patience "with poor clients who are impaired emotionally, socially, economically or intellectually because I see them just as valuable as people as myself"; another mentioned patience together with the ability to stand in adversaries' or clients' shoes to understand their positions better, and, finally, one, who had patience with peers, was often asked to mediate work-related problems among them. Another advantage, according to one, was that "Quakerism develops an instinct for, and an ability to find, consensus," and one respondent further believed that consensus-based collaborative problem-solving was critical to good lawyering. A woman noted an added value of consensus: one's ego takes a back seat to finding a just resolution.

One of the few respondents who thought being a Quaker lawyer helped in getting new clients wrote, "Most clients are hoping to be treated fairly. A known Quaker will attract this type of client." Another explained that Friends' advantage in counseling and advising was avoiding overoptimism or zealousness. Friends' example of being unafraid to hold minority opinions made it easier for one lawyer to "represent unpopular causes and the underdog." Further advantages of being a Quaker lawyer were Friends' practice of listening and looking for the light within each person; Friends' beliefs that helped transcend the limited view of the legal system as the final resolution to any problem; Friends' practice of truthfulness and respect for that of God in others in helping negotiate clients' claims and having straightforward interaction with other attorneys; and "the remote possibility of remaining human."

Quaker lawyers with such advantages have an abundance of ideas and perspectives to share. A conference at Pendle Hill, or elsewhere, might include a generous number of lawyers who are not Friends. It could also include legal scholars and thinkers mentioned in this chapter and others who are on the forefront of new ideas about law and its practice such as Burke, the Jacks, Noonan, Perry, Presser, Shaffer, Unger, and Wasserstrom. Along with Quaker lawyers and judges, such a mix would certainly result in a rich dialogue out of which still more ideas might emerge, including a consensus on next steps. If that consensus includes a need for certain changes in the practice of law and the legal system, the conferees might take cooperative steps to initiate that process of revision.

Disadvantages of Being a Quaker Lawyer

Question 21 asked respondents if there were any disadvantages in being a Quaker lawyer, and if so, in which areas: getting new clients, settlement negotiations, at trial, counseling/advising, relationships with peers, or other.

Only slightly more than one-half of respondents (54%) answered this question. Of those, 41% thought that Quakers lawyers were most disadvantaged in "getting new clients," and more men than women thought so; in the questionnaire space marked "getting new clients," one wrote "Ha!"

Many responded that the perception of Quaker lawyers was one of goodness or softness—not toughness, a trait that many clients seek in a lawyer, especially a litigator: "If one is . . . known as a Quaker, in some minds he will be 'too good,' sitting too quickly and easily in judgment on the client." Another thought that "people often don't understand Quakers and perceive them as 'soft, less aggressive.'" One wrote in a similar vein, "Perhaps clients feel that peaceable

Quakers are too easy in pursuing their interests." And again, "Some . . . in the community may think that I am not aggressive enough for their needs or temperament." Another agreed: "To many, my integrity is not as desirable as are warrior-like (take no prisoners) skills." And he wrote that he may be a "pushover" and not "tough enough." The Quaker lawyers' perception of these qualities as disadvantageous seems counterintuitive, but perhaps they realize that in the atmosphere of current law practice, they are only being realistic.

Friends' tendency to speak plainly and modestly makes marketing difficult for one: "[t]he projection of oneself in an aggrandizing way seems inconsistent with being a 'Quaker lawyer.' " Another similarly noted this disadvantage, "Quaker reticence about . . . blowing one's own horn, which may be necessary . . . to getting clients."

The next most frequently cited disadvantage was at trial. This finding is not surprising given the public's perception and expectation of heightened aggressiveness and hostility in that setting. One said, "Conflict is hard . . . fighting does not come to me intuitively. It's like speaking a foreign language before you get good enough to think in the language. It takes a lot of work. However, counseling and mediation flow out of my pores without effort." It is unfortunate that a lawyer thinks he has to work hard to become good at fighting and conflict. A challenge is to educate clients and the public that civility and attempts at accommodation do not signify weakness in either the lawyer or the case. Many others acknowledged that being Quaker makes them uncomfortable with the fighting inherent in today's litigation. A man wrote that being a Friend "unstrings you for the aggressive warfare of litigation." Another agreed that trial, the most adversarial part of the legal system, was the most "Quakerly frustrating." One noted that being "one of the boys" is difficult—"being callous, asking sadistic questions at trial, etc." Several women agreed. One disliked the war model of trial and thought that being a Quaker was a disadvantage; another did not want to fight; one found it difficult to be aggressive at trial, especially in cross-examination; another woman noted "the prevailing ethos in [the] legal culture in my city . . . [is] a 'scorched earth' policy [that] collides with Quaker values."

Few respondents thought it disadvantageous to be a Quaker lawyer in counseling and advising. However, one who did wrote: "I'm too willing to see what the other side is saying, perhaps making me less single-minded for my clients." Another noted that "openness probably works to [the] disadvantage of [the] client; nice guys finish last."

Respondents' elaborations on the disadvantages of being a Quaker lawyer are interesting because they would be considered advantages in most other settings. For instance, one thought it disadvantageous in every area because "I can appear more interested in peace than punishment." Another agreed that it was a disadvantage in all areas because in law practice, there is "too much show, status, aggressiveness and questionable behavior."

As for being honest with clients, one respondent acknowledged, "I sometimes do not advocate as strongly as I might if I think it would be a distortion of the truth. Also I don't always take advantage of a weakness . . . of the other side." Another wrote, "prospective clients who know I am a Quaker express the fear I will not 'fight' for them." He added that participation in antiwar activities was politically suicidal. Several saw a financial disadvantage: "[F]inancially, my classmates are rich in money. I'm rich in love." Another noted, "Quakers are no longer industrial leaders and now mostly offer only unprofitable representations"; one wrote: "it became clear that most of the well-paying clients did not want their lawyer to be too honest." Another confirmed this—if a client wants a dishonest lawyer, "he won't seek out a Quaker."

Some respondents realized that their faith commitment to tell the truth and hew to high ethical standards could put clients at a disadvantage. One wrote, "I try to be honest; that often can hurt a potential client who is in denial." Another explained that Quaker lawyers' stronger standards for ethical behavior might disadvantage a Quaker lawyer vis-à-vis an opponent because, at times, the former will have "less room . . . to maneuver legally." One responded that "requirements . . . or knowledge of respect and honesty may limit me in how to deal with others, especially other lawyers." A man realized that "clients feel that a low-key less confrontational approach does not fit their image [of a lawyer] . . . and sometimes a close adherence to ethical standards may not please a client or peer."

Some respondents believed that being Quaker could negatively impact peer relationships. They felt isolated, and one woman admitted, "I am so rigid [that] my peers get disgusted with me." Another wrote that colleagues thought she was too forthcoming about her faith. One wrote that "peers often regard us as namby-pambies, not serious about law practice in the prevailing manner"; one noted a disadvantage with peers because she "won't lie," and a man felt being Quaker "prompts the unscrupulous to take advantage of you."

Another responded, perhaps tongue in cheek, that a disadvantage of being a Quaker lawyer was that it kept him from "being an aggressive son of a bitch who'll do anything to anyone." Asking God's help keeps one lawyer focused on "what is fundamentally important . . . and that, in turn, helps me have the courage to be honest." Having empathy "makes difficult ethical decisions so much easier."

Whether, or How, the Practice of Quaker Lawyers Differs from That of Others

Question 26 asked respondents whether their practice differed from others'. Almost half, mostly women, answered yes.

"Non-Quakers look at a case to see if it's economical. I do too, but I also ask whether it's right." Another noted that her "perception of the issues differs from many other non-Quaker lawyers and clients." A man answered candidly that his practice did not differ as much from non-Quaker colleagues' "as it should. I don't always have the courage of my convictions." Another wrote, "I do more challenging of the status quo than most attorneys I know." One answered, "I believe that I am more likely to advise clients to reach a compromise than [other] lawyers." Another wrote, "my billing practices are different from my partners'." One noted, "For most of my non-Quaker colleagues, money is the only barometer of success." A man explained: "I am an idealist who is principally interested in changing the world radically through non-violence. . . . I am a lawyer second."

Quaker Lawyers Who Changed, or Left, Their Law Practice

Some of the tensions Quaker lawyers articulated caused several to change their area of practice or leave the law entirely. One, who left her Wall Street law firm after five years to become a public interest attorney, wrote that she had experienced tensions not because of decisions "that I was required to make in representing corporate clients, but because I felt that I shouldn't be representing corporations . . . in the first place." Another wrote that he no longer practices criminal law because, as a young public defender, he had problems "defending people [he] knew were . . . perpetrators [or] killers." One took a four-year sabbatical from the practice of law after three years as a legal services staff attorney: "partially because I found some tension between my Quakerism and the nature of the largely litigation practice in which I was engaged. . . . I felt that litigation frequently didn't solve anything, not even when the client "won," and certainly did not often solve an underlying problem. I often felt that I was making matters worse rather than better. In hindsight, I'm sure that too often I limited my clients' choices of remedy to litigation. There was little or no alternative dispute resolution then. . . ."

After 30 years, a woman could "no longer endure the 'war' that civil litigation has become—not just between . . . lawyers but the 'war' of paperwork (mostly unnecessary). I deplore having to confirm the simplest agreement by letter and by fax; a telephone call used to be enough." Her practice "was no longer fun or intellectually stimulating," had become a drag and a bore, and was "too dam aggressively adversarial for my taste."

One stopped practicing for several reasons, not all of which she understood. "I was unhappy practicing law and felt quite a bit of tension between my values and personality (non-aggressive) and law practice (adversarial)." A woman left law practice because she "hated marketing for clients, charging them and keeping my time records to do so, feeling like a fungible worker . . . [and] the acrimony of litigation was disturbing." Still another woman who left law practice had experienced tensions and conflicts because there was "[t]oo much emphasis on winning [and] no focus on . . . what was in the best interest of the parties." Another had "felt extraordinary tension" while practicing because of the perceived need to obscure and dissimulate.

A young woman respondent and interviewee had married an attorney, and, contrary to his counsel, entered law school. After she graduated and had practiced family law for a year, she discovered that there was "no way to be a kind and gentle person and still practice divorce law." She was considered weak when she sought to protect the children by trying to prevent their parents' growing antagonism. She generally found opposing counsels' tactics "very rough"; many seemed exhilarated by game-playing and would "cut you down" before substantive issues were reached.

She also experienced a conflict in regard to Quaker truth-telling, honesty, and plain speech. Because most lawyers are disinclined to reveal their intentions and "language is not used fairly," she felt it nearly impossible to be herself and say what she meant without having opposing counsel take advantage of her. Furthermore, representing her clients zealously while maintaining her integrity was difficult. This respondent makes clear a lawyer's difficulty in simultaneously fulfilling the dual duties as zealous advocate and truthful officer of the court. After becoming a Quaker, her awareness grew, her values became clarified, and her intuitively felt discomfort with law practice crystallized. "To live a Quaker way of life and practice law effectively within the system as it exists are poles apart."

Another discussed his tendency toward openness and plain speech: "Personally, I would probably be more open than I think appropriate when acting as representative of [my] client." His observation is significant in light of the Lawyer's role—when lawyers do not operate as themselves ("I would probably be more open") but in the devised construct of a role ("than I think appropriate when acting as representative of [my] client"). One who no longer has a litigation practice wrote, "[I] am not directly faced with issues of discovery—of making strategic decisions on which information to disclose and which to withhold, how to manipulate the truth-gathering process, etc. I used to do personal injury . . . and divorce cases, . . . and I couldn't take it." Another lawyer explained why she left the practice of law: "I found I couldn't do what I wanted/felt was right and still make a living. Possibly if I'd started earlier, it might have been different. I don't like litigation or 'lawyer' behavior. Also I didn't like working with clients whose desire for $ made them want to get as close as possible to the legal/illegal line. . . ." In addition, the law's demands on her time made living a balanced life difficult.

Two lawyers who were not respondents weighed in with their own reasons for leaving law practice. One left practice to become a law professor. He had once thought that he would be a kind of warrior/artist who fought for his clients but above all fought for justice. Instead, he found himself in a sort of ethical cave where attorneys functioned as shadowy clerks copying documents requested by clients with little regard for concepts of fairness and right. The other who left law practice explained that although some attorneys "do their best to balance . . . conflicts without sacrificing their integrity, . . . the adversarial system makes it inherently difficult to do so. Those who act ethically often put themselves at a competitive disadvantage."[25]

Respondents' Suggested Changes for the Law and Legal System

Respondents reflected on the legal system within the broader society in answering Question 27: "In your opinion, should there be any fundamental changes in the way law functions in our society? If yes, please explain." Of the 86 respondents who answered this question, 73 (or 85%) said yes, and 13 (or 15%) said no.

One had lost respect for the "deeply flawed" adversary system that, as currently constituted, does not have the search for truth as its goal. Another wished the legal system were less crisis-oriented and more oriented toward global problem-solving. One wrote that "[w]e need to move away from a rights-based system which automatically leads toward isolation of self from others towards a recognition of the need for community through collaborative problem solving." This respondent would likely concur with the great chain of being model that legal scholars Unger, Perry, and Presser admire. Another complained, "law now encourages the shifting of responsibility (as in imposing liability without fault) and the lottery concept (as in much tort litigation)."

Some themes recurred. Respondents wrote that, within the laws and legal system, there should be greater truth, fairness, and equality; fewer rules; more trust, caring, and sense of community; greater access for more people, especially the poor; increased emphasis and greater use of mediation, arbitration, or their allies. One thinks that "our legal system is a farce . . . law fails to take into account the feelings of women, minorities, and even a few William Faulkner types like me. Connections, pull, and being white male are important [and there is] too little common sense." One respondent believed that the legal system, as it has evolved over the last millennium, is good and has fulfilled its basic purposes of protecting the individual against the state and avoiding physical violence by providing an avenue for dispute resolution in the courts. However, the legal system may have failed to meet its full potential in proving a real and viable alternative to violence when the system becomes too expensive for the poor and disenfranchised. There may be a connection between poor people's lack of accessibility and a perceived need to settle disputes by violence, the only means not foreclosed to them. There may be a link between the lack of affordable legal assistance and physical violence because the paucity of alternatives results in frustration and anger. This might diminish if more affordable and peaceful methods of dispute resolution were available outside the courts.

Some respondents took a broad view: "First, the society must change to a win-win society, [and] then the legal system can reflect this. . . ." A woman wrote that there should be fundamental changes not in law, "but [in] people." Another pointed out that "most laws are based on reason, common sense, and justice; it's the way we abuse the process that is damaging." A man similarly wrote that law reflects the attitudes prevalent in society: "me first and getting the most bucks for myself," but he believes that greater use of alternative dispute resolution could ameliorate this. Another believes that:

> [c]ulture is collapsing; it is relying on the court system to hold it together and the system is not capable of this. Law needs to think in integrative, holistic . . . not discrete, dissected, narrow disciplinary terms. The law ought to emphasize stewardship over ownership; there is great potential for this in the law of trusts, environmental law, water law, growth of comparative negligence and no-fault divorce, moving away from blame . . . to an equitable adjustment of differences.

Another respondent wrote: "The legal system is part of a broad system of nation-states, industrialism, imperialism, profit-based economy, patriarchy, and exploitation and destruction of the earth, which I consider "living in Babylon" . . . [and] the only way to stop living in Babylon is to stop living in Babylon, stop participating in the guts of this system. . . ."

A few respondents' remarks evinced a certain "aloneness." One noted that clients and colleagues do not share her values and ethics regarding the resolution of problems. Another wrote that others do not seem to understand her feeling of conflict in regard to truth-telling; "Not having found anyone who seems to understand, I tend to withdraw . . . avoided doing the actual litigation. . . ." A respondent who experienced tensions answered that she could not resolve them by talking with Quaker colleagues because "There were none!" One antidote to this loneliness might be participation in Quaker lawyer conferences. Lawyer-Friends have convened at Pendle Hill to discuss and explore common attitudes, goals, or dilemmas, and ponder variations of the question—how Quaker lawyers can practice law in today's legal environment and still be true to Friends' testimonies. At least three such gatherings have taken place at Pendle Hill: Quaking at the Bar in 1982; Quakers at the Bar in January 1988; and An Exploration for Lawyers in April 1993. The time may be ripe for another.

Respondents' Suggestions for Changes to the Practice of Law

Question 28 asked, "What, if anything, would you like to see changed about the practice of law?"

One wrote, "Can I get away with saying *everything*?!" A repeated refrain was "less litigation," "less posturing," less adversariness, and less aggressiveness. However, a firm advertising for an attorney in Baltimore's legal newspaper, *The Daily Record,* apparently thought aggressiveness was an attractive trait. The list of criteria in the position announcement began: "Candidate should be aggressive. . . ." In the same issue, a "[s]mall congenial law firm" advertised for a personal injury lawyer; the copy read "MUST BE AGGRESSIVE." An advertisement on the exterior of a city bus in a southwest city shows two law firm partners outfitted in red boxing gloves with the caption "Serious Injury? We'll Fight for You." The Quaker lawyers, however, wanted the practice of law to be more collegial. One believed the legal system should rely more on alternative processes to "shift from the mentality of winning to one of helping those in conflict resolve their differences fairly."

Some respondents suggested that changes be made to the rules, including evidentiary, procedural, and court rules. One proposed following the British system, that makes pretrial coaching of witnesses illegal. Another wanted a "new code of ethics" including "[p]rocedural changes to eliminate adversary 'bullying' of [the] poor and disenfranchised," and one suggested modifications to the rules of evidence as well. One yearned for "more focus on equity and justice than detail and technicality," and another believed that justice should be a right, not a privilege.

Not surprisingly, several Quaker lawyers believed that the practice of law should emphasize service over commercial gain. One suggested a renewal of professionalism and "permanent leave-taking of the notion that the practice is just another business. Money, necessarily, is in everything. But law, like medicine, primarily is service, or ought to be." Former U.S. Supreme Court Justice Sandra Day O'Connor agrees. She believes that public service differentiates a profession from a business; furthermore, she thinks that law schools should teach the importance of doing good while doing well.[26] Similarly, one respondent wanted the legal profession to abandon its desire for wealth and status and treat the law as a public trust; "We are trustees engaged in a public service, not mercenaries for hire." One agreed that law has become a business rather than a profession, and attributes that in part to lawyers' advertising; another suggested that lawyers' ads be banned. Yet another wanted less emphasis on law as a business, but more on conflict resolution.

Many respondents wished for more civility, collegiality, and professionalism. In addition to a return to civility, one suggested more policing of lawyers' abuses, including their disregard of procedural and ethical rules. One hoped for a better and more effective process for the selection of judges. Judges should be at least partially selected for their willingness and ability to curb lawyers' disregard and abuse of rules. One respondent wrote that she would like to see all clients, victims, offenders, and adversaries treated with respect and equality. Another believed there should be equal respect and funding for prosecutors and defense counsel.

Two wanted lawyers to practice "without stalling, dirty tricks, etc." and without trying to "win at any cost." One voiced familiar dissatisfactions: "[too much] emphasis on earnings, discourteousness, [not being able to] trust another lawyer's word and pit bull clients." Another also wanted less pressure from clients. Two specifically wished for less economic pressure and a de-emphasis on money. One respondent suggested that "[y]oung lawyers should be required to serve internship[s] with experienced practitioners who have demonstrated superior moral judgment." Another disliked the narrow compartmentalization of law practice and wished that it were less complex so that general practice would be more feasible; apropos of this, he suggested a change from the billable hour method of billing because it encourages inefficiency, discourages discussion, and generally corrupts the practice. Another also suggested less emphasis on this billing method.

One echoed many respondents' desire for greater use of alternative methods of dispute resolution. He also advocated abolishment of the death penalty and a "Supreme Court that is not intellectually dishonest." Another believed that in the past two decades, law school admission policies and glamorization of legal practice have had an adverse effect on the profession.

Both judge and lawyer respondents wanted a raising of ethical standards, perhaps recognizing this to be a responsibility of each. A judge wanted the bar to return to "standards of historic morality, ethics and professionalism." A lawyer wished the level of the judiciary were higher, as well as a greater degree of professional courtesy among attorneys. Another wished for an improvement in ethics from both the bar and the bench. Other respondents continued to emphasize ethics and ethics education: "more ethics in corporate practice"; "ethics, values, and psychology should be more extensively taught in law school"; and "more training in ethics, alternative dispute resolution, and pro bono service."

One wanted a quicker resolution of cases and, to this end, suggested more adjudication by qualified nonjudges such as those in one Pennsylvania county. This lawyer's other "totally unrealistic" wishes were "less nastiness, more working to[ward] a goal of compromise . . . and women attorneys not feeling pressured to act like men. . . ." A man wanted to spend less of his time on "salesmanship" and more on thorough preparation, public service, and leisure. One respondent would like to see a substantial change in basic firm management, especially the "master/slave method of training."

The financial cost of legal services had been worrisome to many, as it was to Fox. In fact, one suggested that lawyers' income be limited to the national median "by capping fees at, say, the real income equivalent of $50.00/hour or require one hour of pro bono work for each thousand dollars of legal income"; he also proposed that litigation files be limited to "one inch thick." Two respondents believed that contingent fees should either be limited or abolished. One suggested what he knew was "a fantasy": "take [the] profit motive out of . . . [law practice]." Another ventured that 90% of lawyers serve 10% of the population because their services are too expensive for the rest; he suggested that there be public support for more comprehensive community legal service offices and for class action suits on social issues affecting the poor. One believed that legal advice and representation should be made available to most of the people "who can afford little or no legal representation." One thought that legal services insurance might provide access to a broader spectrum of people who need legal assistance.

A respondent suggested a public advocacy system for children, consumers, and the mentally and physically impaired noting, "[i]f we were civilized, we would fund advocacy for the weak." Like Thomas Shaffer, one believed that the powerful should be sensitive to the powerless, and another supported more equitable treatment for minorities and the poor. For instance, one worried about the large disparity in sentencing between the rich and poor and between the majority and minorities. This sentencing disparity was also stressed in the ABA survey of the public mentioned earlier in this chapter. Evident in these comments is the thread of Friends' testimony that advocates economic justice for the poor. George Fox had an early concern for their inadequate access to the legal system, as others did then and some Friends do now.

The many respondents who wanted an incorporation of real resolution of disputes into the legal system and a greater use of litigation alternatives follow Friends' testimony of harmony and community. They would no doubt admire the Society's historic practice of mediation and arbitration within the meetings and outside them. A respondent wrote that her state's judiciary had declared a completely adversarial approach inappropriate for many domestic cases because it impeded the parents' ongoing relationship with the children: "This recognition of the value of interpersonal relationships should be expressly articulated and elevated to something comparable to the requirement of 'good faith' conduct in contracts cases. Perhaps there should be a rebuttable presumption that there is value . . . in furthering . . . peace between people."

A respondent echoed the sentiment of many: a lawyer's job should be reframed as "equitable dispute resolution, not hired gun advocacy." He suggested that lawyers study and practice psychology and even undergo therapy before practicing. Another believes that lawyers should not have a monopoly on law practice but be open to the appropriate use of certified, licensed, or regulated paralegals. One man wrote there should be fewer lawyers, but more women lawyers, as in Japan.

One wrote that practicing law would be fun if his suggestions were implemented: recognition of all human rights including social and economic rights; replacement of criminal law by a system of medical, psychological, social, and therapeutic communities; and enforcement of court decisions by shunning. Another believes that the adversarial system does not result in truth, its purported goal, and suggests that "trial . . . [be] an effort by the court, with the help of marshals, to gather facts and reach a judicial conclusion based on them . . . without [lawyers] interrogating . . . witnesses [and] arguing to a jury or judge."

The respondents' ideas are thought-provoking. The lawyers have obviously considered improvements to the law, legal system, and practice of law perhaps because of their own discomfort with many of its aspects. This kind of thinking is necessary to any constructive changes that can bring law into clearer alignment with truth and justice.

Legal Ethicists and Quaker Lawyers on Truth-telling

A critical area of inquiry vis-à-vis Quaker lawyers relates to truthfulness, intrinsic and essential to Friends' faith. The lack of truthfulness was anathema to George Fox, and, indeed, the hypocrisy he observed as a youth in his church was the imperative that compelled his search for an alternative. In the context of Quaker lawyers, we have seen how difficult it is to maintain a primary focus on truthfulness while practicing a profession that, more than occasionally nowadays, calls for the practitioner to engage in some dissimulation, chicanery, or outright deception. According to Professor Burke, the effectiveness of the broad prohibition in lawyers' rules of professional conduct against engaging in conduct involving dishonesty, fraud, deceit, or misrepresentation has been de minimus. "For years, we have 'winked, blinked, and nodded' at blatant, if not outrageous, lying and deception in pleading, negotiating, investigating, testifying, and bargaining. In almost every aspect of our professional practice we have come to accept, in fact to expect, a certain amount of lying and deception."[27]

Burke believes that lawyers' current codes of legal ethics and rules of evidence and procedure frustrate and inhibit truth-telling and truth-finding:

> Whether predicated on the seemingly sacrosanct grounds of lawyer-client privilege, client confidentiality, or zealous advocacy, or on the less hallowed grounds of "puffing," "bluffing," and accepted conventions, lawyer lying and deception cannot be squared with any principled statement of the purposes and goals of the profession. And we should say so.[28]

If there is a modicum of truth in this assessment that "we [lawyers] have come to accept . . . a certain amount of lying and deception," if truth-telling is the quintessential core of Quaker belief, and if Friends generally try to live their beliefs ("so say and so do"), then Quaker lawyers are especially vulnerable to tension created by these countervailing forces. Indeed, many survey respondents identified the difficulty of maintaining truthfulness as a frequent source of tension. One believed that Friends' "single standard of truth . . . often conflicts with some principles of American jurisprudence." Another wrote, "Quaker testimonies of plain speaking and honesty seem to be in conflict with the way trial and pretrial practice is conducted. . . ." One went even further: "the adversarial system promotes . . . dishonesty. . . ."

Others, too, concede that the adversary system, the cornerstone of the U.S. court-based dispute resolution, tolerates deception and concealment. When the moral assumptions of a profession and associated institutions are at odds with the everyday life morality of the profession's practitioners, a moral tension will exist.[29] The Quaker lawyers' comments appear to confirm this. One wrote that in practicing law, an attorney often has to "avoid or hide the truth, which is counter to Friends testimony to seek and speak truth." However, the fact that new legal thinkers are sparking a resurgence of interest in morality and spirituality in the sphere of law is a hopeful sign, and like-minded lawyers should support and encourage that interest.[30]

Two attorneys, who were not respondents to the survey, spoke about truth-telling in relation to law practice: "Speaking is a very powerful thing. Speaking something you don't believe—even though it's socially acceptable to do that—creates an internal tension," and "It felt sleazy to cut the truth that finely."[31] Quakers lawyers are not alone in recognizing the moral costs of "cutting the truth" but they, and these two lawyers may be among the relatively few who acknowledge it outright. If it were otherwise, more voices would be demanding change in the profession and its rules.

In his 20 years of practicing law, Mohandas K. (Mahatma) Gandhi came to realize the foremost importance of facts in the preparation of an argument: "Facts mean truth, and once we adhere to truth, the law comes to our aid naturally."[32] In this sense, if facts are presented truthfully, practicing law does not have to conflict with truthfulness. However, Gandhi's statement was made more than 100 years ago, and he was no ordinary lawyer; his words still resonate and are food for thought for today's lawyers. One respondent does find it hard to be an advocate and still maintain truthfulness: "[The] quest for truth [is] a challenge. . . . I never tell (knowingly) a falsehood, but I sometimes withhold information which [would] weaken my client's case and which arguably is not the 'complete' truth." As the respondent implicitly recognized, Quakers aim not only to tell the truth but to tell the complete truth. Omission of a relevant fact compromises truth-telling, because truth is truth only in its wholeness.

It is significant, and not merely coincidental, that the oath or affirmation administered to court witnesses requires that they tell "the truth, the whole truth and nothing but the truth." The nondisclosure of a relevant fact, intent, or consequence is a passive form of deceit. One respondent felt tension when pressured by other attorneys to "make sure that half truths are revealed (or not revealed) at depositions."

Scholars and law professors at a Yale Law School symposium once discussed truthfulness as it pertained to similar tensions an academician may experience when he or she is both a scholar and a law professor. The scholar's devotion to the discovery of truth and his duty as a law professor to teach students effective advocacy skills can conflict; a habitual indifference to truth that advocates learn to cultivate in their professional lives can result in a certain carelessness about it.

Robert Rodes, a law professor who has developed a theory of Christian jurisprudence, has acknowledged similar incongruities in the professional lives of law professors who have one foot in the university and the other in the marketplace. "In one society we may be too academic—so sophisticated in our analysis of the transcendent that we lose track of what is actually going on. In another, we may be too pragmatic—so aware of the things we can make happen that we hardly stop to think whether they *ought to happen* or not."[33] In the fast-paced legal "marketplace," a lawyer rarely has, or takes, the opportunity to contemplate "shoulds" and "oughts." Lawyers, like many amid the hurly-burly of contemporary life, are inundated by deadlines, meetings, and other pressures. The "should" is displaced by "what is"—"it is what it is."

Some critics of Rodes's reformism worry that when bright students, taught according to his model, are unable to implement it in the real world of law practice, they will become disillusioned and unhappy. However, a critical mass of Rodes's "bright students" might feel more fulfilled if they and other like-minded lawyers could create a groundswell of support for the implementation of some of Rodes's reformist ideas. Quaker lawyers, as members of a community that has for centuries sought to bring about justice, could lead or make important contributions to this effort. Although small in numbers, Friends have been bold and forthright pioneers in defending unpopular causes, perhaps because of their beginnings as a persecuted minority. After many of their initial reformative efforts "have received the support of larger groups, they have withdrawn. . . . In all of their major efforts at social betterment the Quakers [have received backing from the Society and from] many like-minded persons outside their membership." With this historical tradition as part of their heritage, Quakers should not shrink from taking their place in the vanguard of U.S. law reform along with the scholars of "Christian jurisprudence" who remain optimistic about the place of law and lawyers in society. They believe that a drive for social justice can be institutionalized through law, and the lawyers who try to effectuate this engage in a blessed calling.

In a 1982 commencement address at John Marshall Law School, Gerhard Casper[34] warned graduates to shun the manipulative aspects of law practice because neither "law nor its history can be infinitely manipulated to suit our own views. Those who believe otherwise will simply be bad lawyers, in every sense of the word." Two respondents agreed and expressed discomfort with this practice. One wrote, the "adversarial process is not always above board and I don't like being manipulative." Another hated "manipulation for the sake of advantage."

Burke demands that both bench and bar shed the toleration of dishonest and deceptive practices hidden under the benign cloaks of conventional practice, confidentiality, and rights of the accused. He is saddened that the profession has become inured to white lies and duplicity and so has attempted to stir it from complacency: "While observation of current practices may make one despair about the efficacy of strict rules and high standards, a public profession such as ours should not countenance a code of ethics based on the lowest common denominator, [that is], common practices or conventions."[35] To counter this state of affairs, Burke advocates a change in the rules—the requirement of full disclosure of relevant facts and law and truth-telling and fairness in all legal environments. He believes that lax rules of professional conduct and lax enforcement appear to place a higher priority on loyalty to the client than to the profession and the public, and on zealous representation and confidentiality than to truth and fairness. Such skewed priorities cannot be squared with the public's rightful expectation of a fair justice system and the bar's declared dedication to principles of honesty and fairness.

Burke confronts the most sacred of sacred cows—the client's right of confidentiality. Because he believes that maintaining a confidence can sometimes fly in the face of a lawyer's responsibility to be fair and truthful and to prevent harm, he advocates a broad rule of mandatory disclosure to prevent significant harm. Rules of professional conduct inadvertently aid lawyers' escape from this responsibility by protecting a client's desire for harmful and deceitful conduct under the cloak of confidentiality. Burke's proposal would eliminate this protection by mandatory disclosure of that conduct. Under current rules, disclosure is only permissive, and, even then it is limited to the prevention of criminal acts. Arguing that moral considerations should not be optional, Burke also asserts that disclosure is the best and only response to perjured testimony. He believes a rule change requiring disclosure would raise standards and have very little deleterious effect on open communication necessary to lawyers and their clients. "Neither zealous advocacy nor client confidentiality can justify winning by lying. Our priority of values in the adversary process should make clear that the values of truth and fairness override those of confidentiality and zealous representation."[36] If Burke's recommendations were implemented, Quaker lawyers might experience fewer tensions.

John Noonan, currently a judge on the Court of Appeals for the Ninth Circuit, also regards the privilege of confidentiality a significant barrier to the search for truth; he wrote "absolute confidentiality is inimical to a system which has as its end rational decision-making."[37] A respondent who practices criminal law acknowledged that most of his tension "involves a conflict between my truthfulness and my client's right to expect information to remain privileged. This . . . arises in situations . . . where my client admits guilt to me and then I am called on to cross-examine an eyewitness to cast doubt on that person's credibility." Another wrote, "in small business counseling, [I] often find I'm being asked to cover for dubious activities." If the declared goal of the justice system is truth, then it is lawyers' individual and collective responsibility to refuse to participate in lying, falsification, deception, and misrepresentation in all aspects of law practice. Nor must they allow the demands of the Lawyer's "role" to justify deviations from the truth-telling responsibility that undergirds the system. It has been said that in our adversary system where truth and falsehood grapple freely, truth will overcome. But if two lies grapple freely, no truth can emerge.[38]

As George Fox did more than 350 years ago, Burke complains of deceit in pleadings and pretrial procedure. Legal procedures were abused for purposes of delay in Fox's time, but today the larger array of pretrial motions increases opportunities for obstruction and delay. And, like Fox, Burke believes that allegations, admissions, and denials in pleadings can and must be honest. A Quaker lawyer wrote, "all persons engaged in the trial should be seeking only the truth," and if this happens too rarely, the adversarial system cannot often result in truth and fairness. Burke believes that law's truth-seeking goal should be emphasized and reiterated in lawyers' code of professional conduct and rules of evidence and procedure. The first of the federal civil rules of procedure[39] states: These rules . . . should be construed and administered to secure the just . . . determination of every action and proceeding." The federal rules of evidence are to "be construed to secure fairness in administration . . . to the end that the truth may be ascertained and proceedings justly determined."[40] But the actual realization of abstract concepts of truth and justice are left to the discretion and judgment of the court and to lawyers as officers of the court. One respondent wrote, "Justice does not always triumph but the law should be designed to that end."

Judge Noonan has observed that users of any system, be it scientific, theological, or legal, encounter points where premises and practices are inconsistent. When that occurs, one of two things must happen: either the gaps must be bridged or the system must be changed. When there is acceptance instead of change, the gaps must be bridged by employing fictions.[41] A fiction in the current U.S. jurisprudential system is that lawyers can play games, dissimulate, mislead, and still reach the truth and achieve justice. Another fiction is that a lawyer can zealously advocate in the customary way and still perform as an officer of the court. One respondent said so:

> I don't like the hypocrisy [of] . . . having lawyers . . . deemed "officers of the court" as if they are really truth-seekers, when in fact lawyers are really agents of their clients and are promoting their clients' interests over their adversaries' interests. I'd like to have that . . . image of righteousness stripped away so that people in general would be more aware of the reality.

The inherent tension in lawyers being zealous advocates and officers of the court is disturbing. As zealous advocates, lawyers must be highly partisan, but, as officers of the court, they must be neutral enforcers of justice. In current practice, the former usually prevails, and the result is a weakening and distortion of the lawyer's equally important duty as an officer of the court. The gap widens when the role of zealous advocate requires the lawyer to say or do things that would be unacceptable if done by nonlawyers.[42]

Highly publicized trials, such as that of O. J. Simpson, have exposed a few judges' toleration of game-playing and dissimulation that accompanies overzealous advocacy. The timidity of the bench in enforcing rules allows this tomfoolery to become an accepted course of behavior. Judges must be chosen with extreme care because they have substantial discretion in determining "what justice may require," and those chosen should exercise that discretion by enforcing all rules, most importantly, those of truth-telling and sanction lawyers who deceive. Lawyers have the primary responsibility to follow rules of court, but if they do not, judges must intervene to ensure that the court system functions fairly. One jurist, with more than 25 years' experience in criminal law, believes that the search for truth should be courts' guiding principle because without it there can be no justice. However, he found that in reality, "the law is not necessarily a search for the truth. Indeed, it is often *not* a search for truth. Our system is a carefully crafted maze, constructed of elaborate and impenetrable barriers to the truth."[43]

A respondent was troubled by the public perception that lawyers will lie for clients. This concern was borne out by results of a 1995 poll[44] of 1,000 American adults about their thoughts on the legal system; 69% believed that lawyers were "not usually honest" or only "sometimes honest." According to one Quaker lawyer, this view is shared by lawyers. She described her frequent clashes over ethics with attorneys who "perceive lying to be the equivalent of good advocacy." Another agreed that the "name of the game is to dissimulate when the truth is on the other side, to obscure rather than reveal." One felt "pressure to stretch the facts for the benefit of the client. . . ." Another complained that "the adversary system tends to place one's sights on winning at all costs." More than a few expressed discomfort with this attitude because the "cost" is loss of truth-telling and therefore truth-finding. A lawyer who left the practice of law realized that when one must win the battle at all costs and by whatever means, "truth is often the first casualty of [the] war."[45]

In her book *Lying*, Sissela Bok noted that the early-seventeenth-century lawyer Hugo Grotius returned to the discourse about lying the notion, nearly extinguished by St. Augustine, that falsehoods are, at times, justifiable and thus should not count as lies from a moral point of view.[46] Although Bok does not seem to be swayed by Grotius's position, many present-day attorneys could be. Bok believes that the erosion of trust and confidence in public officials and professionals such as lawyers is a natural response to the "uncovering of practices of deceit for high-sounding aims such as . . . the 'adversary system of justice.' "[47]

The loss of trust in lawyers is evident in a plethora of jokes. "How do you know if lawyers are lying?—Their lips are moving." This kind of "humor" attests to a certain cynicism that derives from a sense of powerlessness to improve the situation. Although many acknowledge this by complaining and joking, they nevertheless seem to accept it as lawyers' normal behavior. Burke cautions, however, that lawyers willing to lie or deceive for clients do so at their legal and ethical peril.[48] A change toward greater truth-telling in the legal community would benefit lawyers as well as the public.

Justice Byron White straightforwardly wrote about lawyers' "normal" course of behavior in his dissent in *United States v. Wade*.[49] "Defense counsel need present nothing, even if he knows what the truth is. . . . If he can confuse a witness, even a truthful one, or make him appear at a disadvantage, unsure or indecisive, that will be his normal course." The Jacks would most likely agree with Justice White's observation and further comment that the adversary system of justice imposes a duty of conduct on even the most honorable defense counsel that has little, if any, relation to the search for truth.[50]

Justice White called counsel's behavior "normal" in trying to confuse a truthful witness or otherwise put him at a disadvantage. If this is normal, many lawyers have become inured to dissimulation. In fact, John Dean, President Nixon's White House counsel, testified during the Watergate hearings that an inordinate number of lawyers participated in the Watergate deception. This led him to wonder if lawyers might have been more inclined than others to say or do what was necessary to further the cover-up.[51]

Truth-telling is absolutely critical to the truth-finding process. An important function of the attorney as officer of the court is to help the fact-finder make an impartial determination of the truth. If lawyers are truthful, they can be both a good advocate and a good officer of the court. As Gandhi noted, facts lead to truth, and in adhering to truth, the law comes to our aid naturally. An impartial, informed, and wise decision presupposes that lawyers have truth-fully exposed the facts and the law. To deceive the judge or jury is to mock impartiality, mislead instead of inform, and stultify the decisional process rather than make it an exploration leading to a mature judgment.[52] This principle was confirmed by federal judge Robert Keeton in the 1981 Strasburger Lecture at the University of Texas School of Law.[53] He stated that in most cases, but especially in complex litigation, judges depend on the lawyers to instruct them on the facts and issues of a case, undistorted by deceptiveness borne of excessively zealous advocacy. If, in their zeal to promote a client's cause, advocates polarize issues and thereby stretch the truth, the trier of fact is actually hindered in his task of impartial decision-making. The polarization of issues obscures rather than elucidates the truth and therefore does not aid the judge. Lawyers who are overzealous advocates stray from their equally important duty as officers of the court. One respondent agreed: "litigation and trial process tends to drive people to extreme positions" and thereby casts inaccurate slants on the facts and the law.

Role, Mask, and Self in Relation to Truthfulness and Integrity

The assumption of roles and masks in our lives and in the practice of law implicates issues of truthfulness and responsibility. A person's assumption of the role of Lawyer may make it easier to set aside certain moral considerations[54] because a role by its very nature is pretending to be what one is not, outside oneself, and fake, like a character an actor plays in a performance, a reason why some early Quakers shunned the theater. In terms of responsibility, a "role" becomes a safe haven from the Sturm und Drang of moral dilemma. One's personal authenticity is threatened by allegiance to an externally defined role; a role is assumed as a guise for absolving one of personal moral responsibility for an action. There seems to be a correlation between a high degree of role assumption and low accountability for actions or decisions taken; persons in a "role" are not themselves, not unlike aggressive or rude drivers who feel protected by the near-anonymity of a speeding car.

A role differs from a mask. If a certain dehumanization occurs, a role may progress into a mask. Because a mask further conceals and disguises identity, its assumption for any length of time can be self-alienating. A mask socially fashioned and imposed on oneself may become internalized. "In the making of masks, lawyers have let their fiction-making capacity run amok."[56] Early-twentieth-century lawyer Charles Curtis seems to have accepted the inevitability of the legal mask in that he believed that one of the lawyer's functions is to lie for his client. He wrote that the practice of law is vicarious, not altruistic, and a lawyer must go back of Christianity . . . for the vicarious detachment which will permit him to serve his client.[56] More than a few Quaker lawyers would be uncomfortable with Curtis's view.

In their work *Moral Vision and Professional Decisions*, the Jacks thoroughly address a potential tension between the external commands of professional responsibility and the internal demands of personal morality. Since the role of the Lawyer establishes the rules of the game, a person's close identification with this role and its commands increases the likelihood of success in law and simplifies the spectrum of moral considerations.[57] A reason for this gap is that an advocate, by role, is required to do things that would be morally unacceptable if done by another. For example, when most people see another person approach danger, they feel morally bound to give warning, but often an advocate not only watches with glee when an opponent moves toward danger but also does everything possible to lubricate his progress, including the setting and disguising of the trap.[58] This example shows how being solidly "in role" can insulate one from otherwise censurable behavior, but such a gap between personal and professional morality can also tear the fiber of individual personality.

The Jacks identify four positions along a spectrum of moral distance between role and personal morality: (1) lawyers who identify most strongly with role and therefore experience little or no moral tension; (2) lawyers who experience some disharmony but tend to subjugate moral concerns to the professional role; (3) lawyers who experience still more conflict but follow their professional obligations while understanding the moral cost; and (4) lawyers who experience extreme conflict and therefore sometimes abandon their professional obligations altogether.[59] Lawyers in the first category see commitment to their client as the primary value and role morality as the standard of acceptable conduct. Those in the second accept as a requirement of the profession the ability to mute their moral voices while they continue to carry out the role's commands. In the third, lawyers' personal morality demands a greater share in decision-making, and the lawyers begin to see and accept responsibility beyond the immediate demands of the client. In this position, more productive of tension, there is also a tempering of the lawyer's neutrality and detachment, and personal morality becomes a continuing touchstone for decision. In the fourth position, lawyers retain their capacity and willingness to define themselves independently of professional norms. Although the 100 Quaker survey respondents might be represented throughout these four positions, the greatest numbers would most likely be in the third and fourth positions; the fourth fits some respondents who left the practice of law and even some who have remained in practice.

Atticus Finch, the lawyer-protagonist in *To Kill a Mockingbird*[60] seemed intuitively to understand and manifest the integration of profession and self. He believed that what a person is and does must be closely meshed; he told his daughter Scout that a man cannot be one person in town and another at home.[61] Finch's near-instinctive morality is akin to more Quakers' strivings for integrity or integration of self. A Quaker lawyer echoed Fox's early observations in his village church: "I find it difficult to rationalize how I can espouse one set of beliefs on Sundays and act differently during the work week." However, to remain apart from the institutionalized identity of Lawyer may well impair a lawyer's ability to act effectively within the current legal system. Apropos of this, a respondent wrote, "I do what I find to be morally right and often take the consequences," perhaps meaning that this lawyer, by doing what feels "morally right," weakens his efficacy or "success" as a lawyer.

The Jacks believe that lawyers who maintain a broad moral landscape and stave off atrophy of moral sensitivity pay a price by living with tension—in the words of one respondent, tension "every minute of every day." Another thought that being a Quaker lawyer created "internal conflict and turmoil!" Only a few lawyers in the Jacks' study succeeded in avoiding tension between personal and professional moral considerations despite "the attractiveness of the relatively simple and unambiguous moral world of client allegiance and the code of professional conduct."[62] The tensions among those lawyers were similar to those of many in the survey of Quaker lawyers. One who often experienced tensions wrote, "Clients come to me for help in *getting* justice, money, whatever; I find myself counseling them . . . to find their answers within themselves, not in trying to force someone else to do something differently—which is probably a violation of the lawyer code of zealous representation." She too recognized that the professional responsibility of zealous advocacy can often conflict with a lawyer's own personal moral compass.

Thomas Shaffer, a Notre Dame Law School professor and legal scholar, believes that a lawyer's avoidance of ethical choices by ignoring this moral compass is corruptive. Lawyers cannot and should not avoid responsibility by taking refuge in zealous advocacy demanded by the adversarial system. Of the lawyer's many responsibilities, he thinks the one to self and conscience is frequently forgotten. Yet the ability to live with oneself should be foremost. Atticus Finch, who Shaffer considers a fitting hero for American lawyers, thinks similarly: "Before I can live with other folks I've got to live with myself. The one thing that doesn't abide by majority rule is a person's conscience."[63] Finch's defense of the black man Tom Robinson, accused of raping a white girl, had caused him to consider this dilemma, heed his conscience, and resolve to represent Tom. The town folks who attended Robinson's trial certainly recognized and respected Finch's integrity. At the conclusion of Robinson's trial, Finch's daughter Jean Louise (Scout) remembers: "All around us and in the balcony on the opposite wall, the Negroes were getting to their feet. Reverend Sykes's voice was as distant as Judge Taylor's: 'Miss Jean Louise, stand up. Your father's passin'.' "[64] Shaffer asserts that whenever lawyers take positions, file claims, or make statements that violate their consciences, they lie to themselves. One respondent tried to avoid doing this by being "careful not to take or apply for jobs I couldn't feel comfortable with . . . I took only cases I could make a contribution to. . . ."

Robert Rodes, who has studied and written about the interface of religion and law, disapproves of the principle that those who act in accordance with approved procedures are not to be held accountable for the consequences of their actions. This principle, dear to bureaucrats, leads a lawyer to feel no responsibility for succeeding by superior advocacy in returning an abused child to an abusive parent's custody.[65] What about a sense of responsibility for degrading a truthful but bewildered witness with a skilful but overaggressive cross-examination, for deliberately confusing a deponent so that he will say what the lawyer wants, deliberately misspelling a name so an opposing lawyer's research will take longer or be less thorough, or for deliberately misquoting that lawyer's brief so that meanings of words or quotations are skewed? More often than not, under the rubric of zealous advocacy, these are not even considered a de minimus infraction. Lawyers' rules should be balanced so none gain dominance over others. The question legal ethicists raise is important: has the professional rule of zealous advocacy come to trump truthfulness and fairness? Perhaps the time has come for the entire legal profession to grapple with this imbalance and its continued potential for harm and begin to act to rectify it. Quaker lawyers and scholars such as Burke, Noonan, and Shaffer who are not Friends, agree that the practice of law should be brought into greater balance with the legal system's stated goals and with less disparity between earnest advocacy and service as an officer of the court. Burke has suggested modifications to the rules of procedure, evidence, and professional responsibility. Quaker lawyers too have thoughts and ideas on carving a more spacious place for truth-telling in courts and lawyers' practices. One respondent suggested adopting the British prohibition against "preparing" or coaching witnesses before trial. Several suggested that a new and fairer method of billing clients be devised. Many respondents suggested greater use of alternative dispute resolution.

A comprehensive reform task will not be easy, but it can be accomplished with the help of several groups within the profession. For instance, an important and necessary first step would be to assemble a group of qualified, serious, intelligent, and open-minded men and women with no self-serving agendas in a concerted, coordinated, and cooperative effort. This group of about 30 might include law professors, judges, legal scholars, ethicists, lawyers (including Quakers), and alternative dispute resolution professionals. The group's critical first step would be to define, or redefine, the goals of the legal system in straightforward terms; a century ago, Justice Oliver Wendell Holmes Jr. believed that the legal profession should do more to determine the goals of the law and the reasons behind them.[66]

After the group completes that large and important task, it might undertake the drafting of additions and deletions to the rules of procedure, evidence, and professional responsibility to be disseminated for review and consensus. Rule changes would of course have to be accepted by the state and judicial systems. When the group finishes these and any other necessary steps, law school curricula could be coordinated to reflect these changes that, it is hoped, would result in a more humane system of court-based dispute resolution that honors and values truthfulness. The bar would need to be educated about this new thrust and be specifically educated about new and revised rules and expectations. The judiciary would have a renewed opportunity to effectively enforce the new rules and impose sanctions against lawyers who remain intransigent. In sum, this endeavor would reset the court system's compass toward its purported goal—the search for truth. A simultaneous and parallel effort could focus on the coordinated promotion and support of extrajudicial dispute resolution by persons trained, qualified, and certified in its various methods, including mediation and arbitration and who could be lawyers or laypersons. Such an integrated dual approach to judicial and extrajudicial dispute resolution could be beneficial in that it would encourage the use of case-appropriate methods of alternative dispute resolution and relieve overloaded court dockets.

Equality in the Legal System

Besides truthfulness, equality is of significant importance to Friends, and its deficiency in the legal system troubled the Quaker lawyers. Respondents' concerns for greater equality in the legal system centered on access to legal services, the lawyer-client relationship, and the nature of the adversary system. One, when asked whether fundamental changes should be made in the way law functions, answered the way George Fox might have: "Yes, yes, yes. The legal system has a monopoly . . . justice should be easily accessible to all (and lawyers' fees and other legal expenses should be much less)." Another believes that law, which is based on wealth and power, perpetuates inequality. Other respondents believe that the economic issue of better and broader access is critical. One wrote that participation in the legal system has become too expensive effectively foreclosing it to a large part of the middle class and virtually all of the poor; this lawyer suggested that less costly and less adversarial methods be further developed and used. One thought that legal services should be available to people even if they are unable to pay. Another agreed, suggesting that indigent clients be entitled to court- or agency-appointed counsel not only in criminal cases but also in civil cases. A woman thought the present power imbalance gives rise to "unjust results." A man wrote, "law is fact and rule-based, and often is a tool of an unfair social/economic system to enforce classist power and privileges." He believed that Friends' testimony of equality often conflicts with some principles of U.S. jurisprudence.

In this same vein, Rodes discusses the accountability of the "ruling classes," which he believes include lawyers and most clients. The law and the courts seem unaware that a grant of the same protections to corporations as to natural persons only inures to the benefit and profit of corporate managers and their attorneys, and he believes that lawyers, as members of this "ruling class," should help solve the problem. His theory of Christian jurisprudence embodies compassion for the poor and exploited members of society and stresses lawyers' duty of service to them. He believes that lawyers can help by directly serving the poor or they can indirectly exert moral influence by advocating on behalf of poor people to their influential business clients, thereby confronting the power elite and holding them accountable.[67] Like some Quaker lawyers, he places great emphasis on the common good and has called for the reform of institutions that have enriched the ruling class and impoverished the poor.

Like Rodes, Wasserstrom has discussed equality in terms of the legal system, albeit in the context of the lawyer-client relationship. He regards the inequality between dominant lawyer and dependent client as an intrinsic part of a lawyer's role-differentiated professionalism and morally objectionable when lawyers treat clients in a paternalistic or impersonal way.[68] To address this inequity, he advocates a sustained effort to simplify legal language and to make legal processes less mysterious and more accessible to laypersons. Another respondent repeated this echo of George Fox: "The law should not be a magic language understood only by lawyers. . . ." Inequality concerned several others. One believes that being Quaker influences her to "try for more equal treatment of all—judges, lawyers, litigants." Another enlisted her clients, as far as reasonable, to work with her on their cases: "[t]his is more honest, also more simple and bridges a bit [of] the 'power-gap' between us. . . ." A particularly bothersome aspect for an interviewee was the treatment of clients as objects rather than persons.

A Lawyer's Responsibility

This power imbalance between lawyer and client is sometimes reversed so as to impact the former's judgment and sense of responsibility. This occurs when a client becomes the dominant orchestrator of the case. Many clients want to bring adversaries quickly to their knees, so they may encourage or demand bullying behavior from their lawyers, perhaps partly attributable to the high cost of legal advocacy. Nevertheless, attorneys who accede to such client demands act merely as functionaries or "hired guns." Professor Glendon believes that "the professional ideal of [lawyers'] independence has begun to recede while the client loyalty ideal has advanced."[69] Legal ethicists like Burke believe too that many lawyers abdicate responsibility by giving clients' wishes more primacy than necessary. Experts generally agree that lawyers should advise clients to act within the bounds of the law, but some think their responsibility is less clear when clients desire conduct that is legal, but unethical and morally irresponsible. It is clear enough for most Quaker lawyers and ethicists like

Burke. A client's desire for less-than-ethical behavior should be subordinated to the system's assumed goals of truth and justice, and ensuring that these goals are more than abstractions is the individual and collective responsibility of the bench and bar. One respondent noted resignedly: "you just do what the client wants—which is not always coterminous with the larger needs of society," the common good. Another was balkier: "clients want to win at all costs and I won't play that way."

Lawyers should take a greater lead in guiding their clients to act ethically because lawyers must be held accountable not only for selecting clients but also for their actions during each representation. To make lawyers aware of this wider responsibility, some scholars have called for reform and revision of legal education. For example, Shaffer believes that moral questions have an important place in the curricula and can be explored with the same analytical rigor as substantive legal issues.[70] In fact, he believes the irrelevancy of moral convictions runs deep in U.S. legal education and has been profoundly corrupting.[71] Although Justice Holmes distinguished between morality and law in legal practice, he acknowledged that law is the witness of our moral life, and its history is the history of man's moral development.[72]

Thinkers such as Roberto Unger, Michael Perry, and Stephen Presser have offered some interesting views on morality and law. Unger, for example, maintains that the nineteenth-century focus on possessive individualism permitted and enabled by the law's concept of private property and further encouraged by advanced industrial capitalism has made us lose sight of the spiritual aspects of community and fraternity enjoyed in earlier eras.[73] Like other scholars, he dislikes the barriers between morality and law and believes that these should be broken down so that law and courts can follow a more holistic and communitarian approach that stresses peoples' linkages and connections. Unger, with Perry and Presser, favor a "great chain of being" model, which encourages greater preoccupation with community. This recognition of interdependence would likely lead to more cooperation and less confrontation and antagonism in dispute resolution in the courts.

Perry also believes that courts could aid in an evolution of a morality of law, which might help untangle difficult constitutional issues involving freedom of speech and free exercise of religion as well as due process and equal protection; he considers the application of morality to be an articulation of God's will on earth. Other scholars such as Shaffer and Noonan, also disfavor barriers between law and morality. These scholars are right that there should be a paradigm shift in thinking in law. Some legal scholars should revisit and challenge assumptions inherent in our Anglo-American system of jurisprudence. "The image in the Common Law was one of self-interest, of pressing one's legal rights against any individual or against society, in personam and in rem, regardless of the morality of one's cause. It is the image of a man not bound by any ethical or moral consideration, but only the law."[74] If this view has merit, it confirms the need for a system of law which de-emphasizes self-interest and emphasizes community such as the "great chain of being" model. Some of its valuable insights and ideas could be incorporated into a more just U.S. legal system for the twenty-first century.

Noonan, like Shaffer, believes that moral education is essential to a lawyer's professional preparation. Because lawyering is a human activity, it affects both the actors and those acted upon. The primary teaching tools of U.S. legal education—casebooks and hornbooks—hone a law student's technical skills by shedding light on a rule, but they do not sufficiently emphasize the important participants—lawyers and clients—in the process.[75] His book, *Persons and Masks of the Law*, written some 30 years ago, discusses litigants in several well-known legal cases as the individuals they were.

In addition to casebooks, some law professors such as Shaffer teach legal ethics by analyzing novels such as Kazuo Ishiguro's *Remains of the Day* and Harper Lee's *To Kill a Mockingbird* because they illustrate moral dilemmas similar to those lawyers will likely face. In Ishiguro's novel, the butler Stevens can be an analogue of the Lawyer. Stevens's professional role allowed, or forced, him to avoid moral choices. His duty to execute his master's order to dismiss two girl servants because they were Jewish took precedence over his own personal instinct for what was right and fair. In justifying this action, the butler said that "professional duty is not to our own foibles and sentiments, but to the wishes of our employer."[76] Like Stevens, many lawyers believe that their foremost professional duty is to the employer-client, a clear illustration of the shielding effect of professional role-differentiation and another abdication of their responsibility, lawyers ceding their independence to clients. Unlike Atticus Finch, Stevens disregarded his conscience, which he calls "foibles and sentiments." However, conscience connotes a force considerably more powerful than those words indicate. Derived from *conscire*—to know inwardly—conscience is knowing in the inner self the distinction between moral right and wrong. Ishiguro's book raises an important question—whether the butler, or lawyer, can or should be held accountable for the aims of his master, or client. Like Stevens, some lawyers tend to avoid considering such questions. The more they cloak themselves in the professional role of Lawyer, the more they rationalize their behavior and avoid pondering the distinction between what the law allows and what is fair or right. In addition to a disavowal of responsibility, a subjugation of one's personal morality results in distress and tension.

The Jacks pose an important question from a different vantage point: can a culture afford to place people with the ability, skills, training, experience, and authority of lawyers in a central decision-making arena and then neutralize their moral concern and judgment as they operate there?[77] Many Quaker lawyers would answer no.

Lawyers' Conflict of Interest

Professor Glendon writes approvingly in *How the Crisis in the Legal Profession Is Transforming American Society* of an earlier era when much lawyering consisted of advising potential clients to stop being damned fools by furthering disputes through legal action.[78] If that kind of advice were common today, a lawyer should have so counseled the client who wished to sue for a collarbone fracture received while playing in a YMCA softball game. Instead, the lawyer filed a six-figure damages suit against the manager of the player who collided with his client, the graphics firm that printed team T-shirts, and the umpire.[79] Glendon would have also disapproved of the lawyer who sued a surfer for taking his client's wave and another who threatened suit against his client's neighbor for ivy creeping across the common boundary allegedly damaging his shrubbery. There is a growing recognition that inciting persons to sue at every discomfort may be debilitating to the whole society. A respondent indicated that she often counseled clients, according to Glendon's memory of lawyers of an earlier era: "to forget, forgive, and let go. . . ." Such lawyering decreases lawyers' opportunities to file suit and thus reduces income, perhaps one reason it is now rarely done. Glendon argues that a serious problem is that many lawyers nowadays act solely in their own interest. A 1995 poll of 1,000 adults confirmed this: 56% believed that lawyers use the legal system to protect the powerful and to enrich themselves.[80] Two Quaker lawyers agreed. "I would like lawyers . . . to conduct themselves more professionally and civilly with the interests of their clients, rather than their own, governing their actions." Another wished more lawyers would "single-mindedly promote their clients' interest [instead] . . . of their own."

Formal legal ethics standards seem to have dispensed with, or at least blurred, the conceptual boundaries of right and wrong. Examples of self-serving and wrong conduct related to lawyers' monetary gain are: in a major bankruptcy case, a law firm that billed its bankrupt client $177, 844 for time spent preparing the bill; the attorney in a large asbestos case who drafted a motion applicable to thousands of individual cases defended by his insurer-client and then billed 3,000 separate times for the same twelve minutes; and a lawyer who billed clients for 62 hours of work in a single day.[81] One respondent noted that the "legal profession assumes that one's goal is making a lot of money . . . and living a lifestyle that corresponds to that." Another disliked the "pressure solely to pursue money for self and client," and one complained that the practice of law had become a "commercial enterprise."

Law as Battle

The parallel between law and fighting is frequent, familiar, and appropriate as applied to current trial practice. Settling disputes in a court of law was intended to be vastly superior to the use of physical violence to settle scores, but unfortunately, litigation today can include its own kind of violence. The earliest notion of law was not the enumeration of a principle but the judgment in a particular case. In earlier ages, the law issued from the sovereign. When a king pronounced the law, it was considered the result of direct divine inspiration. Later, law came to signify a custom that a judgment affirmed or punished in its breach,[82] an emphasis on decision rather than advocacy.

Among other factors, demographic conditions and environment can have an effect on lawyers' actions and behavior. For instance, a study of urban lawyers and their country counterparts showed less of a "scorched-earth" mentality among the latter.[83] The win-lose scenario was less prevalent among rural and small-town lawyers, and, in general, they got along well and frequently settled cases prior to trial;. in fact, these lawyers did not regard litigation as the best way to resolve disputes. The rural and small-town lawyers are loathe to risk community disapproval, and indeed the study revealed that some impetus for cooperation is peer acceptance and approval. Their more cooperative stance may also be explained by a deeper interconnectedness of professional and personal relationships as a smaller population increases the likelihood of acquaintance or friendship. One Quaker lawyer responded that he wanted to practice in a small community "where lawyers and judges confront one another repeatedly, and reputations for fair dealing are meaningful."

Conversely, the more distant personal and professional relations are, the greater the opportunity for blurring moral boundaries and the greater the potential for confrontation. The study found that urban lawyers litigated more and fought harder, partly due to the likelihood that they would not again face the same adversaries. This distancing principle that begets harder-fought battles is akin to the professional role and mask.

A woman respondent wrote, "the adversarial quality required in litigation feels like a constant violation of my peace testimony. With time, I . . . have been able to minimize [it] in some areas. . . . But it is very difficult to actively challenge the dynamic in action." Another felt tension because "law is fighting [and] I don't like to argue." Several such responses from women bear out the Jacks' contention that women lawyers with a greater "care" orientation are, as a result, more bothered by the aggressiveness of contemporary law practice.

Justice Sandra Day O'Connor, the first woman to sit on the U.S. Supreme Court, has suggested that legal arguments and trials need not be battles. Instead of preparing for a fight, she advised lawyers to use their energies to win cases by diligent work instead of Rambo-style tactics that "work over" their opponents. She believes that such tactics contribute both to a decline in the professionalism of the bar and public dissatisfaction with the legal system.[84] She and many Quaker lawyers probably would agree with Abraham Lincoln: "As a peacemaker the lawyer has a superior opportunity of being a good man [or woman]. There will still be business enough."[85]

Discomfort with aggressiveness in law practice was largely expressed by women respondents, although a man wrote as a Quaker, he "did very little litigation [and] . . . attempted mediation and non-aggressive type work." Another tries to "find ways to avoid conflict . . . [but] most of our legal system promotes conflict. . . . Litigation is institutionalized fighting." One felt conflicted by the perceived requirement to practice law with "aggressiveness and competitive[ness]," echoing the view that practicing law has become a series of skirmishes and battles.

Law as battle conflicts with Friends' peace testimony and is generally distressing to them, reasons why they developed dispute resolution methods outside the courts. However, important issues with potentially broad societal impact must be brought to the courts because of their precedent-setting value that may effect change in unjust and oppressive laws. Mediation and arbitration can play an important part in resolving disputes in myriad matters of more localized concern where precedent is less important.

Conclusion

The Quaker lawyers surveyed for this work were generous with their comments and ideas. They were frank and truthful in describing their assessment of the current legal system and practice as it relates to them personally and to the society as a whole. Most were disinclined to adopt the role of Lawyer and to heed a "professional morality" in their practices. Instead, the Quaker lawyers were primarily guided by a "personal/faith-based morality" which, in the current environment of legal practice, tended to cause them significant tension.

More than 60% of the 100 Quaker lawyers surveyed had been Friends for more than 20 years, and slightly more than 40% had practiced law for that length of time. Although all respondents had once practiced law, eight were no longer practicing at the time of the survey. Thirty-five percent of the respondents were women who had attended law school later than men and had practiced less time.

More than 90% identified either very strongly or strongly with Quaker beliefs and testimonies, and an equal percentage wrote that being a Friend influenced their practice of law. Quaker influence on men's practice was less than on women's.

Respondents' reasons for becoming lawyers varied, but most cited was altruism, followed by prestige, and intellectual interest. More than 60% practiced alone or in small firms. The largest number practiced corporate law, followed by real estate, civil rights, and probate. Only eight were litigators. Sixty-two percent of respondents experienced tensions or conflicts as practicing Quakers and lawyers. The most often-cited source of these was the lack of truthfulness followed by aggressiveness and adversariness. Most worked through their tensions by conferring with Quaker colleagues, although a few went to Meetings or clearness committees. The advantages most saw in being Quaker lawyers were in the areas of counseling and advising and settlement negotiations. The disadvantages were a perceived softness, gentleness, and lack of toughness. Many revealed feelings of frustration about the current legal system and practice of law, and a few believed that being a faithful Friend *and* a successful lawyer were nearly irreconcilable.

Suggestions for change included more truthfulness, less aggressiveness, more civility and collegiality, more emphasis on service rather than moneymaking, and more concern for society's poor and disadvantaged. Some wanted a change in rules of court to effect improvement in these areas. One suggested that ". . . there should be a rebuttable presumption that there is value . . . in furthering . . . peace between people."

These lawyers evinced a longing to do "good," and Friends' principles were patent in their thoughts and suggestions. They are a gentle lot who greatly dislike aggressiveness and deceptiveness in today's legal environment. Many look forward to increased use of alternative dispute resolution, which could diminish or eliminate a perceived need to be aggressive and deceptive in order to "win." We will see in the next chapter that these traits are neither necessary nor effective in mediation, a process that works best when disputing persons can speak directly and truthfully to each other.

Although buffeted by the prevailing customs of contemporary law practice, most Quaker lawyers remain mindful of Quaker principles—truthfulness, peace, equality and community, the light of God residing in each and every person, and concern for society's poor and oppressed. Many believe that the cost of "winning at all costs" is too high—the loss of truth of verifiable facts and their complete and accurate transmission—justice is truth in action. Reverend Martin Luther King Jr. once noted that those who let religion impinge in a major way on their professional activities are considered eccentric.[86] If so, this fine band of Quaker lawyers is indeed an odd lot!

The Quaker lawyers who appear the most content and comfortable in their practice are those who have deliberately limited cases to ones less likely to conflict with their Quaker faith. In doing so, they have limited their income. Some are volunteer lawyers with the American Civil Liberties Union, others teach law, advise prisoners, mediate, or lobby the legislature under the auspices of FCNL. Many chafe under the burden of trying to be good Quakers and good lawyers, but many have learned to cope with a contradiction they did not expect to encounter. What can be done about the tensions and frustration many Quaker lawyers feel? Should they leave the practice of law, as Quaker legislators left the Pennsylvania Assembly in the mid-eighteenth century? One hopes they will continue to practice as valued members of the legal profession, but in a way that produces less tension and conflict. They might engage with others in a movement for constructive change in the legal system by devising a model for resolving differences with greater truthfulness and conciliation.

6

Mediation and Arbitration: Past and Future

My joy was boundless. I had learnt the true practice of law . . . to find out the better side of human nature and to enter men's hearts. I realized that the true function of a lawyer was to unite parties riven asunder.[1]

The great Indian civil rights leader Mohandas K. (Mahatma) Gandhi practiced law in South Africa around the start of the twentieth century. Once, while preparing a case, he realized that the facts strongly favored his client. However, Gandhi knew that if litigation were carried through, it would ruin both the client and his opponent. As the case progressed, legal fees and mutual ill will began to mount, and the time and energy the two parties had to spend on the case left little time for other matters. Because he felt it his duty to befriend and bring the parties together, Gandhi advised his client's opponent to obtain counsel and to consider submitting the case to arbitration. In suggesting this, he identified less with the role of Lawyer than with his personal morality. The parties did agree to arbitration, and Gandhi's client won handsomely. However, the arbitration award was so large that the losing party could not pay the entire amount without going bankrupt, and in the particular culture of his South African group, death was considered preferable to bankruptcy. After some effort, Gandhi persuaded his client to accept long-term installment payments, and "both were happy over the result, and both rose in the public estimation."[2] Gandhi then realized that one of the most important accomplishments of a lawyer was to "unite parties riven asunder," a succinct rationale for the use of a gentler means of settling disputes through alternatives to litigation.

Like Gandhi, a Quaker lawyer wrote, "It is my hope that all lawyers, not just us few Quaker ones, are seeing how much more successful we can be for our clients if we see our role as solving problems of clients rather than just acting as their 'hired gun' to seek some short-term gain through litigation. Negotiation [and] mediation (and even some of the expedited litigation methods) all have their place as alternatives to confrontational litigation." Early Friends thought similarly.

Mediation and Arbitration as Quaker Gospel Order

The early fundamentals of Friends' communitarian justice derived from the New Testament. Matthew's caution against going to law[3] was the genesis of Quaker "gospel order," a gentle means of resolving disputes and reuniting members. In his epistles, Paul too warned against suing.[4] The maintenance, or restoration, of peace and harmony was important to Friends, and as early as 1659 English Quaker Edward Burrough had advised that Friends settle differences "not in the way of the world by hot contests, [and] by seeking to outspeak or overreach one another in discourse."[5] In addition to a scriptural impetus for gospel order, the Society, with its early history of persecution in England, naturally wanted to keep any differences within its confines so that the truth did not suffer because of a member's deviant behavior.[6] Not long after Burrough's caution, Friends developed a comprehensive intra-Quaker dispute resolution process outside the courts to which aggrieved members could bring their "differences." By 1679 the London Six Weeks Meeting had already established a permanent arbitration committee to deal with a wide range of intra-Quaker disputes, including those of a commercial nature.[7] In 1681 George Fox described the skeletal framework of the process in his Epistles and Advices to Birmingham Meeting: "If there happen any difference between friends and friends of any matter, if it cannot be ended before the general meeting, let half a dozen of friends from the general meeting be, once in every quarter of the year, appointed in such places as may be convenient for most friends to meet in."[8] In that same year Friends introduced gospel order to Pennsylvania and West New Jersey in the New World where its primary value lay in the promotion of harmony and community. There, the principles of gospel order were articulated in a Philadelphia Yearly Meeting minute of August 28, 1681. A Friend was not to sue another Friend without necessity and without the consent of the meeting. Burlington Monthly Meeting issued a similar Advice that year, echoing the passage in Matthew: "if anything fall [sic] out, by way of controversy, between Friend and Friend, that if they cannot end the matter between themselves, then they should refer it to two or more Friends, to see if they can end it, then if not, to bring it to the Monthly Meeting, to be ended there."

The Society's 1692 Rules of Discipline and Christian Advices in Pennsylvania and West New Jersey explained that gospel order was to be the primary means of dispute resolution within the Quaker community because of its emphasis on peacemaking: "in all cases of controversy and difference, the persons concerned therein, either speedily compose the difference between themselves, or make choice of some faithful, unconcerned, impartial friends, to determine the same. . . ." This was repeated four years later with the additional mention of sanctions for those who refused to comply. If Friends sued directly without first proceeding in gospel order, they were considered to have departed from the principle of truth, and they risked disownment if they did not quickly discontinue the suit. On the tenth day, seventh month of 1683, Burlington Meeting arranged arbitration between William Cooper and Daniel Wills with Thomas Olive as arbitrator, and another between Samuel Jenings and Daniel Leeds.[9] The Radnor (Pennsylvania) Monthly Meeting also established within each local meeting a standing two-person arbitration committee with the authority to settle differences. Only those that proved intractable were to be referred to the Monthly Meeting.[10] Because there were no formally admitted attorneys in West New Jersey before 1702, Quaker arbitral procedure filled a gap in the legal system and thus was a major influence in the commercial development of the region.[11]

In accordance with gospel order, William Penn's brother-in-law, Edward Penington, in a February 28, 1701, letter, asked Philadelphia Monthly Meeting for assistance in his dispute with William Say:

> I am forced to complain to you against a troublesome Neighbour . . . wearing the mark of a Quaker (though I fear little in reality). . . . I cannot take those Legal courses whereby I could soon bring him to a just compliance with my reasonable demands; and the breach being lately widened between us, so that it seems not likely to be made up by ourselves, I intreat this meeting to take cognisance of the things in difference.[12]

The dispute resolution Matthew advised embraced what today would be termed negotiation, mediation, and arbitration—in that sequence. "[G]o and tell him his fault between thee and him alone" is equivalent to a first attempt at conciliation and negotiation by the parties. At this stage, they control the process as well as the substantive outcome. The complaining person's first step was to speak calmly and, in the parlance of the early Rules of Discipline, in a "brotherly" manner to effect direct but gentle conciliation.

If this failed to solve the dispute, the complainant would "take . . . one or two more" Friends to help work toward a just and expeditious settlement; this is comparable to today's mediation. At this stage, the mediator controls the process, but the disputants determine the substantive outcome by working together toward a mutually agreeable solution.

If this also failed, arbitration was next: "tell it to the church." Friends would ask the parties to choose a number of impartial Friends to arbitrate the dispute. As Paul suggested to the Corinthians, the "people" themselves should "judge," not the state-appointed judiciary. In arbitration, the parties control neither the process nor the outcome, but they have more latitude than in a court of law. Arbitration is more informal and private than a court action and less constrained by formal rules of evidence and procedure. In Quaker arbitrations, relevancy standards were broad and rarely were witnesses or evidence rejected or withheld. Any pertinent matter was introduced that might benefit the outcome or better explain the parties' respective needs and interests. The arbitral process ensured that parties had an opportunity to speak, listen, and answer. Parties could also speak in court but there they were subject to more constraints. In court, nonsuits and defaults could also prevent parties' interaction.

If disputants could not agree to refer the dispute to arbitration, after notice to his opponent, the complainant could take the dispute before Monthly Meeting. The meeting would ask if gospel order had been observed. If it had, the Monthly Meeting would set a time for hearing, but if it had not been, the complainant was required to observe it. After the hearing, arbitrators would bring the decision to meeting for review and implementation. Their determination was binding, and the parties were expected to perform accordingly. The meeting would then report the arbitral decision to the court.[13] If recalcitrant members refused to attend a hearing or unreasonably refused to abide by an arbitral award, Friends would "labour" with them. If they persisted in refusing, "after the exercise of due care," the meeting would "testify to its disunion" with the conduct and could disown the member.[14] The complying party could then take the matter to court with the blessing of the meeting.

Publication was an important aspect of Friends' system of justice. Once it had been determined that a member had wronged another, the Monthly Meeting would publish a public condemnation.[15] Part of the efficacy of this process within the Society was the assurance that the meeting's decisions would be enforced through the threat, and possible imposition, of sanctions.[16] Friends chosen as arbitrators were expected to serve conscientiously, and those who agreed to serve and then declined had to explain their reasons. If the meeting considered the explanation insufficient, it would attempt friendly persuasion, but if the members remained intransigent, the meeting could disown them. This rather harsh sanction for refusal to participate as disputants or arbitrators indicates the importance Friends attached to gospel order and members' obligation to it. However, keeping peace within the broader community was also important. Later Rules of Discipline—such as one from 1719—revealed Friends' duty to observe the peace testimony by applying gospel order to everyone:

> It is our duty to seek peace with all men, and avoid giving provocation or offense to any, it is advised, that Friends be careful not to go to law with others without urgent necessity, nor in a vindictive disposition of mind, nor give them just occasion to sue or implead us; endeavouring, in both cases, to shew a becoming temper of justice and uprightness, by a pacific disposition, [and] to refer our differences . . . to prudent and just arbitrators. . . .

Arbitration then became the preferred way to resolve disputes with both fellow Quakers and "the world's people." A 1737 Advice was accompanied by an Old Testament verse, Deut. 1:16: "Hear the causes between your brethren and judge righteously between every man and his brother, and the stranger that is with him." The Advice suggested, "it would be well that friends were at all times ready to submit their differences, even with persons not of our religious persuasion, to arbitration, rather than to contend at law." Although Friends were encouraged to submit disputes with those outside the Society to arbitration, suing them did not incur community disapproval, especially if gospel order had first been tried.[17]

Despite fundamental dissimilarities, the Quaker process of gospel order did borrow some elements from the traditional legal system, especially legal terminology in pleadings and evidentiary and appeal procedures.[18] Friends who participated in meeting arbitrations were required to sign a bond like those in arbitrations prescribed under Pennsylvania provincial law. Like judges, meeting arbitrators were to disregard all prior information about a case, although they could consult "council learned in the law" to help them reach just and lawful judgments. And, like judges, arbitrators were to be unbiased and "judge righteously, fearing the Lord."[19]

Like the courts, the Society provided an appeal process. Within three months, an aggrieved Friend could appeal the Monthly Meeting's arbitral award to the Quarterly Meeting. After the appeal had been noted, that meeting would appoint twelve impartial Friends to hear and decide the appeal with each party having the right to strike a certain number. The meeting then set the time and place of the appeal and notified the parties. At the convening of the hearing, a clerk would read the appeal, and after each party had presented its "case," the arbitration committee began deliberations. After all, or most, arbitrators had agreed, they prepared and signed a report either confirming or annulling the Monthly Meeting's prior decision, usually without a rationale. The decision was then read before the parties, recorded, and adopted. The party who "lost" the appeal could then appeal to the Yearly Meeting; its decision was final and binding, ending Friends' dispute resolution process. If an appeal concerned an issue of faith and practice, the appellant could require that the *entire* Yearly Meeting hear it.

English and American Quaker meetings of the seventeenth and eighteenth centuries were more cohesive communities than those today. This is largely due to enormous economic, sociological, and demographic changes that have occurred during the past two centuries. Early English Friends were bound together as a persecuted minority whereas the Quaker vanguard of Penn's "holy experiment" was bound by forging together a new society in a new land. The concern, support, and sense of community, especially evident in early Friends meetings, made Quakers' comprehensive peacemaking system especially viable and appropriate. This strong system of support and cohesion within meetings was a cogent force in mediating members' disputes. The loving concern and oversight of Friends who knew each other well went far to mitigate the animosity inevitable to disputing parties and provided a climate in which accommodation and agreement were apt to flower. The intimacy inherent in earlier Friends meetings enabled Quaker mediators and arbitrators to be aware of the total circumstances surrounding members' disputes and therefore treat them comprehensively and in context. This is less likely to occur in courts where issues are more narrowly framed. Loving and gentle, yet firm, pressure to effect reconciliation could be brought to bear on members who could be persuaded through patience, reason, and compassion. The meeting's more intimate and informal environment was generally more conducive to reconciliation than the more formal and combative atmosphere of a law court. The need for judicial intervention was obviated as many disputes were arbitrated within this flexible and well-designed internal system within Friends meetings.

Geographical proximity also contributed to the early success of gospel order. With the exception of Philadelphia, most early American Quakers lived in rural areas; whereas farms may have been relatively distant, a family's land was often contiguous or near that of another Friend. In the first three decades of Penn's province, more than two-thirds of all disputes between persons living near one another were successfully resolved. However, if people rarely saw their adversaries, the incentive to win at the expense of a harmonious future increased.[20] This remains true; accommodation and agreement are most likely to occur between persons who know each other well and are likely to interact again. It is partly due to lack of members' physical proximity that close-knit meetings of earlier years are rare today.

Alternative Dispute Resolution
Is Particularly Attuned to the Testimonies

Gospel order was, and is, especially attuned to Friends' faith and practice of their testimonies and was the primary reason for its extensive use in earlier years in England and America. Even centuries ago, legal rules and procedures placed constraints on what could be said in court. Such restrictions made it more difficult for disputing parties to be as open in court as they could be in meeting arbitrations. As more Friends become further aware of the possibility and promise of alternative dispute resolution, they will recognize its compatibility with their testimonies.

The survey of Quaker lawyers showed that many prefer alternatives to the polarizing combativeness of litigation. One wrote, "the legal system is about having some external "objective" expert . . . make the critical decisions in someone's life, and have the authority/power to enforce compliance with that order. . . . Quaker process is about decisions being made in a gathered community, with all involved participating in a transforming experience under the tutelage of the Holy Spirit, and in that process feeling ownership of the outcome."

This Quaker process of community decision-making is akin to mediation in its collaborative search for agreement. Because of this affinity, Quakers might make more frequent use of mediation and arbitration and recommend these alternatives to others in their meetings and communities. Quakers might go further by resurrecting and adapting these early mediation and arbitration processes for use in today's meetings.

Community

The high value Quakers place on community made it natural to prefer a dispute resolution method that attempted to preserve cherished communal bonds. The hostility engendered by most lawsuits does not further community but instead weakens it. Most lawyers trained in our adversary-based system of justice feel obliged to take strong and aggressive stands on their clients' behalf. These lawyers become Lawyers, forced into roles and positions from which they cannot retreat and that could, if prolonged, ultimately damage their individual identities.

As early as 1653, Quaker James Nayler intimated this tendency of lawyers: "you who should instruct people in the ways of truth and peace, do not you by your wisdom teach lies and strife: advis[ing] your plaintiffs . . . to declare in bills, things that are not true, and make small offences seem very great by false glosses? . . . Is this the way to make up the breach, and preserve peace and truth amongst people?"[21] Nayler argued that law should be an instrument of preserving peace rather than destroying it; the aggrandizement of differences and augmentation of adversaries' offenses was divisive. Because of its "deceits, delays, and expenses," use of the law was worse than the disease it attempted to cure.

It is remarkable that Quakers' complaints about the ills of seventeenth-century law, lawyers, and courts—"deceits, delays, and expenses"—are strikingly similar to those of Quaker lawyers today. Moreover, litigation's potential for increased dissension has likely grown since Nayler's time. Today various forms of discovery not only cause delay but often create fresh discord. Moreover, the judiciary, bar, and the public, in descending order of responsibility, have passively tolerated this obfuscation, posturing, and delay. Most litigators have embraced the old precept, military in tenor, that the best defense is a strong offense. The most "successful" litigators are often the most gladiatorial.

Quaker lawyers wrote of the importance of community: "Law should not continually undermine 'community' as it promotes triumphant 'individualism.' " Another respondent believes that we "need to move away from a rights-based system which automatically leads toward isolation of self from others, towards recognition of the need for community through collaborative problem solving." For instance, community is affirmed when parties enter into mediation together in an interactive problem-solving mode that fosters personal accountability and responsibility. In mediation, the parties are directly involved with, and accountable to, each other, whereas in court they are necessarily more passive and dependent. Another community-affirming aspect of mediation is that after resolution, parties can continue to act as caretakers of each other and their whole relationship. One of the highest and best aspects of community is being our brother's keeper.

Equality

Many Quaker lawyers confirmed the idea that mediation is more consonant with equality than is litigation. In the former, no person in special regalia sits elevated above the parties. Mediators are not called "your honor," an unequal form of address disliked by many early, and a few modern, Friends. Disputing parties are full and equal participants in mediation, mutually empowered and encouraged to work collaboratively toward solutions. And because an agreement is not imposed but self-constructed, it tends be more workable and durable. A study of the durability of mediated settlements revealed that most successfully mediated cases remained resolved. Even though some disputes had not been settled during mediation sessions, they were resolved before trial; the conciliatory atmosphere of mediation may have had a delayed effect so that after mediation and before court, the parties communicated more seriously and thoughtfully and even reconsidered earlier proposals made during mediation.[22] In the face-to-face proximity of mediation, parties' humanity and vulnerability are more evident, perhaps furthered by the absence of lawyers' protective combativeness. In this atmosphere of equality and possibility, labels of "plaintiff" and "defendant" are shed.

Harmony

The testimony of harmony causes Quakers to be naturally supportive of more conciliatory methods of resolving disputes and promoting reconciliation. Friends' early development of a gentler way stemmed from their desire as peacemakers to minimize strife and preserve harmony.[23]

Friends further believed that a less confrontational way of settling disputes could be relevant to nation-states as well. For example, in his *Essay towards the Present and Future Peace of Europe* (1693), William Penn urged the use of international arbitration agreements. A decade later, John Bellers, a wealthy

Quaker merchant and social reformer, proposed an international council for the peaceful settlement of disputes among nations in *Some Reasons for a European State proposed to the Powers of Europe* (1710).[24] Other early examples of Quaker involvement in international peacemaking are Rhode Island Quakers' arbitration efforts to prevent King Philip's War in 1675; Joseph Sturge's attempted mediation between Denmark and Schleswig-Holstein in 1850 and his peace delegation four years later to Nicholas I, Czar of Russia; Member of Parliament John Bright's successful efforts in 1861 to secure arbitration between England and the North at the outbreak of the American Civil War; John Fothergill's assistance to Benjamin Franklin in drafting a reconciliation plan between England and the American colonies; and George Logan's successful efforts in 1798 to prevent war between the United States and France after the latter failed to release imprisoned American sailors.[25]

During the last century, Quakers' peacemaking efforts occurred in many parts of the world.[26] Some were led by a small cadre of Friends who work toward reconciliation through Quaker Peace and Service (QPS), an English group with nineteenth-century origins. Formerly called British Friends Service Council, QPS shared the 1947 Nobel Peace Prize with the American Friends Service Committee (AFSC). During presentation of the 1947 Peace Prize, Nobel Committee Chairman Gunnar Jahn commended Quakers for showing it is "possible to carry into action something that is deeply rooted in the minds of many: the desire to help others . . . feelings which, when carried into deeds, must provide the foundations of a lasting peace," and for demonstrating "strength which is founded on the faith in the victory of spirit over force."[27]

Henry J. Cadbury, Chairman of the American Friends Service Committee, had been invited to Oslo to accept its share of the Peace Prize. A formal suit with tails was de rigueur at the Peace Prize ceremony, but Cadbury did not own one. He had apparently heeded London Yearly Meeting's 1691 Advice to keep to plainness and "avoid pride and immodesty in apparel and all vain and superfluous fashions." Nor did he feel justified in buying one just for this occasion. Fortunately, AFSC kept used clothing in a storeroom in its Philadelphia office, collected for distribution to the needy around the world. Indeed, a "magnificent garment for the chairman" was found there! The fit was perfect, and, after its use at the ceremony, it was left in Europe. Thus elegantly outfitted, he delivered his remarks.[28]

Both Nobel Peace Prize recipients, the AFSC and QPS have worked in humanitarian relief, community development, war relief, peacemaking, and reconciliation throughout the world including India and Pakistan, China, Nigeria, North Vietnam, East and West Germany, Biafra, and the Middle East. The QPS staff has also served in Northern Ireland, where in the early 1990s it worked to help ease the Catholic-Protestant conflict. Friends' reputation for impartiality helped them first to work to understand the views and experiences of the disputing persons and groups. They initially engaged in "shuttle" diplomacy to relay various views, but later they arranged face-to-face meetings.

After the times, places, and agendas of the meetings had been set, the Quakers would customarily leave the parties to continue on their own, although occasionally, they would stay to initiate the dialogue. Confidentiality was extremely important and, although they informed one side of their meeting with the other, they promised to maintain confidentiality by not telling others that a meeting had occurred. Nor would Friends discuss the meetings' substantive content even with their oversight committee. The QPS staff was able to achieve a fair measure of success because it was neutral and perceived to be so, small in number, and therefore virtually unnoticeable. Quakers' established connections with those in high positions of authority were also important in arranging meetings with persons who could make a difference. The Quaker process was almost as important to the negotiations as any specific "solution."[29]

Proscription against Going to Law Is Not Absolute

Quakers cannot be peacemakers in every instance if they are also to witness other testimonies. Harmony is practiced at all possible times but not always at the cost of equality and community. After a period of individual discernment, communal discernment, or both, a Friend or group of Friends may be led to suspend harmony in favor of a plain-spoken struggle for tolerance or justice. Several Quakers did this in the court cases they brought or defended, discussed in chapter 4.

Although early Friends were cautioned against going to law "without urgent necessity," wisely this restraint was not absolute (although at certain times, some were disowned for doing so). Whereas Paul seemed to encourage the Corinthians to suffer a wrong rather than go to law, Quakers did not follow this advice unconditionally. They approved an aggrieved member's going to court if the other's behavior was sufficiently egregious and if more "peaceful" alternatives had been explored and exhausted. Their encouragement of active peacemaking could not justify preventing members from seeking redress of their grievances in court—a state institution with powers of enforcement. In fact, the lack of specific and easily executed penalties for noncompliance was said to have been a salient weakness of Friends' gospel order[30] and perhaps why some defendants tried to take advantage of it.

In *The Courage of Their Convictions, Sixteen Americans Who Fought Their Way to the Supreme Court,* the author profiles people who took their search for justice to the nation's highest court; four of the cases involved Friends. Despite Quaker tradition, Barbara Elfbrandt,[31] Gordon Hirabayashi,[32] Mary Beth and John Tinker,[33] and Daniel Seeger,[34] brought or defended actions at law and prevailed. The common thread among these cases was a triggering act of intolerance or injustice that each resisted.[35]The subsequent vindication of the rights they fought for not only benefited them but others also. Their moral courage and perseverance in these multiyear cases, and the Supreme Court precedents they created, resulted in constructive changes and a greater measure of justice. Courage is an important adjunct to compassion because it alerts those who would be discriminatory or unjust to the imperative of more honorable alternatives. Kindness is courage.

When Lawsuits Are Valuable

A former state supreme court justice,[36] a Quaker, once stated that advocacy for the rights of the underprivileged is integral to Friends' tradition, and courts are often proper fora for redress for the infringement of these rights.[37] Lawsuits are the most appropriate vehicle for the adjudication of public policy issues that have broad repercussions for the society at large. For instance, *Brown v. Board of Education*,[38] the U.S. Supreme Court decision that struck down racial segregation in public schools, involved important public policy and civil rights issues. These are more appropriately aired in a public forum where the constitutional principles at stake can be explored; was "separate but equal" truly equal? *Brown* educated citizens on the necessity and moral rightness of racially integrated education through means of a constitutionally mandated precedent, a deterrent to those who might resist school integration. As valuable as it is, alternative dispute resolution, such as negotiation, mediation, and arbitration, cannot accomplish this because it functions privately and results in individually tailored solutions without precedential value.

Nevertheless, there are no doubt thousands of cases filed each year in state and federal courts that do not need publication because they do not involve public policy questions of far-reaching import. Such cases could be better and more efficiently handled by mediation or arbitration with less attendant cost and rancor. In fact, the adversary system may be ill-suited to many disputes. Then-Attorney General Janet Reno, in a February 1996 speech to the American Bar Association, urged lawyers to be peacemakers—to have courage to stop short of litigation and to use more "low-key" methods to solve disputes. A Quaker lawyer wrote, "Litigation is an all or nothing, yes or no, zero-sum game in most of its forms. Sometimes the situation calls for that and it's important for societies to set certain standards or precedents through this [method]." However, this respondent also noted that many situations do not require suits but "can be appropriately dealt with by sorting out issues to give positive feedback to both disputants so everyone can win something." Mediation or arbitration can do this.

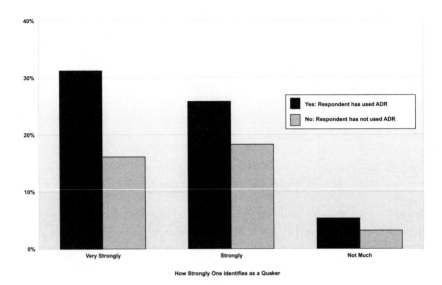

Figure 9. Strength of Identification as Quaker with Use of ADR

The Lawyer's "Philosophical Map"

According to Leonard Riskin, a primary and perhaps inevitable assumption of a lawyer's standard "philosophical map" is the adversarial win-lose thinking that disputes can and should be resolved solely through a court's application of rules of law. The lawyer's map and litigation paradigm on which it is based has power out of proportion to its usefulness and differs radically from that of the mediator.[39] Several factors have intensified lawyers' inclination to view disputes solely in terms of winning and losing. One is the dominance of the adversary model in U.S. legal education and practice. Another is Americans' cultural tendency toward competition rather than cooperation, which naturally fosters a conscious or unconscious preference for court-based dispute resolution where one party competes to win at the other's expense. Law students develop cognitive skills to "think like a lawyer"—to be logical, analytical, and rational. Although logic and common sense form the basis of the best laws and are also important to good alternative dispute resolution, the ability to empathize is equally critical to understanding parties' emotional needs. Lawyers' cognitive capabilities can become overdeveloped to the detriment of their empathetic sensibilities.

The propensity of Americans to view concepts dichotomously (win-lose rather than win-win) is not wholly unique to lawyers although their legal training no doubt increases the tendency. Our tendency to see the world, its concepts, and its phenomena as *either-or* rather than *both-and* contrasts with the more inclusive, if less precise, approach of some Asian cultures. The American view is more apt to lead to polarization rather than toleration, and it accords with the adversarial 'we-they' model of traditional court-based conflict resolution. Many American lawyers seem to find accommodating to the win-win concept of mediation difficult because of the societal and professional tendency toward dichotomization. Even attorneys who have mediated tend to favor rights-based over interest-based mediation because rights are highly valued and actively pursued in the adversary system. One Quaker lawyer noted: "Law is about people standing up for their rights—the right to be paid . . . to custody . . . to privacy. . . ." Another wrote that "ADR [alternative dispute resolution] is appropriate when the dispute involves conflicting interests. When, however, rights are at stake, especially when they must be articulated by a Court in order to be enforceable, then litigation is essential."

A study of 195 lawyers in three states used psychologist Lawrence Kohlberg's theory that persons develop along a psychological continuum of six advancing ethical stages.[40] The results showed that more than 90% of the lawyers displayed Kohlberg's Stage Four, a law-and-order orientation that emphasizes authority, fixed rules, and maintenance of the social order. Right behavior consists of doing one's duty, showing respect for authority, and maintaining the status quo of the given social order, and lawyers in this stage thought less about revising the legal system ("ought") than working within its existing principles and boundaries ("is"). "Law and order oriented people will not change from a competitive posture to a cooperative one for the good of law or society because they fail to recognize that the system is not functioning as it was designed to function."[41] "Moving the individual's cognitive orientation from Kohlberg's Stage Four to Stage Five, the social contract, which emphasizes changing the law for rational considerations, would enable lawyers to understand why cooperation can provide greater gains."[42] If this analysis is correct, then lawyers committed to the status quo of a Stage Four orientation will find encouraging alternatives to litigation difficult—at least until they are able to reach the next stage.

The source of a tendency to resist cooperation and collaboration is likely in our upbringing and culture if certain research is accurate. Psychological studies of American children have shown that creating a cooperative "win-win" situation is difficult for these children to accept because competition is so firmly rooted in cognitive development and culture.[43] A study of cooperation and competition in Mexican- and Anglo-American children, for example, revealed that almost all of the Anglo children found it reinforcing to try to reduce the gains of their peers.[44] Another study showed similar results, finding that children in the United States tend to irrationally compete even when cooperation is a more rational choice.[45] Even legal scholars have theorized about sources of American competitiveness. Presser of Northwestern University cites legal philosopher Unger's view that Americans have lost sight of community and fraternity in the competition to acquire material goods caused by American law's "possessive individualism" of the past 150 years, enabled and permitted by our legal concept of private property and promoted by an economic system of advanced capitalism.[46]

A Quaker lawyer wrote about his clients, "The ideal of win-win is foreign to them. [A] considerable number . . . want a very zealous assertion of their rights [and] want to prevail over those blocking them. . . ." Lawyers have generally been slow to refer cases to ADR, which may be partly due to unfamiliarity with mediation and arbitration processes and resources. Some lawyers also believe that certain disputes should be handled only by lawyers. Referrals mean relinquishing fees. However, with encouragement from bar associations and others, ADR use may increase. Staff of a state mediation program noted that it took time for attorneys accompanying clients to mediation to change from being adversarial to being more cooperative. However, once they did, they became more effective in advising and preparing clients for various alternative resolutions that might be offered.[46] One writer believes that the future of mediation rests heavily on the attitudes and involvement of the legal profession. If mediation is to be well utilized, lawyers must better understand it and when it can best be used. "And a substantial number of lawyers must begin to function explicitly as mediators."[48]

The Mediator's "Philosophical Map"

A mediator's philosophical map employs different assumptions from those of a lawyer, and therefore mediation, unbound by procedural and evidentiary rules or substantive law, requires a radical shift in thinking. One assumption of the mediator's map is that many disputes are not amenable to resolution by a general principle of law. Another is that both parties can benefit from a mutually agreed-upon solution. This is a primary advantage of mediation, that parties can cooperatively devise their own resolution. Because a win-win concept may be counterintuitive to many, a major task of mediation proponents is to reeducate lawyers, courts, parties, and the public to make this alternative an integral part of their thinking on how to resolve conflict.

A good mediator must be aware of the interconnections between disputants and the quality of such interconnections. In addition, he or she must be sensitive to parties' emotional needs and be able to recognize the importance of their desire for mutual respect, equality, security, and other nonmaterial interests.[49] One Quaker lawyer touched on the nonmaterial interests that mediation can address: "parties are given opportunities to recognize the humanity of the person sitting across the table (again, cf. litigation where the opponent is a monster)." A proponent of ADR, she described mediation as a process of recognition and empowerment. Mediation allows parties to take responsibility for the conflict and its resolution in contrast to litigation where parties give control to lawyers and judges. Recognition of the interests, needs, and connectedness of disputing parties fits rather easily with most Quaker lawyers' zeitgeist; several respondents wrote that mediation is a natural fit. One wrote that she "wanted to do mediation, which is compatible w[ith] Quaker values." Another noted, "When I was trained as a mediator; I knew I'd found my calling."

A law professor related his experience in teaching a first-year contracts class. One day he posed a hypothetical involving a buyer and a seller, whose widget delivery was short by one. The professor hoped that students would recite legal doctrines allowing the seller to "crush" the buyer. As he searched the class for a volunteer, all were furiously writing or "inspecting their shoes." But one eager hand shot up, belonging to a student's eight-year-old son. The professor, anxious to reward participation in any form, asked the boy what he would say if he were the seller. The boy answered, "I'd say 'I'm sorry.' "[50] The exquisite simplicity of such a solution speaks volumes and is sometimes all that is necessary to resolve a dispute. It is mediation's emphasis on individual persons qua persons, rather than on roles that enlarges the opportunity for such a solution. Some lawyers

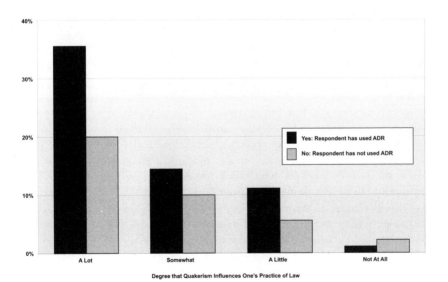

Figure 10. Quaker Influence on Practice with Use of ADR

would do well to realize, as the eight-year-old did, that a simple "I'm sorry" might be sufficient to assuage a person locked in conflict.

Mediation often includes a holistic approach to resolving disputes, which takes into account both the situation of the parties and the circumstances surrounding the dispute; this contrasts with a lawyer's more atomistic approach to a client's situation.[51] This kind of approach may also increase the likelihood of a longer lasting resolution. Mediation strengthens community by stressing interconnectedness, interdependence, and cooperation in defining parties' overlapping needs and interests.

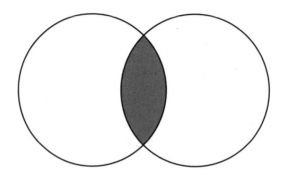

Quaker Lawyers and Mediation or Arbitration

A survey question asked respondents if they had used ADR; 58 responded affirmatively and 35 negatively, more or less equally divided between men and women, and 7 did not answer. The next question asked if they thought ADR was superior to litigation, and 55% thought so, whereas 4% did not. Twenty-two percent were neutral, and the remaining did not answer. The lawyers who considered mediation and arbitration superior were asked to identify the types of cases appropriate for these processes; almost one-half (48%) of those who answered replied *all*; next was domestic relations. Respondents who thought ADR superior to litigation were asked whether they preferred mediation or arbitration; twice as many preferred the former.

Quaker lawyers are more likely to have heightened aptitude for some important elements of good mediation: an ability and willingness to respect both parties, to look beyond roles to individual circumstances, to listen, and to empathize. One Quaker lawyer believed that game playing and unnecessary confrontation in law practice actually hampered the resolution of disputes, and she searched for other lawyers who shared her desire for alternative approaches. She thinks that a primary advantage of mediation is allowing disputants to work as partners toward a resolution. She believes that, at its best, mediation can establish a measure of reconciliation between the parties by replacing the polarization and animosity engendered by most litigation. Lawyers who realize the interconnectedness of people are "less vulnerable to the . . . overenthusiasm with the adversary role that has brought about much of its sinister reputation."[52] Respondents were enthusiastic about alternative dispute resolution and many thought it should be more heavily used. Several respondents specifically suggested that education on mediation be mandatory in every case before the courts, whereas others suggested that conflict resolution be required in schools from elementary through graduate school. If Quaker lawyers foster the use of collaborative methods of dispute resolution, they might influence other lawyers to do so. As we have seen, mediation and arbitration have been time-honored means of dispute resolution for Friends because these processes are conceptually consonant with their testimonies. The survey has shown that Quaker lawyers have a greater affinity for these more cooperative models because, by virtue of their faith, it is natural for them to think in terms of connections and linkages. Friends' belief that there is that of God in every person also reinforces a feeling of kinship.

Mediators can help disputants determine their goals and interests and then together identify areas of common interest. By doing this, they enhance the likelihood of an agreement. Mediation trainers frequently pose a hypothetical in which two parties are disputing over a shipment of oranges. Both want, and believe they need, the oranges and argue over them at great length. When the mediator helps each probe the reasons for wanting the oranges, they discover that one wants peels from the oranges to make marmalade while the other wants the juice from the fruit. A mediator-aided dialogue reveals each party's real interest, the resulting accommodation meets the needs of each, and an agreement results.

Programs that Promote Alternative Dispute Resolution

During the last half-century, the waning of traditional mediating entities such as the church, family, and community together with an expansion of statutory and constitutional rights, has driven a search for alternatives to litigation as the primary means of resolving disputes.

The Civil Rights Act of 1964 created a Community Relations Service intended to aid in the settlement of disputes based on race, color, or national origin. It continues within the Department of Justice its original mandate to perform mediation or mediation training in the context of incidents of intolerance within communities. The 1991 amendments to Title VII of the Civil Rights Act of 1964 explicitly encourage the use of mediation to settle employment complaints brought pursuant to that title.

The Department of Justice under Attorney-General Janet Reno published an order[53] promoting the broader use of ADR within the Department, applicable to all litigating divisions and U.S. attorneys. Beginning in fall 1995, these lawyers were expected to use ADR in appropriate cases as an alternative to litigation. This order also established a senior counsel position for ADR in the Department of Justice.

In the last few decades, the use of mediation, arbitration, and other ADR has increased. Various organizations and associations, including the Society for Professionals in Dispute Resolution and the National Institute for Dispute Resolution, have facilitated the increase. Private ADR firms have sprung up, using mediation, arbitration, and hybrid forms to settle a wide variety of consumer, commercial, labor, and employment disputes. Many corporations have signed agreements promising first to use mediation or arbitration to resolve internal disputes. A number of companies have specifically agreed to mediate employment discrimination complaints filed with the Equal Employment Opportunity Commission (EEOC) against them. The EEOC, a creation of the Civil Rights Act of 1964, has a dual mission: to enforce federal laws prohibiting employment discrimination and to resolve employment disputes. To better fulfill the latter mission, it established a mediation program in the late 1990s. The EEOC mediation program is fully consistent with its enforcement mission, and through it, EEOC can provide a quicker, less expensive, and more productive way to help eliminate workplace discrimination.

A Center for Public Policy Dispute Resolution at the University of Texas at Austin provides dispute resolution assistance for Texas state and local government agencies and courts. Specifically, it assists in designing ADR systems, provides third-party services for resolving public disputes, and educates the public about ADR programs and processes.

In 1994 the American Bar Association (ABA) solicited ideas from a "public jury" of nonlawyers on legal system reform including increased use of arbitration and mediation in lieu of trials. In proposing the plan to state and local bar associations, the ABA president stated that justice in the United States takes too long, costs too much, and is virtually inaccessible to many.[54] Many Quaker lawyer respondents agree. This commendable encouragement from the leading lawyers' association has borne fruit. Various bar associations, the very groups who are customarily protective of their lawyer-constituents' turf, have come to encourage alternative forms of dispute resolution. For instance, a county bar association joined with a state bar in a resolution proclaiming a "mediation week," recognizing that many had turned to dispute resolution services with resulting social and economic benefits, and realizing that public consciousness should be further raised about the merits of these services.[55]

Many state bars and bar associations, including those of Texas and Maryland, have established special ADR committees or sections that promote informed use of ADR and have attorney-members who themselves mediate and arbitrate disputes. Bar publications, too, have featured articles on ADR, and some like the Maryland State Bar Association have devoted an entire issue to the subject. This state bar association has for years also sponsored 40-hour mediation training programs especially for lawyers. There are also one or more associations of attorney-mediators; one, the Association of Attorney-Mediators, formed in 1989, is composed of mediators who are licensed attorneys. Its mission is to promote and support qualified attorney-mediators who are committed to achieving prompt, fair, and cost-effective resolution of disputes through mediation. Pennsylvania's state bar association is one that has required intralawyer disputes be mediated before they are sent to arbitration.

In recent years, mediation projects and settlement programs have been created and based in municipal and county courts, schools, universities, and neighborhood associations across the nation. A peer-based conflict mediation program was established in the public schools by a Baltimore, Maryland, institution originally founded by Quaker Moses Sheppard. This conflict mediation program, intended to reach all grades in every public school, teaches the need for a shift from traditional thinking that confrontation is the sole mode of conflict resolution. It promotes mediation as an easily learned skill that is useful throughout one's life. By participating in mediation, the disputants together learn to untie the rope wrapped around them. If the young are familiar with mediation and feel empowered to work out a solution, they are more likely to continue to use these skills through adulthood. To better educate students interested in ADR, colleges and law schools now also offer mediation courses. Several scholarly journals are devoted to ADR as well.

Because many still perceive courts to be the principal channel of justice, it is important that ADR be made part of state and federal court systems. Maine accomplished this in 1980 when its supreme court established a mediation service to serve its courts. In 1991 a Department of Dispute Resolution Services was created within the supreme court of Virginia. This department, once directed by a Quaker lawyer, was created in response to a *Report of the Commission on the Future of Virginia's Judicial System*, a document that stressed the importance of extensive education on alternative conflict resolution:

> Resolving disputes in a peaceful manner is a paramount obligation of government to its people. To offer the most effective, responsive and appropriate methods for resolving disputes, our justice system must be able to offer alternative dispute resolution programs along with adjudication. . . . Because disputes differ widely in nature, adjudication is not always the most appropriate means of resolving all cases. In fashioning non-traditional dispute resolution alternatives . . . means must be developed that offer an opportunity

to deal with the cause of the underlying issues in a dispute. New approaches must find ways to reduce hostility between disputants, to gain acceptance of the outcome and to restore a sense of control to the parties.[56]

The Virginia report recommended a wide array of dispute resolution services including adjudication, negotiation, mediation, summary jury trials, mini-trials, and binding and nonbinding arbitration. This "multidoor" approach allows flexibility to fashion the most appropriate process for a particular dispute. Similar programs have been implemented in Washington, D.C., and in Burlington County, New Jersey, one of the first Quaker settlements in America.

The number of states that have enacted statutes specifically pertaining to the mediation or arbitration of disputes has grown in recent years. Some of the earliest statutes were those of California, Florida, Maine, Minnesota, Oklahoma, Oregon, and Texas. For example, Texas has had an Alternative Dispute Resolution Procedures Act since 1987.

Quaker Involvement in Alternative Dispute Resolution

Some years ago, a leader in the field of conflict resolution noticed very little Friends' involvement at a national peacemaking and conflict resolution conference. Quaker organizations such as the AFSC were notable by their absence.[57] He concluded that perhaps individual Friends were ahead of their institutions in recognizing opportunities for building peacemaking processes in communities. The nexus between peacemaking in the Quaker tradition and Quaker groups' active sponsorship of peacemaking in the context of ADR should be strong because a vital correlation exists between long- and short-term peacemaking. Quaker groups could make valuable contributions if they were active in conferences that promote a greater understanding of and accessibility to various kinds of ADR. One such group active in promoting and encouraging alternative conflict resolution is the Friends Conflict Resolution Programs (FCRP) of Philadelphia Yearly Meeting. For many years, FCRP programs have provided mediator training as well as conflict intervention services and mediation programs in schools.

Conclusion

This chapter concludes by offering some thoughts to Quakers, Quaker lawyers, and readers interested in just legal systems, law, or peace and peacemaking.

The Quaker internal dispute resolution process created in Fox's time had its origins in scripture, and thus gospel order became an alternative to court-based resolution as Friends were discouraged from going to law. Although this aspect of gospel order later fell into disuse in Quaker meetings, this kindlier way of resolving disputes is no less important today.

Friends' prohibition against going to law cannot, and does not, make sense without meeting members' care and concern for those involved in dispute, joined with an active and focused effort to help end it. Discouraging a member from suing simply by advising, "Don't sue!" is not enough. Meetings must be willing to give its members spiritual and emotional support as well as the requisite procedural tools to make real resolution possible. If there is a disincentive to Friends going to law, it is essential that it be paired with a support structure for those in difficult disputes. As they had done two centuries ago, Friends might consider developing again a clear, simple, yet comprehensive internal dispute resolution process as a viable alternative to suits in court. Quarterly or Yearly Meetings could lead in resurrecting and updating these Quakers' traditional and preferred alternative dispute resolution processes, and Monthly Meetings could implement them for the benefit of members. Then, working both individually and communally, with the help of others, Friends could initiate a broader peacemaking effort around the use of alternative dispute resolution within the larger community by further educating members and others to the possibilities and promise of extralegal alternatives to resolving conflict—a parallel to what might be Quaker lawyers' involvement and leadership in a thrust toward legal reform. Quakers' revival and adaptation of their early practice of "gospel order" would be a powerful witness of the testimonies of harmony and community and a valuable contribution to twenty-first century dispute resolution.

Quaker lawyers could make an immense contribution by leading or joining with other ADR proponents to educate a wider segment of society about its advantages. This could be accomplished by acting as pro bono mediators in courts, community justice centers, schools, and neighborhood associations. Lawyers could also refer disputes to mediation or arbitration or use fee-based alternatives to litigation in their own practices.

By assuming a higher profile in support of ADR, Quaker lawyers could also encourage constructive change in contemporary law practice, change that many appear to long for. From such a platform, lawyer-Friends might become the vanguard of a movement for law reform. Burke's call for substantial change in the rules of procedure, evidence, and professional responsibility could be an important beginning, and revised rules might specify what lawyers must do rather than what they must not do. To begin, Quaker lawyers might again gather for conferences at places such as Pendle Hill and launch a discourse with other lawyers, law professors, and scholars. Those at such a gathering could initiate a dialogue and forthright analysis of current flaws in the legal system and devise a plan for improvement and coordination of courts and ADR programs. Reformulation of rules together with reinvigorated efforts at appropriate case referral to ADR can reemphasize and reprioritize truth and justice in the courts. By a careful and methodical diversion of cases to ADR, overburdened U.S. courts could focus their considerable judicial talent and limited resources toward fewer summary dispositions and more thorough hearings of cases appropriate for courts of law.

The paraphrase of Henry J. Cadbury's words at the 1947 Nobel Peace Prize ceremony[58] is addressed to Quaker lawyers and indeed to all who believe in the possibility inherent in these words:

> I am saying here today that common folk—not Supreme Court justices like Douglas or Black, nor Harvard law professors like Tribe or Miller, nor great legal scholars like Burke or Wright—but just simple plain men and women like the few hundred fine Quaker lawyers can do something to build a better, more truthful and peaceful legal and extra-legal system. To this idea lawyers everywhere can contribute.

Epilogue

Friends' Contributions to Laws and the Legal System, Past and Future

"Friends have always believed . . . that an aim of religion is to change this world for the better, to shape human institutions, including government, to be more responsive to human needs."[1]

Over the centuries, Quakers have made numerous contributions to the "human institution" of law as they have engaged it from their seventeenth-century beginnings. For several decades, they disobeyed English laws requiring oaths out of an allegiance to scripture and to a deep and abiding commitment to truth-telling. George Fox and other Quaker contemporaries authored numerous tracts and treatises on law, lawyers, and judges. They "spoke truth to power" by sending pleas and petitions to Parliament and the King about the suffering of Quakers under the injustices of praemunire laws, laws requiring attendance at Church of England services, and the many English laws requiring oaths. Almost five decades later their efforts bore fruit in the latter regard when Parliament passed a law that permitted Friends' affirmation in lieu of swearing. Friends changed English law with *Bushell's Case*, which originated from the 1670 trial of Quakers William Penn and William Mead and created the principle of independence of juries from manipulation and threats from the judiciary. Thus, their interaction with the law in its many manifestations—their early and frequent appearances as defendants in court, their writings on laws and lawyers, and their persistence in seeking changes to laws—has made the Society unique among religious groups in such engagement, and its written record.

Quaker William Penn had significant influence on the laws of Pennsylvania as its Proprietor. He drafted more humane laws, which provided for prison reform, reduced the number of capital crimes, and instituted peacemaking by arbitrators to settle differences among the early inhabitants. These new laws and changes to existing laws of the Duke of York illustrate Friends' concern for prisoners, the poor and disadvantaged, the sanctity of all life through the Inner Light in every person, and harmony and peace—the highest and best values of the good society Penn hoped Pennsylvania province would be.

Despite proportionately small numbers, Quakers have often been the vanguard of social reform, as the "loyal opposition" and "Lord's advocate," always remembering the primacy of God's laws when they conflict with those of any human authority. Friends' early opposition to slavery began more than 150 years before the American Civil War. Other Friends have continued to "lay bare" the shortcomings of laws and policies regarding war and those that disregard the needs of society's minorities and poor.

From time to time, Friends have bypassed the traditional caution against "going to law" in order to pursue justice in the courts. Individual Friends and some Yearly Meetings did so in the last half of the twentieth century by bringing actions and submitting amici curiae briefs on behalf of Quakers and others. The actions they brought concerning race, immigration, government surveillance, and government coercion were conducted in the public eye where members of the public could consider and discuss them. Naturally, Friends brought or defended many suits that concerned the peace testimony and their conscientious objection to war.

The "divine lobbyists" continue work through the Friends Committee on National Legislation (FCNL) in trying to persuade Congress to enact more socially just legislation that will, in turn, lead to a more peaceful society. In its lobbying efforts, the FCNL works to prevent incipient misunderstandings that might lead to more serious conflict, and to accomplish that, it encourages talks with other nations with whom the United States has differences. First, it was a staunch supporter of the League of Nations and subsequently the United Nations. Quaker concerns travel past Washington, D.C., and U.S. borders to other nations in the form of support for international treaties and relief for people and societies damaged by war. At the periphery of the law, Friends have been leaders in alternative forms of dispute resolution since the seventeenth century when they used them to solve conflict within their meetings. They continue through various programs to give attention and support to this more gentle way of resolving conflict and thereby helping to better realize harmony and community. Quaker contributions and endeavors surrounding matters of law have sprung from their testimonies and Fox's words "so say and so do."

The 100 Quaker lawyers surveyed for this book offer many good insights into the current practice of law and suggestions for its improvement. They were discomfited by the aggressiveness, ruthlessness, and lack of truth-telling, and several aptly emphasized the conflict between lawyers' positions as officers of the court and as zealous advocates of their clients' causes. Polarization of these has been exacerbated in recent years by the ascendancy of zealous advocacy, but the two can be brought into greater balance, that is, unless something inherent in the practice of law makes it bound to foment dissent and distress. One must consider whether this tendency is an inherent characteristic of the profession because many thinkers and writers, from early times to the present, have regarded lawyers with disdain and worse. Or is this state of affairs amenable to change? If it is, the time to start the process of change is now, before some habits of aggressiveness, incivility, and dissimulation become yet more ingrained and widespread.

The goals of our legal system are purportedly truth and justice, but these twin goals must be more than abstractions. If truth-telling is made the essential element of truth-finding, courts will clearly advance to reach the primary goal of justice. When this becomes more fully realized, the inconsistency of lawyers' dual positions as earnest advocates and court officers will be lessened.

In recent years, overzealous advocacy has grown to overshadow lawyers' other professional obligations and is the source of many tensions Quaker lawyers cited with regard to current law practice. Zealous advocacy discourages truth-telling and proper regard for the rules of court and breeds other problems as well. This kind of advocacy and disregard of rules can worsen as lawyers compete hard to win; more believe they must practice in this manner to gain the advantage, a slippery slope on which it becomes increasingly difficult to rebalance. If lawyers' professional obligations and actual workaday practice can be better balanced, their work can be more principled and attuned to the moral imperatives of conscience. If law practice can be synchronized with these obligations, truth-telling can take its essential and rightful place in the law offices and courts. Truth-telling is the central pivot on which truth-finding and justice balance.

The time is ripe for a new direction in the U.S. legal system and practice of law. This book challenges the small but hardy band of Quaker lawyers to lead their colleagues in this blessed calling.

Appendix

The Questionnaire

QUESTIONNAIRE FOR QUAKER LAWYERS   NO. _____

1. Are you: a(n) __ attender __ birthright Quaker __ convinced Quaker __ no longer a Quaker or attender

2. How long have you been a Quaker or Quaker attender? __ less than a year __ 1–5 years __6–10 years __11–15 years __16–20 years __ more than 20 years

3. Do you attend a(n) __ programmed meeting __unprogrammed meeting

4. How strongly do you identify yourself as a Quaker and with Quaker beliefs and testimonies?

    __ very strongly __ strongly __ neutrally __ not much __not at all

5. How long have you been a lawyer? __ less than 2 years __ 2–5 years __ 6–10 years __11–15 years __ 16–20 years __ more than 20 years

6. Did you attend law school immediately upon graduation from college? __ yes __ no; If not, how soon after graduation? __ within 2 years __ within 5 years __ within 10 years __ within 15 years__ more than 15 years after graduation from college

7. Why did you want to become a lawyer? (Check all that apply) __ prestige__ money __altruism __family pressure __ family connections __ intellectual interest __ other (please specify)

8. Are you __under 30 years old __31–40 __41–50 __51–60 __more than 60

9. Do you practice __solo __in a small firm (less than 15 lawyers) __in a large firm (more than 15 lawyers); __please state how many __in government service (local, state, federal) __ other (please specify)

10. Please indicate the type of law you practice by indicating beside each type the approximate percentage of the time you spend on it: __ civil rights __corporate __criminal __domestic __employment discrimination __ immigration __ labor __ patent and copyright __ personal injury __tax __ torts (other than personal injury) __wills and estates__ other (please specify)

11. Please explain your motivation for taking these types of cases.

12. Do you think that your being Quaker influences the type of law you practice (as described in question 10)? __ yes __ no; if yes, please explain as specifically as you can.

13. (a) Do you do pro bono work? __ yes __ no

    (b) If yes, approximately how many hours per month? __1–5 __6–10 __11–15 __16–20 __more than 20

    (c) If you answered yes to 13(b), does your being Quaker influence your doing pro bono work? __yes __no

    (d) If you answered yes to 13(c), why and how?

    (e) If you answered no to 13(c), why do you do pro bono work?

14. Does your being Quaker influence the way you practice law? __not at all __a little ___somewhat ___a lot; if your answer is affirmative, please explain how, as specifically as you can.

15. If your answer to 14 was "not at all," please explain.

16. Do you think that being a Quaker *should* influence the way you practice law? __ yes __no

17. Do you experience any tension and/or conflicts between your practice of law and your Quaker beliefs and testimonies? __ yes __ no; if your answer is yes, please describe these tensions and/or conflicts as specifically as you can.

18. If your answer to 17 was affirmative, how do you try to resolve these tensions and/or conflicts?__ talk with Quaker colleagues __ talk with non-Quaker colleagues __ through my Monthly Meeting __ through a Clearness Committee __ other (please explain).

19. If your answer to 17 was negative, please elaborate.

20. (a) Do you perceive any advantages in being a Quaker lawyer (check all that apply): __ in getting new clients __ in settlement negotiations __ at trial __ in counseling/advising __ in relationships with your peers __ other (please explain)

    (b) Please describe these advantages as specifically as you can.

21. (a) Do you perceive any disadvantages in being a Quaker lawyer: __in getting new clients __ in settlement negotiations __ at trial __ in counseling and advising __ in relationships with your peers __other (please explain)

    (b) Please describe these disadvantages as specifically as you can.

22. Have you ever employed alternative dispute resolution techniques? __ yes __no; If yes, in what kinds of cases? (Check all that apply) __ domestic __ landlord-tenant __ torts __ other (please specify).F

23. Vis-à-vis litigation, do you view alternative dispute resolution as __ superior __ inferior __ neutral as a means of settling disputes?

    If superior, in which types or cases? (check all that apply): __ domestic __ landlord-tenant __ torts __ all __ other (please specify)

    If superior, which kinds of alternative dispute resolution techniques do you prefer? __ arbitration __ mediation __ other (please specify)

24. If you think alternative dispute resolution techniques are superior to litigation, please explain why as specifically as you can.

25. If you think alternative dispute resolution techniques are inferior to litigation, please explain why as specifically as you can.

26. Do you think that your practice of law differs from that of your non-Quaker colleagues? __ yes __ no; if yes, please explain how as specifically as you can.

27. In your opinion, should there be any fundamental changes in the way *law functions in our society*? __ yes __no; if yes, please explain.

28. What, if anything, would you like to see changed about the *practice of law*?

29. If you had absolutely no constraints, what would be *your preferred way of practicing law?*

30. If there is an aspect of Quakers and the law that has not been covered but that you think pertinent, please contribute your thoughts.

31. Please list any other Quaker lawyers you know who might be willing to participate in this project (with their addresses and/or telephone numbers if you know them)

32. Do you know any Quaker lawyers who have left the practice of law? __ yes __ no;

If yes, how many? ___; if yes, and, if you know, please state the reason(s).

If yes, please list the names of any who might be willing to participate in this project (with their addresses and/or telephone numbers if you know them).

33. Please list a telephone number and the times you are most likely to be available in case I need to call you to clarify any of your responses.

Because my sample of Quaker lawyers is small your response is very meaningful. Thanks very much for your cooperation. *Please return by January 30. 1992* to: Nancy Black, Pendle Hill, 338 Plush Mill Rd., Wallingford, PA 19086.

Notes

Introduction

1. Gary B. Madison, ed., *Working through Derrida* (Evanston, IL: Northwestern University Press, 1993), 1.

Chapter 1

1. George Fox, *The Journal of George Fox*, ed. John L. Nickalls (Cambridge, UK: Cambridge University Press, 1952), 263.

2. John 15:15, *Holy Bible*, Authorized (King James) Version (Nashville, TN: Holman Bible Publishers, 1998).

3. George Fox, *The Journal of George Fox*, ed. Rufus Jones (New York: Capricorn Books, 1963), 125.

4. John 1: 6-9.

5. Benjamin Disraeli (Earl of Beaconsfield), Speech before English Parliament, February 11, 1851, in *Selected Speeches of the Earl of Beaconsfield*, 2 vols. (London: Longmans, Green, 1882).

6. The primary Quaker testimonies are harmony or peace, simplicity, equality, and community; each is discussed in detail in this chapter.

7. Plato, *Phaedrus* 272d, quoted in Malcolm Clark, *The Enterprise of Law: Questions in Legal Experience and Philosophy* (St. Paul, MN: West Publishing, 1987), 7.

8. Ibid.

9. Lucius Annaeus Seneca, *Moral Epistles*, 3 vols. trans. Richard M. Gummere (Cambridge, MA: Harvard University Press, 1917–1925), vol. 1, XLI.

10. Ps.15:1–2.

11. Howard H. Brinton, *Friends for 300 Years* (New York: Harper, 1952), 137.

12. Margaret Hope Bacon, *The Quiet Rebels: The Story of the Quakers in America* (Philadelphia: New Society Publishers, 1985), 44–45.

13. James 2:12: "So speak ye, and so do."

14. George Fox, *A Collection of Many Select and Christian Epistles, Letters and Testimonies Written by . . . George Fox*, 2 vols. (Philadelphia: Marcus T. Gould, 1831), vol. 1, 111.

15. Sophocles, *Oedipus at Colonus*, trans. Eamon Grennan and Rachel Kitzinger (New York: Oxford University Press, 2005), 720–721.

16. John Woolman, *The Journal of John Woolman*, ed. Philip P. Moulton (New York: Oxford University Press, 1971), 88.

17. London Yearly Meeting, A selection from the Christian advices issued by the Yearly meeting of the Society of Friends, held in London. From its early establishment to the present time (London: E. Marsh, 1851).

18. Paul Lacey, "Quakers and the Social Testimonies: Servants, Prophets, Reconcilers" (AFSC-IRCA Consultation, Pendle Hill, Wallingford, PA, September 22, 1990), 2.

19. James 3:18.

20. James 3:17.

21. Ibid.

22. James 2:8.

23. James 1:22.

24. James 2:14.

25. James: 2:26.

26. Matt. 5:16.

27. Matt. 7:12; and Luke 6:31, "And as ye would that men should do to you, do ye also to them."

28. Brinton, 174.

29. Matt. 5:9.

30. Fox, *Journal of George Fox*, 65.

31. Fox, *Journal of George Fox*, 399–400. Some historians use 1660 and others, 1661. The discrepancy occurs because until 1752 England used the Julian rather than the Gregorian calendar, so that dates from January 1 until March 25, the beginning of the new year, often had double numerals.

32. *Packard v. United States*, No. 98–6223, (2d Cir. June 1, 1999), *Amicus curiae* brief, New York Yearly Meeting of the Religious Society of Friends, 13.

33. Gunnar Jahn, speech at the presentation of the 1947 Nobel Peace Prize (Oslo, Norway, December 10, 1947).

34. Philadelphia Yearly Meeting of the Religious Society of Friends, Faith and practice, . . . A book of Christian discipline. 1955. (Philadelphia: [Friends Central Bureau, 1955]).

35. Fox, *Journal of George Fox*, 250.

36. Many Friends in the Midwest and West attend "programmed" meetings in Quaker "churches" with minister, music, sermon, and a period of silence. Evangelical Quaker groups are primarily found in other parts of the world. This book, however, is concerned only with Friends' unprogrammed meetings, most closely akin to the kind brought earlier from England.

37. Brinton, *Friends for 300 Years*, 11.

38. Ibid., 145.

39. James 1:9–10.

40. Lev.10:6.

41. 2 Sam. 15:30.

42. Daisy Newman, *A Procession of Friends: Quakers in America*, Religion in America Series, ed. Charles W. Ferguson (Garden City, NY: Doubleday, 1972), 10. A few still spoke in this manner in some late twentieth century Pennsylvania meetings.

43. Richard T. Vann, *The Social Development of English Quakerism 1655–1755*, (Cambridge, MA: Harvard University Press, 1969), 90.

44. "A Minute against Slavery, Addressed to Germantown Monthly Meeting, at Richard Worrell's," 18, 2, 1688, in Joseph Walton ed., *Incidents Illustrating the Doctrine and History of the Society of Friends* (Philadelphia: Friends Book Store, 1897).

45. An Act respecting Fugitives from justice, and persons escaping from the service of their masters, Act of Feb. 12, 1793.

46. Brinton, *Friends for 300 Years*, 104, note.

47. Ibid., 147.

48. Ibid., 11.

49. Lacey, "Quakers and the Social Testimonies," 4.

50. Do unto others as you would have them do unto you is a paraphrase of Luke 6:31: "And as ye would that men should do to you, do ye also to them likewise." See also Matthew 7:12.

51. Jerold S. Auerbach, *Justice without Law?* (New York: Oxford University Press, 1983), 16.

52. 1 Thes. 5:5.

53. Fox, *Journal of George Fox*, 33.

54. William Charles Braithwaite, *Memoirs and Papers*, ed. Anna B. Thomas and Elizabeth B. Emmott (London: Longmans, Green, 1931), 153.

55. Brinton, *Friends for 300 Years*, 28.

56. Isaac Penington, *Naked Truth or Truth nakedly manifesting itself in several particulars . . . Isaac Penington*, vol. 3 (London: S.n., 1674), §2, 332.

57. Amicus curiae brief, New York Yearly Meeting of the Religious Society of Friends, *Packard v. United States*, No. 98-6223 (2d Cir. June 1, 1999), 6.

58. Hugh Barbour, *The Quakers in Puritan England* (New Haven, CT: Yale University Press, 1964), 98.

59. Brinton, *Friends for 300 Years*, 28.

60. Ibid., 44.

61. Ibid., 4.

62. 1995 New York Yearly Meeting *Faith and Practice*, 21, quoted in *amicus curiae* brief of New York Yearly Meeting in *Packard v. United States* No. 98-6223, (2d Cir. June 1, 1999), 12.

63. *Christian Faith and Practice in the Experience of the Society of Friends*, London Yearly Meeting, (London: Headley Brothers, 1960), no. 182.

64. Brinton, *Friends for 300 Years*, 29–30.

65. New York Yearly Meeting amicus curiae brief, *Packard v. United States*, 3.

66. John Munson, Quaker lawyer, letter to author, May 15, 1999.

67. Fox, *Journal of George Fox*, 33.

68. Unprogrammed Friends generally do not proselytize.

69. *Faith and Practice* was earlier called *Book of Discipline;* occasionally both names are used.

70. 1995 New York Yearly Meeting *Faith and Practice*, 6.

71. These queries appeared in a monthly meeting newsletter of Stony Run Friends Meeting, Baltimore, MD.

72. Anabaptists, a sixteenth-century sect that rose in Switzerland during the Reformation, advocated social and religious reform and practiced pacifism and adult baptism.

73. *Amicus curiae* brief, New York Yearly Meeting, *Packard v. United States*, 4.

74. Ibid., 11, quoting Gray Cox, *Bearing Witness: Quaker Process and a Culture of Peace*, Pendle Hill Pamphlet 262 (Wallingford, PA: Pendle Hill Publications, 1985) 4, 6.

75. Acts 5:29.

76. Philadelphia Yearly Meeting of the Religious Society of Friends, *Faith and practice: a book of Christian discipline* (Philadelphia: Philadelphia Yearly Meeting, 1972).

77. Samuel Janney, *The Life of William Penn*, 2nd ed. (Philadelphia: Lippincott, 1852), 51. Janney's account of Penn's life provides context. On an earlier trip to Paris, Penn had carried his sword. With it, he had disarmed a challenger-opponent in a duel, thus saving his life. He may have known Luke 22:36: "He that hath no sword, let him sell his garment, and buy one."

78. Brinton, *Friends for 300 Years*, 113.

70. William Penn, *Works*, 225, quoted in Melvin B. Endy Jr., *William Penn and Early Quakerism* (Princeton, NJ: Princeton University Press, 1973), 116.

80. Bacon, *The Quiet Rebels: The Story of the Quakers in America* (New York: New Society Publishers, 1985). The quotation was taken from a passage in which Bacon was discussing the Nazis of Germany.

81. *Journal of George Fox*, ed. Rufus Jones, 541.

82. Auerbach, *Justice without Law?* 4.

83. Matt. 18:15–17.

84. Philadelphia Yearly Meeting, 1681 minute, at Burlington.

85. Both cases are discussed in chapter 5.

86. Robert Barclay, *Apology for the True Christian Divinity*, 1678, in *Truth Triumphant*, vol. 2 Proposition XI, § VII, 357 (1692).

87. Ibid., Proposition XI, § IX, 360.

88. *Faith and Practice*, Phildelphia Yearly Meeting 1972, 9.

89. Christian Faith and Practice in the Experience, London Yearly Meeting, No. 246.

90. Thomas L. Shaffer, "Should a Christian Lawyer Sign Up for Simon's Practice of Justice?" *Stanford Law Review* 51 (1999): 903, 917.

91. Fox, *Journal of George Fox*, 263.

92. In the past, this caution was more emphatic, and indeed some early Quakers were disowned for this infraction.

Chapter 2

1. Edward Burrough, "A Declaration to All the World of our Faith and What we Believe. And this is written that all people upon earth may know by whom and how we are saved, and hopes for eternal life & what we believe concerning God, Christ & the spirit, and of the things that are eternal appertaining to all mankind to know

& believe. Concerning God, Christ, and the Spirit, this we believe" (London: Thomas Simmons, 1660), 7, quoted in Bacon, *The Quiet Rebels*, xi.

2. However, after the 1676 establishment of Meeting for Sufferings, Friends used the legal system in order to combat their persecution more effectively.

3. Joseph Besse. *A Collection of the Sufferings of the People called Quakers, for the testimony of good Conscience, from . . . 1650, to . . . the Act of Toleration . . . 1689*, 2 vols. (London: Luke Hinde, 1753).

4. Matt. 5:33–37. See also James 5:12: "But above all things, my brethren, swear not, neither by heaven, neither by the earth, neither by any other oath: but let your yea be yea and your nay, nay; lest ye fall into condemnation."

5. Margaret Fell, Works, 95, 136, quoted in Hugh S. Barbour, *The Quakers in Puritan England* (New Haven, CT: Yale University Press, 1964), 98.

6. Vann, *The Social Development of English Quakerism*, 90.

7. An Act for preventing the Mischiefs and Dangers that may arise by certaine Persons called Quakers and others refusing to take lawfull Oaths, 14 Car. II c. 1.

8. Besse, *A Collection of the Sufferings*, vol. 1, 397.

9. 16 Car. II c. 4.

10. Craig W. Horle, "Changing Quaker Attitudes toward Legal Defense: The George Fox Case 1673–75 and the Establishment of Meeting for Sufferings," in *Seeking the Light: Essays on Quaker History in Honor of Edwin B. Bronner*, ed. William J. Frost and John M. Moore (Wallingford, PA: Pendle Hill Publications and Friends Historical Assoc., 1986), 22, 26.

11. Besse, *Collection of the Sufferings*, vol. 2, 166.

12. Craig W. Horle, *The Quakers and the English Legal System 1660–1688* (Philadelphia: University Pennsylvania Press, 1988), 172.

13. Nicholas J. Morgan, "Lancashire Quakers and the Oath 1660–1722," *Journal of Friends Historical Society* 54 (1976–1982): 235, 238, Table A.

14. 30 Car. II c. 3.

15. The four legal societies of London—Gray's Inn, Lincoln's Inn, Inner Temple, and Middle Temple—have the exclusive right of admitting persons to the English bar.

16. Arnold Lloyd, *Quaker Social History 1669–1738* (London: Longmans, Green, 1950), 81.

17. Morgan, "Lancashire Quakers and the Oath 1660–1722," 237.

18. An Act for restraining Non-Conformists from inhabiting in Corporations, Five-Mile Act of 1665, 17 Car. II c. 2.

19. 29 Car. II c. 7.

20. Exod. 20:10.

21. Horle, *Quakers and the English Legal System*, 130.

22. Besse, A Collection of the Sufferings vol. 2, 142.

23. 23 Eliz. I c .1 and 29 Eliz. I c. 6.

24. Besse, *Collection of the Sufferings*, vol. 2, 112.

25. 14 Car. II, c. 1.

26. 13 Car. II, c.1.

27. 25 Car. II c. 2.

28. To distrain is to seize and hold property as security or indemnity for a debt.

29. Besse, *Collection of the Sufferings*, vol. 2, 97.

30. Barbour, *Quakers in Puritan England,* 223.

31. Praemunire or praemunire; literally "to warn"; a legal writ charging an offense of procuring translations, processes, excommunications, bulls, or other actions or benefits from the pope against the king or generally obeying an authority other than the Crown by introducing a foreign power into the kingdom. It was construed to include Friends.

32. Richard and Mary Maples Dunn, eds. *The Papers of William Penn.* 5 vols. (Philadelphia: University of Pennsylvania Press, 1981–1987), vol. 1, 291, n.11.

33. Besse, *Collection of the Sufferings,* vol. 1, 314.

34. Besse, *Collection of the Sufferings,* vol. 2, 106.

35. Some 300 years later, the judge in *United States v. Snider,* discussed in chapter 4, issued a contempt citation for the Quaker defendants' refusal to stand as he entered and left the courtroom.

36. Besse, *Collection of the Sufferings,* vol. 2, 99.

37. The historic criminal court on London's Old Bailey Street. The Penn-Mead trial is described in detail later in this chapter.

38. Besse, *Collection of the Sufferings,* vol. 1, 418.

39. Besse, *Collection of the Sufferings,* vol. 2, 157.

40. Horle, *Quakers and the English Legal System,* 265.

41. Craig W. Horle, "Judicial Encounters with Quakers 1660–1688," *Journal of Friends Historical Society* 54 (1976–80), 85.

42. Horle, *Quakers and the English Legal System,* 107–108.

43. Ibid., 110.

44. Ibid., 115.

45. Alfred W. Braithwaite, "Early Friends Experience with Juries." *Journal of Friends Historical Society* 50 (1962–1964): 217, 224–225.

46. Besse, *Collection of the Sufferings,* vol. 1, 49.

47. Ibid., vol. 1, 48.

48. Horle, "Judicial Encounters with Quakers 1660–1688," 85, 87.

49. Ibid., 90.

50. Besse, *Collection of the Sufferings,* vol. 1, 416.

51. Besse, *Collection of the Sufferings,* vol. 1, 419–420.

52. Ibid.

53. Besse, *Collection of the Sufferings,* vol. 1, 420.

54. Ibid.

55. Besse, *Collection of the Sufferings,* vol. 1, 421.

56. The fourteenth and twenty-ninth articles of the Magna Carta are in part sources for the right of due process in the U.S. Constitution.

57. Besse, *Collection of the Sufferings,* vol. 1, 426.

58. George Fox, *The Law of God, the Rule for Law-Makers, the Ground of all just Laws, and the Corruption of English Laws and Lawyers Discovered* (London: Giles Calvert, 1658), 4.

59. Hugh S. Barbour, "The Early Quaker Outlook upon 'the World' and Society 1647–1662" (Ph.D. diss., Yale University, 1952), 414.

60. One such proposal was "That no persons whatsoever, who have persecuted any for their conscience, shall be . . . elected into any place of Trust within . . . this Common-wealth." Edward Billings (Byllynge), *A Mite of Affection, Manifested in 31 Proposals* (London: Giles Calvert, 1659), 2.

61. Edward Byllynge [Billing], *A Word of Reproof and advice*, (London: Printed for Thomas Simmons, 1659), 20

62. Robert Barclay, The Anarchy of the Ranters and other libertines (London: N.p., 1676) in *Truth Triumphant* (London: Printed for Thomas Northcott, 1692), 209.

63. Christopher Hill, *The World Turned Upside Down: Radical Ideas during the English Revolution* (London: Viking, 1972), 219.

64. Quaker lawyers expressed similar thoughts in their survey responses reported in chapter 5.

65. Dunn and Dunn, *The Papers of William Penn*, vol. 1, 221.

66. Ibid.

67. George Fox, *The Law of God, The Rule for Law-makers, The Ground of all just Laws, and the corruption of English Laws and Lawyers Discovered* (London: Giles Calvert, 1658), 27.

68. William Penn echoed Fox's thought in a Frame of Government for Pennsylvania, discussed in chap. 4.

69. Sir Edward Coke, *The Second Part of the Institutes of the Laws of England*, (London: W. Rawlins for Thomas Basset, 1681), 625.

70. Besse, *Collection of the Sufferings*, vol. 1, 49.

71. George Fox, *To the Parliament of the Comon-wealth of England Fifty-nine particulars laid down for the regulating things and the taking away of oppressing laws and Oppressors and to Ease the Oppressed* (London: N.p., 1659), 3.

72. Fox, *To the Parliament*, 4.

73. Fox, *To the Parliament*, 12.

74. William Shakespeare, *Romeo and Juliet*, 1:4: 73, *The Complete Plays and Poems of William Shakespeare*, William A. Neilson and Charles J. Hall eds. (Cambridge, MA: Riverside Press, 1942).

75. Fox, *Instruction to Judges*, 39.

76. Ibid.

77. Vann, *Social Development of English Quakerism*, 49.

78. Besse, *Collection of the Sufferings*, vol. 2, 145.

79. Lloyd, *Quaker Social History*, 71.

80. Shakespeare, *Timon of Athens*, 4.3.153, *The Complete Plays and Poems of William Shakespeare*, William A. Neilson and Charles J. Hall eds. (Cambridge, MA: Riverside Press, 1942).

81. Fox, *Instruction to Judges*, 2.

82. Braithwaite, "Early Friends Experience with Juries," 219.

83. Ibid., 221.

84. Horle, *Quakers and the English Legal System*, 172.

85. A prohibited meeting of any group or sect that disputed the authority of the Church of England. Two Conventicle acts were added during the late seventeenth century to one enacted during the reign of Elizabeth I.

86. Fox, *Instruction to Judges*, 36–38.

87. Fox, *Instruction to Judges*, 26.

88. Ibid., 39.

89. Horle, *Quakers and the English Legal System*, 130.

90. Fox, *Instruction to Judges*, 40.

91. Vann, *Social Development of English Quakerism*, 74, table 7.

92. Horle, *Quakers and the English Legal System*, 187.
93. Ibid., Appendix 2, 285–91.
94. Vann, *Social Development of English Quakerism*, 51, table 1.
95. Horle, 15.
96. Horle, *Quakers and the English Legal System*, 18.
97. Horle, "Changing Quaker Attitudes toward Legal Defense," 18.
98. Matt. 18:15–17.
99. 1 Cor. 6: 1–7: "Dare anyone of you, having a matter against another, go to law before the unrighteous, and not before the saints? Do ye not know that the saints shall judge the world? And if the world shall be judged by you, are you unworthy to judge the smallest matters? Know ye not that we shall judge angels? How much more things that pertain to this life? If then ye have judgments of things pertaining to this life, set them to judge who are least esteemed in the church? I speak to your shame. Is it so, that there is not a wise man among you, not one that shall be able to judge between his brethren? But brother goeth to law with brother, and that before the unbelievers. Now therefore there is utterly a fault among you, because ye go to law one with another. Why do ye not rather take wrong? Why do ye not rather suffer yourselves to be defrauded?"
100. Titus 3: 9–11: "But avoid foolish questions, and genealogies, and contentions, and strivings about the law; for they are unprofitable and vain. A man that is an heretick after the first and second admonition reject; knowing that he that is such is subverted, and sinneth, being condemned of himself."

Chapter 3

1. Letter from William Penn to James Harrison, August 25, 1681, Mary Dunn and Richard Dunn, *The Papers of William Penn*, 5 vols. (Philadelphia: University of Pennsylvania Press, 1982), vol. 2, 108.
2. Dunn and Dunn, *The Papers of William Penn*, vol. 5, *William Penn's Published Writings 1660–1726, An Interpretive Bibliography* (Philadelphia: University of Pennsylvania Press, 1981–1987), 264–265.
3. Edwin B. Bronner, *William Penn's Holy Experiment: The Founding of Pennsylvania 1681–1701* (Philadelphia: Temple University Publications, 1962, distributed by Columbia University Press, New York), 11.
4. Dunn and Dunn, vol. 2, 82.
5. Ibid., 81.
6. William Penn, *No Cross, No Crown*, in Two Parts, Part 1. (London: Office of the Society of Friends, 1896), 29.
7. Dunn and Dunn, vol. 5, 330.
8. Dunn and Dunn, vol. 2, 82. This First Frame of Government was rejected in December 1682. The Second, Third, and Fourth Frames were written in 1683, 1698, and 1701 respectively.
9. Gal. 3:19: "Wherefore then serveth the law? It was added because of transgressions, till the seed should come to whom the promise was made; and it was ordained by angels in the hand of a mediator" and 1 Timothy 1:8–9: "we know that

the law is good, if a man use it lawfully; . . . the law is not made for a righteous man, but for the lawless and disobedient, for the ungodly and for sinners. . . ."

10. Penn, in an April 1, 1700, speech to the Provincial Council of Pennsylvania, Dunn and Dunn, *The Papers of William Penn,* vol. 3, 591.

11. Luke 6:31.

12. Dunn and Dunn, 2:87.

13. 1 St.L. Appendix 1, Charter of the Province of Pennsylvania, 1682, 306. II Pa. Stat. § 2, Appendix I, March 4, 1680.

14. William H. Loyd, *The Early Courts of Pennsylvania,* (Boston: Boston Book Co., 1910), 71.

15. Dunn and Dunn, vol. 2, 234.

16. *The Law about Forms of Writs, Plainness and Brevity* (May 31, 1693), *The Statutes at Large of Pennsylvania in the Time of William Penn,* vol. 1, 1680–1700 (New York: Vantage Press, 1976).

17. Dunn and Dunn, vol. 2, 141. *The Fundamentall Constitutions of Pennsilvania* is believed to have been written in summer 1681.

18. William McEnery Offutt, "Law and Social Cohesion in a Plural Society: The Delaware Valley, 1680–1710" (PhD diss., Johns Hopkins University, 1987), 23, 170.

19. Fox's analogy of the joiner and the lawyer is described in chapter 2.

20. Act of March 30, 1722–1723, An Act for Regulating and Establishing Fees (3 St.L. 367, Ch.270).

21. Dunn and Dunn, vol. 2, 232

22. Ibid., 148–149.

23. Act of Jan. 12, 1705–1706, An Act Against Burning of Houses (2 St.L. 184, Ch. 125).

24. III Pa. Stat. 236 (May 31, 1718). Act of May 31, 1718, Act for the Advancement of Justice, and more certain Administration Thereof (3 St.L. 141, Ch. 236).

25. Loyd, *Early Courts of Pennsylvania,* 86.

26. Ibid., 87.

27. Richard Bauman, *For the Reputation of Truth: Politics, Religion, and Conflict among the Pennsylvania Quakers 1750–1800* (Baltimore, MD: Johns Hopkins University Press, 1971), 32.

28. Law Concerning Liberty of Conscience (1 St.L. 28, Ch. 1).

29. Ibid., II Pa. Stat. c. 115 § 2, Appendix I.

30. Edwin Bronner, *William Penn's Holy Experiment,* 56.

31. Jack Marietta, "The Growth of Quaker Self-Consciousness in Pennsylvania 1720–1748," in *Seeking the Light: Essays on Quaker History in Honor of Edwin B. Bronner,* eds. William J. Frost and John M. Moore (Wallingford, PA: Pendle Hill Publications and Friends Historical Association, 1986), 92.

32. Act of 1693, "The Law about the Registry Kept by Religious Societies" (1 St.L. 189, Ch. 85).

33. An Act to Prevent the Importation of Negroes, 10 Anne 10, *The Earliest Printed Laws of Pennsylvania 1681–1713* (Cushing), 165.

34. An Act for the Gradual Abolition of Slavery, *The First Laws of the Commonwealth of Pennsylvania* (Laws Enacted in the Second Session of the Fourth General Assembly

of the Commonwealth of Pennsylvania which commenced on Wednesday, January 19, 1780) (Wilmington, DE: Glazier,1984), 282, 284.

35. Dunn and Dunn, *The Papers of William Penn*, vol. 2, 150–151.

36. Act of May 28, 1715, An Affirmation Act for Such "Who for Conscience Sake" Cannot Take an Oath (3 St.L. 39, Ch. 204).

37. Act of May 9, 1724, An Act Prescribing the Forms of Declaration of Fidelity, Abjuration and Affirmation . . . (3 St.L.427, Ch. 281). The allowance of affirmation in lieu of oath continues to the present day. See Fed. R. Civ. Pro. 43(b).

38. Act of February 28, 1710–1711, An Act against Riotous Sports, Plays and Games (2 St.L. 360, Ch. 174).

39. 2 St.L. Appendix 3, 550.

40. Act of November 27, 1700, An Act to Prevent Immoderate Fines (2 St.L. 44, Ch. 37). "Wainage" are carts or wagons pulled by horses or oxen often necessary to Quaker farmers.

41. Act of November 27, 1700, An Act for the Names of Days and Months (2 St.L. 44, Ch. 37).

42. Jerold S. Auerbach, *Justice without Law?* (New York: Oxford University Press), 8.

43. Gabriel Thomas, *An Historical Description of Province of Pennsylvania and County of West New Jersey in America* (London: 1698), quoted in Loyd, *Early Courts of Pennsylvania*, 109–110.

44. *Pennsylvania Packet*, July 12, 1785.

45. "Instructions of the Town of New-Braintree to Its Representative," *Worcester Magazine*, vol. 1, 9 (June 1786): 106.

46. Benjamin Austin, *Observations on the Pernicious Practice of the Law* (Boston: Adams and Nourse, 1786), 6.

47. "Observations on the Propriety of Extending the Powers of the Justice of the Peace," *National Gazette*, vol. II, 31 (February 13, 1793): 121.

48. Stephen Presser, "Critical Legal Studies Movement and the New Great Chain of Being: An English Legal Academic's Guide to the Current State of American Law," *Northwestern University Law Review* 79 (1984–1985): 869, 899, n. 83.

49. Michel-Guillaume-Jean de Crevecoeur, also known as J. Hector St. John de Crevecoeur, *Letters from an American Farmer* (New York: Dutton, 1957), 135.

50. Maxwell Bloomfield, *Lawyers in a Changing Society 1776–1876* (Cambridge, MA: Harvard University Press, 1976), 39; John Robert Aiken, "Utopianism and the Emergence of the Colonial Legal Profession: New York 1664–1710, A Test Case" (Ph.D. diss., University of Rochester, 1967), vii–viii.

51. Offutt, *Law and Social Cohesion,* 143–144, table 3.2.

52. Bronner, *William Penn's Holy Experiment*, 47.

53. Craig W. Horle, ed., *Lawmaking and Legislators in Pennsylvania, A Biographical Dictionary*, 3 vols. (Philadelphia: University of Pennsylvania Press, 1991), 1:490.

54. Craig W. Horle, ed., *Lawmaking and Legislators in Pennsylvania: A Biographical Dictionary,* 3 vols. (Philadelphia: University of Pennsylvania Press, 1997), 2:591.

55. Offutt, *Law and Social Cohesion*, 170.

56. Charles P. Keith, *Provincial Councillors of Pennsylvania 1733–1776* (Philadelphia: 1883), 126.

57. Thomas R. Meehan, "Courts, Cases, and Counselors in Revolutionary and Post-Revolutionary Pennsylvania," *The Pennsylvania Magazine of History and Biography,*

vol. 91, No.1 (1967): 4, quoting James L. Whitehead, "Notes and Documents." "Autobiography of Peter Stephen Du Posceau," *The Pennsylvania Magazine of History and Biography*, 63 (1939): 436.

58. Lloyd, *Quaker Social History*, 4.

59. *The Duke of York's Laws 1665–75, Easthampton copy, Earliest Printed Laws of New York 1665–1693*, (reprint, Wilmington, DE: Glazier, 1978), 111.

60. Dunn and Dunn, vol. 2, 100.

61. Loyd, *Early Courts of Pennsylvania*, 15–16.

62. Auerbach, *Justice without Law?* 4.

63. George S. Odiorne, "Arbitration and Mediation among Early Quakers," 9 *Arbitration Journal* (1954): 161.

64. Offutt, "Law and Social Cohesion," 233.

65. Ibid., 234. table 4.2.

66. Albert C. Myers, *The Immigration of Irish Quakers into Pennsylvania 1682–1750*, (Swarthmore, PA: Author, 1902), 228–229.

67. William M. Offutt, *Of "Good Laws" and "Good Men": Law and Society in the Delaware Valley, 1680–1710* (Champaign: University of Illinois Press, 1995), 129.

68. Jack Marietta, *The Reformation of American Quakerism* (Philadelphia: University of Pennsylvania Press, 1984).

69. Offutt, *Of "Good Laws" and "Good Men,"* 154.

70. Alan Tully, *William Penn's Legacy, Politics, and Social Structure in Provincial Pennsylvania 1726–1755* (Baltimore, MD: Johns Hopkins University Press, 1977), 143.

71. Ibid., 181–184, table 3.10.

72. Ibid., 244, 249, 252.

73. Odiorne, "Arbitration and Mediation among Early Quakers," 164.

74. Marietta, "The Growth of Quaker Self-Consciousness," 80.

75. I Annals of Congress 434 (1789).

76. Marietta, *The Reformation of American Quakerism*, 233–234.

77. Ibid., 234.

78. The Fugitive Slave Act of 1793, Statutes at Large, Session II, Chap. 7, 302 (February 12, 1793).

79. Besse, *A Collection of the Sufferings*, 2:240.

80. Ibid., 179–180.

81. Ibid., 189.

82. Ibid., 183.

83. Daniel Boorstin, *The Americans: The Colonial Experience* (New York: Random, 1958), 69.

84. Besse, *A Collection of the Sufferings*, 2:185.

85. Ibid., 185.

86. Ibid., 236.

87. Ibid., 202–207. These pages provide a detailed narrative of Dyer's execution and events surrounding it.

88. William J. Weston, "Between the Spheres: A Weberian Study of the Friends Committee on National Legislation" (PhD diss., Swarthmore College, April 30, 1982), 41, 117–118.

89. Besse, *A Collection of the Sufferings*, vol. 2, 387.

90. Chap. 2 contains a short description of *Bushell's Case*.

91. Braithwaite, "Early Friends Experience with Juries," 227.

92. 18 Car. I, 268–269 (1642–1643).

93. "An Act for the Suppressing the Quakers (March 1659–1660)," in *The Statutes at Large; Being a Collection of All the Laws of Virginia from 1619 . . .* , ed. William Waller Hening, 11th of Commonwealth, vol. 1, reprint (Charlottesville: University Press of Virginia, 1969), 532–533.

94. Some contemporary Quaker lawyers have been unaware of this restriction.

Chapter 4

1. Larry Ingle, *Living the Truth, Speaking to Power*, a review of Hans A. Schmitt, *Quakers and Nazis: Inner Light in Outer Darkness* (Columbia: University of Missouri Press, 1997), in Chuck Fager, *The Best of Friends*, vol.1 (Fayetteville, NC: Kimo Press, 1998), 1.

2. Frederick B. Tolles, "Quakerism and Politics" (The Ward Lecture, Guilford College, Greensboro, NC, November 9, 1956).

3. The years between the execution of King Charles I in 1649 and the restoration of Charles II to the throne in 1660.

4. Fox, *The Journal of George Fox*, 274.

5. Margaret Fell, *Works*, 95, 136, quoted in Hugh S. Barbour, *The Quakers in Puritan England* (New Haven, CT: Yale University Press, 1964) 98.

6. Peter Irons, *Justice at War* (New York: Oxford University Press, 1983), 93.

7. Oliver Wendell Holmes Jr., "The Path of the Law," *Harvard Law Review* 10 (1897): 457

8. "Congress shall make no law respecting an establishment of religion, or prohibiting the free exercise thereof; or abridging the freedom of speech, or of the press; or the right of the people peaceably to assemble, and to petition the Government for a redress of grievances." U.S. Constitution, amend I.

9. *The Burlington Court Book: A Record of Quaker Jurisprudence in West New Jersey 1680–1709*, ed. H. Clay Reed and George J. Miller (N.p.: American Historical Association, 1944), xi. This book is the primary source of records of early court cases involving Friends.

10. *Burlington Court Book*, 178.

11. Ibid., 41–42.

12. Ibid., 132.

13. Ibid., 293.

14. Ibid., 299.

15. 2 N.H. 268, 9 Am. Dec. 61 (1820).

16. 1 N.H. Laws 350 (February 1791).

17. 20 F.Cas. 281 (D.R.I 1884).

18. 127 Mass. 459, 34 Am. Rep. 411 (1879).

19. Mass. Stat. of 1786, c. 3 § 97.

20. 25 F. Cas. 650 (D.R.I. 1820).

21. 25 F. Cas. at 655.

22, 14 F. Cas. 520, 3 Cranch C.C. 435 (D.D.C. 1829).

23. ". . . the people called Quakers . . . holding it unlawful to take an oath on any occasion shall be allowed to make solemn affirmation as witness . . . which shall be of the same avail as an oath to all intents and purposes whatever." Maryland Declaration of Rights, § 33.

24. 162 A. 909 (Sup. Ct., N.J. 1932).

25. See Howard Brinton, *Friends for 300 Years* (Wallingford, PA: Pendle Hill Publications, 1965), 112.

26. *Sparrow v. Goodman*, 361 F.Supp. 566 (W.D. N.C. 1973).

27. 361 F.Supp. at 573.

28. 361 F.Supp. at 583–584.

29. 361 F.Supp. at 585.

30. *Quaker Action Group v. Hickel*, 421 F.2d 1111, 1117 (D.C. Cir. 1969).

31. 361 F.Supp. at 586.

32. 376 F.Supp. 1268 (W.D.N.C. 1974).

33. *Sub.nom. Rowley v. McMillan*, 502 F.2d 1326 (4th Cir. 1974).

34. 421 F.2d at 1118.

35. *Philadelphia Yearly Meeting of the Religious Society of Friends v. Tate*, 382 F. Supp. 547 (E.D.Pa 1974).

36. *Philadelphia Yearly Meeting v. Tate*, 519 F.2d 1335 (3d Cir. 1975).

37. *James v. Board of Education of Central District No. 1*, 385 F.Supp. 209 (W.D.N.Y. 1974).

38. 385 F.Supp. at 211, n.2.

39. *James v. Board of Education of Central District No. 1*, 461 F.2d 566 (2d Cir. 1972).

40. 385 F.Supp. at 216.

41. Ibid.

42. *Tinker v. Des Moines Independent Community School District*, 393 U.S. 503 (1969).

43. 393 U.S. at 514.

44. 393 U.S. at 511.

45. *Straut v. Calissi*, 293 F.Supp. 1339 (D.N.J. 1968).

46. *American Friends Service Committee v. United States*, 368 F.Supp. 1176, 1178 (E.D. Pa. 1973).

47. 293 F.Supp. at 1346.

48. Barbara Elfbrandt was a respondent to the Quaker lawyer survey and was interviewed by the author.

49. Peter Irons, *The Courage of Their Convictions: Sixteen Americans Who Fought Their Way to the Supreme Court* (New York: Free Press, 1988), 193.

50. *Elfbrandt v. Russell*, 384 U.S. 11 (1966).

51. Approximately 500 teachers did lose their jobs in the ten-year period 1948–1958 for refusing to sign loyalty oaths or answer questions of loyalty boards. Irons, *The Courage of Their Convictions*, 185.

52. Irons, *The Courage of Their Convictions*, 183.

53. Ibid., 186.

54. *First Unitarian Church of Los Angeles v. County of Los Angeles*, 357 U.S. 545 (1958).

55. Amicus curiae brief for Petitioner, Philadelphia Yearly Meeting of the Religious Society of Friends, 6, 357 U.S. 545 (1958).

56. Ibid., 10, 12.

57. *In re Petitions for Rulemaking* 223 N.J. Super. 453 (1988).

58. 117 N.J. 311 (1989), 566 A.2d 1154.

59. 443 F.2d 720 (D.C. Cir. 1971).

60. 22 D.C. Code § 1107 (1967).

61. *Hobson v. Wilson*, 556 F.Supp. 1157 (D.D.C. 1982).

62. *Hobson v. Wilson*, 737 F.2d 1 (D.C. Cir. 1984).

63. *United States v. Lansdowne Swim Club*, 713 F.Supp. 785 (E.D. Pa 1989).

64. An allegation of discrimination against black children resurfaced in July 2009 at a Pennsylvania swim club of the same name.

65. 42 U.S.C. §2000a–2000a-6. (1964).

66. *United States v. Lansdowne Swim Club*, 894 F.2d 83 (3d Cir. 1990).

67. Act of Congress, March 21, 1942, 77 Public Law 503, 56 Stat. 173, issued pursuant to President Roosevelt's Executive Order 9066 of February 19, 1942, on protection of war resources against espionage.

68. *Hirabayashi v. United States*, 320 U.S. 81 (1943).

69. 320 U.S. at 110.

70. Irons, *Justice at War*, 93.

71. *Hirabayashi v. United States*, 828 F.2d 591, 607 (9th Cir. 1987).

72. *Scull v. Virginia*, 359 U.S. 344 (1959).

73. Ibid. at 353.

74. *Seattle School District No. 1 of King County, Washington and ACLU v. State of Washington*, 473 F.Supp. 996 (W.D. Wash. 1979).

75. Ibid. at 999.

76. *Seattle School District No. 1 v. State of Washington*, 633 F.2d 1338 (9th Cir. 1980).

77. *Washington v. Seattle School District No. 1*, 458 U.S. 457 (1982).

78. Paul Lacey, "Quaker Beliefs and Immigration Law" (Philadelphia: AFSC Immigration Policy Issues, March 1991), 7.

79. Lacey, "Quakers and the Social Testimonies," 19. A more detailed discussion of the prophet and reconciler can be found at 17–19.

80. Lacey, "Quaker Beliefs and Immigration Law," 8.

81. Lacey, "Quakers and the Social Testimonies," 22.

82. Paul Lacey, telephone interview by author, June 23, 1999.

83. Lacey, Quaker Beliefs and Immigration Law, 8.

84. Before the Immigration and Naturalization Service was abolished in 2002, it was under the jurisdiction of the U.S. Department of Justice.

85. 718 F.Supp. 820 (C.D. Cal. 1989), aff'd, 941 F.2d 808 (9th Cir. 1991), rehearing en banc, 951 F.2d 957 (9th Cir. 1991).

86. 8 U.S.C. § 1324a (1986).

87. The I–9 form facilitates the enforcement of employer sanctions through 8 U.S. C. §1324a (e) and (f) by requiring employers to complete it and, after inspecting documents of employees, attest that they are legally authorized to work.

88. 718 F.Supp. at 822.

89. *American Friends Service Committee v. Thornburgh*, 951 F.2d 957 (9th Cir. 1990).

90. *Employment Division v. Smith*, 494 U.S. 872 (1990).

91. *Sherbert v. Verner*, 374 U.S. 398 (1963).

92. *Wisconsin v. Yoder*, 406 U.S. 205 (1972).

93. *Summary Judgment at Sixty*, 76 Tex. L. Rev. 1897 (1998).

94. Fed. R. Civ. Pro. 56. (1937).

95. 76 Tex. L. Rev. at 1897.

96. 76 Tex. L. Rev. at 1905.

97. Ibid.

98. *Anderson v. Liberty Lobby*, 477 U.S. 242, 249 (1986).

99. *Selective Service Draft Law Cases.* 245 U.S. 366 (1918),consolidating *Arver v. United States, Grahl v. United States, Wangerin v. United States* (two cases), *Kramer v. United States*, and *Graubard v. United States.*

100. *An Act to Authorize the President to Increase Temporarily the Military Establishment of the United States*, te Draft Act of 1917, 40 Stat. 76 (1917).

101. Senate Comm. on Military Affairs Hearings before the Committee on Military Affairs, on Senate Bill 4164, 76th Cong., 3d Sess. July 3–5, 10–12, 1940.

102. *United States v. Flower*, 452 F.2d 80 (5th Cir. 1971).

103. 452 F.2d at 90, 93.

104. *Green v. F.C.C*, 447 F.2d 323 (D.C. Cir. 1971).

105. 447 F.2d at 327, n. 6.

106. *Welch v. Shultz*, 482 F.2d 780 (D.C. Cir. 1973).

107. 40 Stat. 415 (1917), as amended, 50 U.S.C.S. App. §§1 et seq. (1970).

108. *Tatum v. Morton*, 562 F.2d 1279 (D.C. Cir. 1977).

109. 562 F.2d at 1282.

110. Exodus 20:13.

111. William Stringfellow, *Keeper of the Word.* ed. Bill Wylie Kellerman (Grand Rapids, MI: Eerdmans, 1994), 70.

112. *Greenham Women against Cruise Missiles v. Reagan*, 755 F.2d 34 (2d Cir. 1985).

113. *Dickinson v. Bell*, 580 F. Supp. 432 (D.D.C.1984); *aff'd without opinion*, 757 F.2d 372 (D.C. Cir. 1985).

114. 20 U.S.C. § 1070 et seq. (1982).

115. 50 U.S.C. § 462(f)) (1982).

116. 580 F.Supp. at 433, n. 1.

117. 580 F.Supp. at 435.

118. The Selective Training and Service Act of 1940, 54 Stat. 889 (1940).

119. *United States v. Seeger*, 380 U.S. 163 (1965).

120. Daniel Seeger, interview by author, Pendle Hill, Wallingford, PA, February 14, 1992.

121. *United States v. Seeger*, 326 F.2d. 846, 855 (2d Cir. 1964).

122. *United States v. Seeger*, 380 U.S. at 170.

123. Act of June 30, 1864, 13 Stat. 9 (1864).

124. Draft Act of 1917, 40 Stat.76 (1917).

125. 380 U.S. at 176.

126. 380 U.S. at 187.

127. *Briggs v. United States,* 397 F.2d 370 (9th Cir. 1968).

128. *United States v. Purvis,* 403 F.2d 555 (2d Cir. 1968).

129. One classified 1–AO was exempt from combatant but not noncombatant service; one classified 1–O was exempt from all military service.

130. *United States v. Nugent,* 346 U.S. 1 (1953).

131. *Gonzalez v. United States,* 348 U.S. 407 (1955).

132. 220 F.2d 114 (7th Cir. 1955).

133. 220 F.2d at 118, 120.

134. Daisy Newman, *A Procession of Friends,* 136.

135. 180 F.2d 711 (7th Cir. 1950).

136. 180 F.2d at 712, 713.

137. 223 F.2d 893 (3d Cir. 1955).

138. 223 F.2d at 896.

139. 509 F.2d 13 (4th Cir. 1974).

140. 435 F.2d 601 (8th Cir. 1971).

141. 435 F.2d at 603.

142. 435 F.2d at 604.

143. John Woolman, *The Journal and Major Essays of John Woolman,* ed. Phillips P. Moulton (New York: Oxford University Press, 1971), 85.

144. 368 F.Supp. 1176 (E.D. Pa. 1973).

145. 26 U.S.C.§ 3402. (I.R.C. 1954).

146. 368 F.Supp. at 1178.

147. 368 F.Supp. at 1177, 1180–81.

148. *United States v. American Friends Service Committee,* 419 U.S. 7 (1974).

149. 26 U.S.C. §7421(a).(I.R.C. 1954).

150. 419 U.S. at 11.

151. 419 U.S. at 13.

152. 753 F.Supp. 1300 (E.D. Pa. 1990).

153. *Employment Division v. Smith,* 494 U.S.872 (1990).

154. 753 F.Supp. at 1306.

155. *United States v. Haworth,* 386 F.Supp. 1099 (S.D.N.Y. 1974).

156. *Autenrieth v. Cullen,* 418 F.2d 586, 588 (9th Cir. 1969).

157. *Orlando v. Laird,* 443 F.2d 1039 (2d Cir. 1971), *cert. denied,* 404 U.S. 869 (1971). In *Orlando,* more than 100 plaintiffs, including singer Joan Baez, sought income tax refunds because of conscientious and religious scruples against payment of taxes for purposes of war.

158. *United States v. Harper,* 397 F.Supp. 983 (E.D. Pa. 1975).

159. 397 F.Supp. at 989.

160. 397 F.Supp. at 990.

161. *United States v. Snider,* 502 F.2d 645 (4th Cir. 1974).

162. 26 U.S.C. § 7205(a) (I.R.C. 1954).

163. 502 F.2d at 647–648.

164. 502 F.2d at 649, n. 8.

165. 18 U.S.C. §401 (1948).

166. *The Crown v. William Penn and William Mead,* 6 Howell's State Trials 951 (1661–1678).

167. 502 F.2d. at 648–49, n. 7A.

168. *United States v. Wilhelm*, 570 F.2d 461 (3d Cir. 1978).

169. Judiciary Act of September 24, 1789, 1 Stat. 73, (1789), codified at 28 U.S.C. § 1654 (1970).

170. 570 F.2d at 465.

171. *Employment Division v. Smith*, 494 U.S. 872 (1990).

172. 494 U.S. at 879, quoting *Minersville School District Board of Education v. Gobitis*, 310 U.S. 586, 594–95 (1940).

173. 42 U.S.C. § 2000bb et seq. (1993)

174. 374 U.S. 398 (1963).

175. 406 U.S. 205 (1972).

176. *Adams v. Commissioner of Internal Revenue*, 170 F.3d 173 (3d Cir. 1999).

177. *United States v. Lee*, 455 U.S. 252 (1982).

178. 455 U.S. at 260.

179. *Browne v. United States*, 22 F.Supp. 2d 309 (D.C. Vt. 1998).

180. *Browne v. United States*, 176 F.3d 25 (2d Cir. 1999).

181. Amicus curiae brief, New York Yearly Meeting, *Packard v. United States*, No. 98–6223, 1–2.

182. Ibid., 2.

183. 7 F.Supp 2d 143 (D. Conn. 1998).

184. *Packard v. United States*, No. 98–6223, amicus curiae brief of New York Yearly Meeting (December 21, 1998), 3.

185. *Packard v. United States*, No. 98–6223 (2d Cir, June 1, 1999).

186. 176 F.3d 25 (2d Cir. 1999).

187. 170 F.3d 173, 173 (3d Cir. 1999).

188. *Jenkins v. Commissioner of Internal Revenue*, No. 05–4756 (2d Cir. March 6, 2007).

189. 42 U.S.C.§ 2000bb et seq. (1993).

190. Henry J. Cadbury accepting the Nobel Peace Prize on behalf of the AFSC (address, Oslo, Norway, December 10, 1947).

191. *In re Summers*, 325 U.S. 561 (1945).

192. 325 U.S. at 570.

193. Amicus curiae brief for Petitioner, AFSC, 9, 15.

194. Ibid., at 26.

195. Ibid., at 45.

196. *In re Summers*, 325 U.S. at 575, 578.

197. Ibid., at 575.

198. Mohandas K. Gandhi, the great Indian civil rights activist was a practicing lawyer in late-nineteenth-century South Africa. His view of lawyering is discussed in chap. 6.

199. Tolles, "Quakerism and Politics." Tolles was the Howard M. Jenkins Professor of Quaker History and Research at Swarthmore College.

200. Every six to eight years, FCNL publishes a long-range position statement that reflects Friends' broad issues of concern.

201. Arthur Boyd, interview by author, Baltimore, MD, May 30, 1999.

202. Edward F. Snyder, Wilmer A Cooper, Stephen L. Klineberg, et al., ed. Tom Mullen, *Witness in Washington: Fifty Years of Friendly Persuasion* (Richmond, IN: Friends United Press 1994), 3.

203. The work of this group, now called Quaker Peace and Social Witness, is discussed in chapter 6.

204. Snyder, Cooper, Klineberg, et al., *Witness in Washington*, 38.

205. Tolles, "Quakerism and Politics." However, it is unlikely that FCNL lobbyists would describe themselves this way today.

206. Ibid.

207. Ibid.

208. As a result of this activism, a committee of the Virginia Legislature subpoenaed Scull to testify. That subpoena resulted in the Supreme Court decision, *Scull v. Virginia*, discussed earlier in this chapter.

209. Brinton, *Friends for 300 Years*, 146.

210. Snyder, Cooper, Klineberg, et al., *Witness in Washington*, 3.

211. *FCNL Washington Newsletter*, "Time to Talk with Iran," April 2007.

212. *FCNL Washington Newsletter*, "Walk and Chew Gum," June 2008.

213. Rachel Brett and Margaret McCallin, *Children the Invisible Soldiers*, 2nd ed. (Stockholm: Radda Barnen, 1998), and Rachel Brett and Irma Specht, *Young Soldiers: Why They Choose to Fight* (CITY: International Labour Organization/Lynne Rienner, 2004).

Chapter 5

1. Richard K. Burke, "Truth in Lawyering: An Essay on Lying and Deceit in the Practice of Law," *Arkansas Law Review* 38 (1984): 1, 11.

2. Thomas L. Shaffer, "Moral Theology in Legal Ethics," *Capital University Law Review* 12 (1982): 179, 181.

3. Ibid., 191.

4. A sample of 100 Quaker lawyers is a significant size if one considers that when the survey was completed in 1992, the percentage of lawyers in the U.S. population was about 0.295%. If this percentage is applied to the approximately 100,000 estimate of Quakers at that time, then the number of Quaker lawyers in 1992 would be approximately 295 (although Quakers probably become lawyers at a lower rate than the general population). Therefore, the 100 Quaker lawyers surveyed in 1992 comprised about 34% of those practicing in the United States. Accurate numbers for U.S. Quakers are elusive because Friends meetings count members variously; some include children, some only adults; some include both members and attenders, and others only members, and so forth. Margaret Fraser, Executive Secretary. Friends World Committee for Consultation (FWCC), Section of the Americas. Telephone Interview by author, August 27, 2009.

5. July 1861 American Civil War battle at Manassas, Virginia, also known as the first battle of Bull Run.

6. Rand Jack and Dana Crowley Jack, *Moral Vision and Professional Decisions: The Changing Values of Women and Men Lawyers* (Cambridge, UK: Cambridge University Press, 1989), 4.

7. Ibid., 149.

8. Stephen Presser, "Critical Legal Studies Movement, and the New Great Chain of Being: An English Legal Academic's Guide to the Current State of American Law," *Northwestern University Law Review* 79 (1984–1985): 869, 899, n. 83.

9. Ibid., 898.

10. Barbara A. Curran and Clara N. Carson, *The U.S. Legal Profession in 1988, Supplement to the Statistical Report* (Chicago: American Bar Foundation, 1991), 2.

11. Ibid., 10.

12. Presser, "Critical Legal Studies Movement," 897.

13. Matt. 25:40.

14. Mic. 6:8.

15. This respondent wrote: "(although I confess that until you asked the question I wouldn't necessarily have expressed it in those terms)."

16. *Model Rules of Professional Conduct,* Comment to Rule 4.1(1983) in *Lawyer's Manual of Professional Conduct* (Chicago: ABA/BNA, 1984).

17. Burke, "Truth in Lawyering." 10-11.

18. Mary Ann Glendon, *A Nation under Lawyers: How the Crisis in the Legal Profession Is Transforming American Society* (New York: Farrar, Straus, and Giroux, 1994), 30.

19. Jack and Jack, *Moral Vision and Professional Decisions,* 108.

20. Richard Wasserstrom, "Lawyers as Professionals: Some Moral Issues," *Human Rights* 5 (1975-1976): 1, 15.

21. A clearness committee is a communal process of discernment, described in chap. 1.

22. Jack and Jack, *Moral Vision and Professional Decisions,* 112.

23. The 1988 study of 207 lawyers was conducted at the direction of the Maryland State Bar Association Special Committee on Law Practice Quality and was reported in 1989 in the *Maryland State Bar Journal.* It is the latest such study of Maryland lawyers.

24. Stephanie Francis Ward, "Pulse of the Legal Profession," *ABA Journal.* October 2007, 30-34.

25. Sam Benson, "Why I Quit Practicing Law," *Newsweek,* November 4, 1991, 10.

26. Sandra Day O'Connor, "Professionalism," *Washington University Law Quarterly* 76 (1998): 5.

27. Burke, "Truth in Lawyering," 2.

28. Ibid., 3.

29. Jack and Jack, *Moral Vision and Professional Decisions,* 97.

30. Presser, "Critical Legal Studies Movement," 899.

31. Jack and Jack, *Moral Vision and Professional Decisions,* 112.

32. Mohandas K. (Mahatma) Gandhi, *Gandhi's Autobiography: The Story of My Experiment with Truth,* trans. Mahadev H. Desai (Washington, DC: Public Affairs Press, 1948), 168.

33. Robert E. Rodes Jr., *Pilgrim Law* (South Bend, IN: University of Notre Dame Press, 1998), 61–62.

34. Gerhard Casper, former dean of the University of Chicago Law School, president emeritus and the Peter and Helen Bing Professor in Undergraduate Education, Stanford University, Stanford, CA.

35. Burke, "Truth in Lawyering," 11.

36. Ibid., 19.

37. John T. Noonan, "The Purpose of Advocacy and the Limits of Confidentiality," *Michigan L. Rev.* 64 (1966): 1489.

38. Burke, "Truth in Lawyering," 19.

39. Fed. R. Civ. Pro. 1 (1948).

40. Fed. R. Evid. 102. (1975).

41. John T. Noonan, *Persons and Masks of the Law: Cardozo, Holmes, Jefferson and Wythe as Makers of Masks* (New York: Farrar, Straus, and Giroux, 1976), 25.

42. Jack and Jack, *Moral Vision and Professional Decisions,* 36.

43. Harold J. Rothwax, *Guilty: The Collapse of Criminal Justice* (New York: Random House, 1996), 18-19.

44. Stephen Budiansky, "How Lawyers Abuse the Law," *U.S. News and World Report,* January 30, 1995, 50-54.

45. Sam Benson, "Why I Quit Practicing Law," *Newsweek,* November 4, 1991, 10.

46. Sissela Bok, *Lying* (New York: Vintage Books, 1978), 37.

47. Ibid., 27.

48. Burke, Truth in Lawyering, 6, quoting Charles Fried, "The Lawyer as Friend: The Moral Foundations of the Lawyer-Client Relation," *Yale Law Journal,* 85 (1976): 1081–1083.

49. *United States v. Wade,* 388 U.S. 218, 258 (1967).

50. 388 U.S. at 258.

51. Wasserstrom, "Lawyers as Professionals," 3.

52. Noonan, "The Purpose of Advocacy and the Limits of Confidentiality," 1488.

53. Robert Keeton, The Henry W. Strasburger Lecture in Trial Advocacy, University of Texas School of Law, March 27, 1981.

54. Wasserstrom, "Lawyers as Professionals," 3.

55. Noonan, *Persons and Masks of the Law,* 26; see also 20-25.

56. Charles P. Curtis, *The Ethics of Advocacy,* 4 Stanford Law Review 3, 9 (1951).

57. Jack and Jack, *Moral Vision and Professional Decisions,* 41.

58. Ibid., 37.

59. Ibid., 99-129.

60. Harper Lee, To Kill a Mockingbird (Philadelphia: Lippincott, 1960).

61. Ibid., 288.

62. Jack and Jack, *Moral Vision and Professional Decisions,* 35.

63. Lee, *To Kill a Mockingbird,* 114.

64. Ibid., 224.

65. Rodes, *Pilgrim Law,* 61-62.

66. Holmes, "The Path of the Law," at 468, 474, 476.

67. Rodes, *Pilgrim Law,* 64.

68. Wasserstrom, "Lawyers as Professionals," 16, 23.

69. Glendon, *A Nation under Lawyers,* 58.

70. Thomas L. Shaffer, "Christian Lawyers Stories and American Legal Ethics," 33 *Mercer L. Rev.* 877 (1982): 877–878.

71. Shaffer, "Moral Theology in Legal Ethics," 190.

72. Holmes, "The Path of the Law," at 459.

73. Presser, "Critical Legal Studies Movement," 881.

74. John Robert Aiken, "Utopianism and the Emergence of the Colonial Legal Profession: New York 1664-1710, A Test Case" (Ph.D. diss., University of Rochester, 1967), vii-viii.

75. Noonan, *Persons and Masks of the Law,* xi, 6.

76. Shaffer, "Moral Theology in Legal Ethics," 191.

77. Jack and Jack, *Moral Vision and Professional Decisions*, 162.

78. Glendon, *A Nation under Lawyers*, 37, quoting Gerard W. Gawalt, *The New High Priest: Lawyers in Post-Civil War America* (Westport, CT: Greenwood Press, 1984).

79. *Baltimore Sun*. "Stumbling around the Base Path; Courtroom Collision: Softball Injury Suit Chills Enthusiasm for Game." February 13, 1996. 14A.

80. Stephen Budiansky, "How Lawyers Abuse the Law," *U.S. News and World Report*, January 30, 1995, 53.

81. Ibid.

82. *Black's Law Dictionary*, 4th ed. (St. Paul, MN.: West Publishing, 1968), 712.

83. Donald D. Landon and John P. Heinz, *Country Lawyers: The Impact of Context on Professional Practice* (New York: Praeger, 1990), 131. Landon studied 201 rural or small-town and 77 urban lawyers.

84. Sandra Day O'Connor, Address, Wake Forest University, Winston-Salem, NC (April 3, 1993).

85. Abraham Lincoln, *Selected Speeches, Messages, and Letters*, ed. T. Harry Williams (New York: Holt Rinehart, 1957), 33.

87. Quoted in Shaffer, "Should a Christian Lawyer Sign Up for Simon's Practice of Justice?" at 917, n.74.

Chapter 6

1. Mohandas K. (Mahatma) Gandhi, *Gandhi's Autobiography: The Story of My Experiment with Truth*, trans. Mahadev H. Desai (Washington, DC: Public Affairs Press, 1948), 168.

2. Ibid.

3. Matt. 18:15–17: "Moreover if thy brother shall trespass against thee, go and tell him his fault between thee and him alone: if he shall hear thee, thou hast gained thy brother. But if he will not hear thee, then take with thee one or two more, that in the mouth of two or three witnesses every word may be established. And if he shall neglect to hear them, tell it unto the church: but if he neglect to hear the church, let him be unto thee as an heathen man and a publican."

4. 1 Cor. 6:1–7 and Titus 3: 9.

5. Lloyd, *Quaker Social History*, 2.

6. Marietta, "The Reformation of American Quakerism," 9–10.

7. Odiorne, "Arbitration and Mediation among Early Quakers," 162.

8. Ibid. "Epistles and Advices to Birmingham Friends by Geo. Fox," cited in Thomas Ellwoods's *Collection of Many Select and Christian Epistles, Letters, and Testimonies*, written by George Fox (London: N.p., 1698).

9. *Burlington Court Book*. Court cases involving Daniel Leeds are mentioned in chap. 4.

10. Offutt, "Law and Social Cohesion," 200.

11. Odiorne, "Arbitration and Mediation among Early Quakers," 164.

12. Bronner, *William Penn's Holy Experiment*, 52–53.

13. J. William Frost, *The Quaker Family in Colonial America* (New York: St. Martin's Press, 1973), 200.

14. 1719 Philadelphia Yearly Meeting minutes, (September 21, 1719).

15. Marietta, "The Reformation of American Quakerism," 10.

16. Offutt, *Law and Cohesion*, 191–192.

17. Ibid., 115.

18. Ibid., 226–227.

19. *Rules of Discipline and Christian Advices of the Yearly Meeting of Friends for Pennsylvania and New Jersey.* . . . (N.p: Printed by Samuel Sansom, June 1797), 17.

20. Offutt, *Law and Cohesion*, 267.

21. James Nayler, "A Call to Magistrates, Ministers, Lawyers, and People to Repentance," in *Collections of Sundry Books, Epistles,* by James Nayler from London edition of 1716 (Cincinnati, OH: Stanton, 1829), 166.

22. Richard V. Wagner, "Mediated Divorces Last—At Least to the Bench," 6 *Negotiation Journal* (1990): 47, 50.

23. This is similar to the Confucianist view that a lawsuit was a disruption of a natural harmony that supposedly existed in human affairs. Law was coercive and thereby tainted. The optimum resolution lay not in coercive force but in moral persuasion. Leonard L. Riskin, "Mediation and Lawyers," *Ohio St. Law Journal* (1982): 29, citing Jerome Alan Cohen, "Chinese Mediation on the Eve of Modernization," *California Law Review* (1966): 1201.

24. Brinton, *Friends for 300 Years,* 169.

25. Ibid.

26. See also C. H. Mike Yarrow, *Quaker Experiences in International Conciliation* (New Haven, CT: Yale University Press, 1978).

27. Gunnar Jahn, Address at the presentation of the 1947 Nobel Peace Prize, Oslo, Norway, December 10, 1947.

28. Daisy Newman, *A Procession of Friends: Quakers in America, Religion in America Series* (Garden City, NY: Doubleday, 1972), 212.

29. Steve and Sue Williams, interview by author, Pendle Hill, Wallingford, PA, May 8, 1992.

30. Offutt, *Law and Social Cohesion,* 242.

31. *Elfbrandt v. Russell,* 384 U.S. 11 (1966).

32. *Hirabayashi v. United States,* 320 U.S. 81(1943).

33. *Tinker v. Des Moines Indep. Community School Dist.,* 393 U.S. 503 (1969).

34. *United States v. Seeger,* 380 U.S. 163 (1965).

35. Peter Irons, *The Courage of Their Convictions: Sixteen Americans Who Fought Their Way to the Supreme Court* (New York: Free Press, 1988), 407.

36. Rosalie Wahl, former associate justice of the Minnesota Supreme Court.

37. Anne Farrer Scott, "Fishing in Troubled Waters," *Friends Journal* (January 1–15, 1982): 10.

38. *Brown v. Board of Education,* 347 U.S. 483 (1954).

39. Riskin, "Mediation and Lawyers," 45.

40. John J. Dieffenbach, "Psychology, Society and the Development of the Adversarial Posture," 7 *Journal on Dispute Resolution* (1992): 261, 275, quoting Lawrence J. Landwehr, "Lawyers as Social Progressives or Reactionaries: The Law and Order Cognitive Orientation of Lawyers," *Law and Psychol. Review* (1982): 39, 40, n.2.

41. John J. Dieffenbach, "Psychology, Society and the Development of the

Adversarial Posture," 275, citing Lawrence J. Landwehr, "Lawyers as Social Progressives or Reactionaries."

42. Ibid., 278.

43. Ibid., 261.

44. Dieffenbach, "Psychology, Society and the Development of the Adversarial Posture," 268, quoting. Spencer Kagan and Millard C. Madsen, "Experimental Analyses of Cooperation and Competition of Anglo-American and Mexican Children," *Dev. Psychol.* 6 (1972): 49.

45. Dieffenbach, "Psychology, Society and the Development of the Adversarial Posture," 265, quoting Millard C. Madsen and Ariella Shapira, "Cooperative and Competitive Behavior of Urban Afro-American, Anglo-American, Mexican-American and Mexican Village Children," *Dev. Psychol.* 3 (1970): 16, 17.

46. Presser, "Critical Legal Studies Movement and the New Great Chain of Being: An English Academic's Guide to the Current State of American Law," 881–882.

47. Wagner, "Mediated Divorces Last," 5–6.

48. Riskin, "Mediation and Lawyers," 42.

49. Ibid., 44.

50. Riskin, "Mediation and Lawyers," 46.

51. Ibid., 44.

52. Riskin, "Mediation and Lawyers," 58.

53. U.S. Department of Justice Order, OBD 1160.1.

54. *Baltimore Sun,* "Lawyers' Group asks for Outside Counsel," January 1, 1994, 3.

55. Proclamation of the Alameda County Bar Association Proclaiming March 22–28, 1992 Mediation Week.

56. *Courts in Transition,* The Report of the Commission on the Future of Virginia's Judicial System, (Richmond, VA: N.p., 1989).

57. Paul Wahrhaftig, "Trends in Peacemaking and Conflict Resolution," *Friends Journal 37* (October 1991): 18–19.

58. Henry J. Cadbury accepting the Nobel Peace Prize on behalf of the American Friends Service Committee, Great Hall, University of Oslo, Karl Johansgate, 47 (Oslo, Norway, December 10, 1947).

Epilogue

1. Lacey, "Quaker Beliefs and Immigration Law," *AFSC Immigration Policy Issues* paper (March 1991), 6.

Glossary

American Friends Service Committee (AFSC). Founded by a group of Friends in 1917, its original intent was to provide conscientious objectors an opportunity to provide alternative service to the nation in wartime. It has since broadened its scope of concerns.

Assizes. Court sessions held periodically in England's counties to try civil and criminal cases.

Bale dock. A cage-like structure where defendants are placed during the trial, usually within the courtroom.

Barrator. One who habitually brings lawsuits against others.

Birthright Friend. One born into the Religious Society of Friends by virtue of both parents being Quakers. Approximately 100 years ago, after coming of age, birthright Friends began to choose whether they wished to become members of the Society.

Clearness Committee. A communal process of discernment, described in chapter 1.

Concern. A weighty matter that disturbs the conscience and impels one to act.

Convinced Quaker. One not born into a Quaker family who chooses after thoughtful consideration to become a member of the Religious Society of Friends.

De minimus. Literally, "of the least"; of trifling or minimal importance.

Distrain. To seize and detain personal property as security for a debt.

Faith and Practice. An evolving guide published by each Yearly Meeting for its members' guidance on matters of Quaker faith and practice.

First Day, First Day School. Sunday, Sunday School. Early, and some contemporary, Friends used numbers to refer to days of the week and months of the year instead of names, as most of the latter derived from pagan deities.

Friends Committee on National Legislation (FCNL). This organization is discussed in chapter 4.

Gathered meeting. A meeting is gathered when individual personalities vanish and one is conscious only of a mystical union of the worshipping group.

Gloss. An annotation or explanation of a passage in a law that elucidates or amplifies.

"Going to law." Suing in a court of law. This term is discussed in chapter 1.

Gospel order. In its broad historical sense, it is a term used to gather many of the most significant elements of Friends' understanding of the meeting community. George Fox used it to more fully describe Friends' practices of worship, the inward life of worship and discernment, decision-making and the functioning of the meeting community, and daily living as it pertained to Friends' social testimonies. In its narrower sense, it is used to refer to the practice of settling disputes outside the courts, usually by mediation or arbitration as prescribed by Matthew.

Hold in the light. To invoke a kind of intercession in support of those who are sick, grieving, or in other difficulty or distress; more positively, to be uplifted and supported in an endeavor.

In personam. Literally, "against a person." Involving or determining personal rights and interests of parties.

In rem. Literally, "against a thing." Involving or determining the rights of a thing and therefore the rights of persons in regard to that thing.

Inner (or Inward) Light. That of God within each person.

Inns of Court. The four legal societies of London—Gray's Inn, the Inner Temple, Lincoln's Inn, and Middle Temple—that have the exclusive right of admitting persons to the English bar.

Intervenor. A third party who is allowed by permission of court to voluntarily join with plaintiff or defendant in a suit.

Law French. A corrupted form of the Norman French language introduced into England by William the Conqueror; for several centuries thereafter it was the primary language of the English legal system.

Lincoln's Inn. One of the four English legal societies founded in the fourteenth century and invested with the exclusive privilege of calling men to the bar.

Memorandum opinion. A unanimous appellate opinion that succinctly states the court's decision without elaboration.

Minute. A writing composed to express the sense of the meeting.

Monthly Meeting. Except for preparative meetings, the smallest and most localized group within the Quaker meeting structure.

Old Bailey. The famous Law Court on Old Bailey Street in London.

Pendle Hill. A Quaker center for study and contemplation founded in 1930 in Wallingford, Pennsylvania.

Per curiam. An appellate opinion that does not identify the particular judge who authored it.

Political question. An issue that the Constitution commits to another branch of government or an issue inherently incapable of resolution by judicial process.

Praemunire (premunire). Literally, "to warn"; a legal writ charging an offense of procuring translations, processes, excommunications, bulls, or other actions or benefits from the pope against the king or generally obeying an authority other than the Crown by introducing a foreign power into the kingdom. English officials broadened the scope of this law to include Friends.

Preparative meeting. A group of persons who meet and prepare to become a recognized monthly meeting of the Society.

Pro bono publico. Uncompensated legal services usually performed "for the public good."

Pro forma. Literally, "for form." Done as a matter of form.

Pro se. Literally, "for oneself"; pleading one's own case without aid of a lawyer.

Programmed worship. Meetings for worship that are similar in form to traditional Protestant services with music, sermon, and presiding minister.

Quarterly Meeting. After the Monthly Meeting, the next largest meeting in numbers of members; it is comprised of several monthly meetings within a certain geographical region.

Queries. Sets of questions issued by Quarterly and Monthly Meetings to challenge and guide faith and practice on such matters as meeting for worship, members' care, faithfulness to the testimonies, and extent to which Quakers' lives agree with what they profess ("so say and so do").

Res judicata. Literally, "a thing adjudicated." A matter already settled or decided.

Silent worship. A gathering of Friends, usually in a meetinghouse, to listen and commune with God in silence. The silence may be lifted by a person who rises to speak words impelled and guided by the Spirit of God or Inner Light.

"Speaking truth to power." Title of a 1955 AFSC publication. This particular configuration of words was first used then, although the concept of taking concerns to the highest level of authority has been vital from the Society's beginnings.

Unprogrammed worship. Meetings for worship that are conducted in silence with no music, presiding minister, or set program.

Weighty Friend. A Friend whose judgment is frequently sought and relied upon.

World's people. A term used by early Quakers for those who were not members of the Religious Society of Friends.

Writ of certiorari. An extraordinary writ from a higher to a lower court directing it to deliver a record of a case for the purpose of reviewing it.

Yearly meeting. The largest configuration of Quaker meetings; it is comprised of numerous Quarterly Meetings, which themselves are composed of smaller Monthly Meetings.

Many of the Quaker terms are from: Mae Smith-Bixby, *One Explorer's Glossary of Quaker Terms*, ed. Warren Sylvester Smith (Philadelphia: Quaker Press of Friends General Conference, 1985).

Selected Bibliography

Aiken, John Robert. "Utopianism and the Emergence of the Colonial Legal Profession: New York 1664–1710, A Test Case." PhD diss., University of Rochester, 1967.

American Friends Service Committee amicus curiae brief, *In re Summers*, 1945.

Auerbach, Jerold S. *Justice without Law?* New York: Oxford University Press, 1983.

Austin, Benjamin. *Observations on the Pernicious Practice of the Law*. Boston: Adams and Nourse, 1786.

Bacon, Margaret H. *The Quiet Rebels: The Story of Quakers in America*. New York: Basic Books, 1969.

Barbour, Hugh S. "The Early Quaker Outlook upon 'the World' and Society, 1647–1662." PhD diss., Yale University, 1952.

———. *The Quakers in Puritan England*. New Haven, CT: Yale University Press, 1964.

Barclay, Robert. *An Apology for the True Christian Divinity*. [Aberdeen]: [John Forbes], 1678. Reprint, Glenside, PA: Quaker Heritage Press, 2002.

———. *The Anarchy of the Ranters*. In *Truth Triumphant*. London: Printed for Thomas Northcott, 1692.

Bauman, Richard. *For the Reputation of Truth: Politics, Religion, and Conflict among the Pennsylvania Quakers 1750–1800*. Baltimore, MD: Johns Hopkins University Press, 1971.

Benson, Sam. "Why I Quit Practicing Law." *Newsweek*. November 4, 1991, 10.

Besse, Joseph. *A Collection of the Sufferings of the People called Quakers, for the testimony of good Conscience, from . . . 1650, to . . . the Act of Toleration . . . 1689*, 2 vols. London: Luke Hinde, 1753.

Bloomfield, Maxwell. *Lawyers in a Changing Society 1776–1876*. Cambridge, MA: Harvard University Press, 1976.

Bok, Sissela. *Lying*. New York: Vintage Books, 1978.

Boorstin, Daniel. *The Americans: The Colonial Experience*. New York: Random House, 1958.

Braithwaite, Alfred W. "Early Friends Experience with Juries." *Journal of Friends Historical Society* 50 (1962–1964): 217.

Brinton, Howard. *Friends for 300 Years*. New York: Harper and Brothers, 1952. Reprint, Wallingford, PA: Pendle Hill Publications, 1964.

Bronner, Edwin B. *William Penn's Holy Experiment: The Founding of Pennsylvania 1681–1701*. Philadelphia: Temple University Publications, 1962.

Budiansky, Stephen. "How Lawyers Abuse the Law." *U.S. News and World Report*, January 30, 1995, 53.

Burke, Richard K. "Truth in Lawyering: An Essay on Lying and Deceit in the Practice of Law," *Arkansas Law Rev.* 38 (1984): 1.

Burlington Court Book of West New Jersey 1680–1709. Edited by H. Clay Reed and George J. Miller. Washington, DC: American Historical Association, 1944.

Burrough, Edward. *A Declaration to All the World of our Faith and what we Believe.* . . . London: Thomas Simmons, 1660.

Burton, John. Lecture at Haverford College, Haverford, PA, November 13, 1991.

Byllynge, Edward. *A Mite of Affection, Manifested in 31 Proposals.* London: Giles Calvert, 1659.

Cadbury, Henry J. Address accepting the Nobel Peace Prize on behalf of American Friends Service Committee, Oslo, Norway, December 10, 1947.

Clark, Malcolm. *The Enterprise of Law: Questions in Legal Experience and Philosophy.* St. Paul, MN: West Publishing, 1987.

Curran, Barbara A., and Clara N. Carson. "Supplement to the Statistical Report." *The U.S. Legal Profession in 1988.* Chicago: American Bar Foundation, 1991.

Coke, Edward. *Institutes of the Laws of England The Second Part of the Institutes of the Laws of England, The Exposition of many ancient, and other Statutes.* . . . London: W. Rawlins for Thomas Basset, 1681.

Courts in Transition. The Report of the Commission on the Future of Virginia's Judicial System, 1989. Richmond, VA: Author, 1989.

Cox, Gray. *Bearing Witness: Quaker Process and a Culture of Peace.* Pendle Hill pamphlet 262. Wallingford, PA: Pendle Hill Publications, 1985.

Crevecoeur, Michel-Guillaume-Jean de [J. Hector St. John de Crevecoeur]. *Letters from an American Farmer.* New York: Dutton, 1957.

Curtis, Charles P. "The Ethics of Advocacy." *Stanford Law Review* (1951): 3, 9.

Dieffenbach, John J. "Psychology, Society and the Development of the Adversarial Posture." *Journal of Dispute Resolution* 7 (1992): 261.

Disraeli, Benjamin (Earl of Beaconsfield). Speech before English Parliament, February 11, 1851. In *Selected Speeches of the Earl of Beaconsfield,* 2 vols. London: Longmans, Green, 1882.

Duke of York's Laws 1665–1675, Easthampton copy, Earliest Printed Laws of New York 1665–1693. Reprint, Wilmington, DE: Glazier, 1978.

Dunn, Mary, and Richard Dunn. *The Papers of William Penn,* 5 vols. Philadelphia: University of Pennsylvania Press, 1981–1987.

Ellwood, Thomas. "Collection of Many Select and Christian Epistles, Letters, and Testimonies Written by George Fox." Birmingham, UK: N.p., 1698.

Endy Jr., Melvin B. *William Penn and Early Quakerism.* Princeton, NJ: Princeton University Press, 1973.

Faith and Practice. New York: New York Yearly Meeting, 1995.

Faith and Practice. Philadelphia: Philadelphia Yearly Meeting. 1972.

FCNL Washington Newsletter. "Time to Talk with Iran." April 2007.

FCNL Washington Newsletter. "Walk and Chew Gum." June 2008.

First Unitarian Church of Los Angeles v. County of Los Angeles, California, Amicus curiae brief of the Philadelphia Yearly Meeting of the Religious Society of Friends.

Fox, George. *The Journal of George Fox.* Edited by John L. Nickalls. Cambridge, UK: Cambridge University Press, 1952.

———. *An Instruction to Judges and Lawyers.* London: Thomas Simmons, 1658. Folio 1848.

———. *The Law of God, The Rule for Law-makers, The Ground of all just Laws, and the corruption of English Laws and Lawyers Discovered.* London: Giles Calvert, 1658.

———. *To the Parliament of the Comon-wealth of England Fifty-nine particulars laid down for the regulating things and the taking away of oppressing laws and Oppressors and to Ease the Oppressed.* (London: N.p., 1659. Folio 1958.

Frost, William J. *The Quaker Family in Colonial America.* New York: St. Martin's Press, 1973.

Gandhi, M. K. *The Story of My Experiments with Truth.* Translated by Mahadev Desai. Washington, DC: Public Affairs Press, 1968.

Glendon, Mary Ann. *A Nation under Lawyers: How the Crisis in the Legal Profession Is Transforming American Society.* New York: Farrar, Straus, and Giroux, 1994.

Hill, Christopher. *The World Turned Upside Down: Radical Ideas during the English Revolution.* London: Viking Press, 1972.

Holmes Jr., Oliver Wendell. "The Path of the Law." *Harvard Law Review* 10 (1897): 457.

Horle, Craig W. *Quakers and the English Legal System, 1660–1688.* Philadelphia: University of Pennsylvania Press, 1988.

———. "Changing Quaker Attitudes toward Legal Defense: The George Fox Case 1673–75 and the Establishment of Meeting for Sufferings." In *Seeking the Light: Essays on Quaker History in Honor of Edwin B. Bronner.* Edited by William J. Frost and John M. Moore. Wallingford, PA: Pendle Hill Publications and Friends Historical Association, 1986.

———. "Judicial Encounters with Quakers 1660–1688" *Journal of Friends Historical Society* 54 (1976–1989): 98.

——— et al., eds. *Lawmaking and Legislators in Pennsylvania, A Biographical Dictionary,* 3 vols. Philadelphia: University of Pennsylvania Press, 1991–2005.

Irons, Peter. *The Courage of Their Convictions: Sixteen Americans Who Fought Their Way to the Supreme Court.* New York: Free Press, 1988.

———. *Justice at War.* New York: Oxford University Press, 1983.

Jack, Rand, and Dana Crowley. *Moral Vision and Professional Decisions: The Changing Values of Women and Men Lawyers.* Cambridge, UK: Cambridge University Press, 1989.

Jahn, Gunnar. Speech at the presentation of the 1947 Nobel Peace Prize, Oslo, Norway, December 10, 1947.

Janney, Samuel. *The Life of William Penn,* 2d ed., rev. Philadelphia: Lippincott, 1852.

Kagan, Spencer, and Millard C. Masden. "Experimental Analyses of Cooperation and Competition of Anglo-American and Mexican Children," *Dev. Psychol.* 6 (1972): 49.

Keeton, Robert. The Henry W. Strasburger Lecture in Trial Advocacy, University of Texas School of Law, March 27, 1981.

Keith, Charles P. *Provincial Councillors of Pennsylvania 1733–1776.* Philadelphia: S.n., 1883.

Lacey, Paul. "Quaker Beliefs and Immigration Law." Paper presented at AFSC Consultation, Pendle Hill, Wallingford, PA, September 22, 1990. Reprinted in *AFSC Immigration Policy Issues paper.* Philadelphia, March 1991.

———. "Quakers and the Social Testimonies: Servants, Prophets, Reconcilers," AFSC-IRCA Consultation at Pendle Hill, September 22, 1990.

Landon, Donald D. *Country Lawyers, The Impact of Context on Professional Practice.* New York: Praeger, 1990.

Lee, Harper. *To Kill a Mockingbird.* Philadelphia: Lippincott, 1960.

Lincoln, Abraham. *Selected Speeches, Messages, and Letters.* Edited by T. Harry Williams. New York: Holt Rinehart, 1957.

Lloyd, Arnold. *Quaker Social History 1669–1738.* London: Longmans, Green, 1950.

London Yearly Meeting. A selection from the Christian advices issued by the Yearly meeting of the Society of Friends, held in London. From its early establishment to the present time. London: E. Marsh, 1851.

Loyd, William H. *The Early Courts of Pennsylvania.* Boston: Boston Book Company, 1910.

Madsen, Millard C., and Ariella Shapira. "Cooperative Behavior of Urban Afro-American, Anglo-American, Mexican-American and Mexican Village Children." *Dev. Psychol.* 3 (1970): 16.

Marietta, Jack. *The Reformation of American Quakerism.* Philadelphia: University of Pennsylvania Press, 1984.

———. *The Growth of Quaker Self-Consciousness in Pennsylvania 1720–1748.* In *Seeking the Light: Essays on Quaker History in Honor of Edwin B. Bronner.* Edited by William J. Frost and John M. Moore. Wallingford, PA: Pendle Hill Publications and Friends Historical Association, 1986.

Meehan, Thomas R. "Courts, Cases, and Counselors in Revolutionary and Post-Revolutionary Pennsylvania." *The Pennsylvania Magazine of History and Biography* 91, no.1 (1967): 4.

Morgan, Nicholas J. "Lancashire Quakers and the Oath 1660–1722," *Journal of Friends Historical Society* 54 (1976–1982): 235.

Myers, Albert C. *The Immigration of Irish Quakers into Pennsylvania 1682–1750.* Swarthmore, PA: Author, 1902.

National Gazette. "Observations on the Propriety of Extending the Powers of the Justice of the Peace." vol. II, 31 (February 13, 1793). American Periodical Series: 18th Century. Reel 33. Ann Arbor, MI: University Microfilms.

Nayler, James. "A Call to Magistrates, Ministers, Lawyers, and People to Repentance," *Collections of Sundry Books, Epistles, and Written by James Nayler from London edition of 1716.* Cincinnati, OH: Stanton, 1829.

New York Yearly Meeting of the Religious Society of Friends *amicus curiae* brief in *Packard v. United States*, No. 98–6223 (2d Cir. June 1, 1999).

Newman, Daisy. *A Procession of Friends: Quakers in America*, Religion in America Series. Garden City, NY: Doubleday, 1972.

Noonan, John T. *Persons and Masks of the Law: Cardozo, Holmes, Jefferson and Wythe as Makers of Masks.* New York: Farrar, Straus, and Giroux, 1976.

———. "The Purpose of Advocacy and the Limits of Confidentiality," *Michigan L. Rev.* 64 (1966): 1485.

O'Connor, Sandra Day. Address at Wake Forest University, Winston-Salem, NC, April 3, 1993.

———. "Professionalism," *Wash. U. L.Q.* 76 (1998): 5.

Odiorne, George S. "Arbitration and Mediation among Early Quakers," *Arbitration Journal* 6 (1954): 161.

Offutt, William McEnery. "Law and Social Cohesion in a Plural Society: the Delaware Valley, 1680–1710." PhD diss. Johns Hopkins University, 1987.

———. *Of "Good Laws" and "Good Men": Law and Society in the Delaware Valley, 1680–1710.* Champaign, IL: University of Illinois Press, 1995.

Penn, William. *No Cross, No Crown.* In two parts, 26th ed. London: Office of the Society of Friends, 1896.

Pennsylvania and New Jersey Yearly Meeting of Friends. *1751 Rules of Discipline and Christian Advices.* Philadelphia: Pennsylvania Historical Society.

Pennsylvania Packet and Daily Advertiser. July 12, 1785. Philadelphia: Historical Society of Pennsylvania.

Philadelphia Yearly Meeting Minutes. Burlington, West New Jersey: N.p. 1681.

Philadelphia Yearly Meeting Minutes. September 21, 1719. PYM Minutes, 1681—1798; Desc.: Affil.: Pre; Repos.: HV; Loc.: 1250/A1.2. Haverford, PA: Haverford College Library.

Philadelphia Yearly Meeting of the Religious Society of Friends. *Faith and practice. . . . A book of Christian discipline.* Philadelphia: Friends Central Bureau, 1955.

Plato. *The Symposium and the Phaedrus: Plato's Erotic Dialogues.* Translated by William S. Cobb. Albany: SUNY Press, 1993.

Presser, Stephen. "Critical Legal Studies Movement and the New Great Chain of Being: an English Legal Academic's Guide to the Current State of American Law." *Northwestern University Law Review* 79 (1984–1985): 869.

Riskin, Leonard L. "Mediation and Lawyers," *Ohio St. L.J.* 43 (1982): 29.

Rodes Jr., Robert E. *Pilgrim Law.* South Bend, IN: University of Notre Dame Press, 1998.

Rothwax, Harold J. *Guilty: The Collapse of Criminal Justice.* New York: Random House 1996.

Scott, Anne Farrer, "Fishing in Troubled Waters." *Friends Journal,* January 1–15 1982, 10–11.

Seneca, Lucius Annaeus. *Moral Epistles,* 3 vols. Translated by Richard M. Gummere. Cambridge, MA: Harvard University Press, 1917–1925.

Shaffer, Thomas L. "Christian Lawyers' Stories and American Legal Ethics." *Mercer L. Rev.* 33 (1982): 877.

———. "Moral Theology in Legal Ethics," *Cap. University. L. Rev.* 12 (1982): 179.

———. "Should a Christian Lawyer Sign Up for Simon's Practice of Justice?" *Stanford Law Review* 51 (1999): 917, n. 74.

———. "The Christian Jurisprudence of Robert E. Rodes, Jr." *Notre Dame Law Review* 73 (1998): 737.

Shakespeare, William. *Romeo and Juliet.* In *The Complete Plays and Poems of William Shakespeare.* Edited by William A. Neilson and Charles J. Hall. Cambridge, MA: Riverside Press, 1942.

———. *Timon of Athens.* In *The Complete Plays and Poems of William Shakespeare.* Edited by William A. Neilson and Charles J. Hall. Cambridge, MA: Riverside Press, 1942.

Snyder, Edward F., and Wilmer A. Cooper, Stephen L. Klineberg, et al. *Witness in Washington: Fifty Years of Friendly Persuasion.* Edited by Tom Mullen. Richmond, IN: Friends United Press, 1994.

Sophocles, *Oedipus at Colonus.* Translated by Eamon Grennan and Rachel Kitzinger. New York: Oxford University Press, 2005.

Stringfellow, William. *Keeper of the Word.* Edited by Bill Wylie Kellerman. Grand Rapids, MI: Eerdmans, 1994.

Tolles, Frederick. *The Ward Lecture*. Guilford College, Greensboro, NC, November 9, 1956.

Tully, Alan. *William Penn's Legacy, Politics, and Social Structure in Provincial Pennsylvania 1726–1755*. Baltimore, MD: Johns Hopkins University Press, 1977.

Vann, Richard T. *The Social Development of English Quakerism 1655–1755*. Cambridge, MA: Harvard University Press, 1969.

Wagner, Richard V. "Mediated Divorces Last—At Least to the Bench." *Negotiation Journal* 6 (1990): 47.

Wahrhaftig, Paul. "Trends in Peacemaking and Conflict Resolution." *Friends Journal*, October 1991.

Wald, Patricia. "Summary Judgment at Sixty" *Texas Law Review* 76 (1998): 1897.

Ward, Stephanie Francis. "Pulse of the Legal Profession," *ABA Journal*, October 2007, 30–34.

Wasserstrom, Richard. "Lawyers as Professionals: Some Moral Issues," *Human Rights* 5 (1975–1976): 1.

Weston, William J. *Between the Spheres: A Weberian Study of the Friends Committee on National Legislation*. PhD diss., Swarthmore College, 1982.

Woolman, John. *The Journal of John Woolman*. Edited by Philip P. Moulton. New York: Oxford University Press, 1971.

Worcester Magazine, June 1786. American Periodical Series: 18th Century. Reels 1–22. Ann Arbor, MI: University Microfilms.

Yarrow, C. H. Mike. *Quaker Experiences in International Conciliation*. New Haven, CT: Yale University Press, 1978.

Index

abolition of slavery, 18, 52
absence from parish church, 32
absolutist, 114
accommodation, 105, 133
accommodation, place of public, 81
Act for Burying in Woolen, 31
Act for the Gradual Abolition of Slavery, 52
Act for the Names of Days and Months, 53
Act for the Relief of Persons who are Scrupulous of Taking an Oath in the Usual Form, 73
activists, antiwar, 80
activists, civil rights, 80
Adams v. Commissioner of Internal Revenue, 105
advice, 180, 185
Advices, 18, 88, 178
Advices, Balby, 21–22
advocacy, over-zealous, 163
affidavits, unprobed, 87
affirmation, 31, 72
Affirmation Act
    England, 31, 45, 52
    Pennsylvania, 51–52
affirmative acts, 85–86
Afghanistan, 113
aggression, 173
Aid to Families with Dependent Children, 80
allegiance, 23
Allison, Samuel, 61

alternative dispute resolution (ADR), 2, 5, 57, 127, 166, 182, 187, 190, 193–97
alternative to war, 119
American Bar Association (ABA), 144
American Civil Liberties Union (ACLU), 82, 174
American Friends Service Committee (AFSC), 13, 22, 69, 82, 95, 102, 108–09, 116, 119
American Friends Service Committee v. Thornburgh, 84
American Friends Service Committee v. United States, 100
American Revolution, 60
amicus curiae brief, 79, 96, 105–06, 108
Anabaptists, 22
Anglo-American system of jurisprudence, 10, 169
Anne (queen), 49, 52
Antigone, 131
Anti-Injunction Act, 100–01
Anti-Jewish Laws, 110
anti-militarism, 88, 92, 95, 112
antiproprietary democratic opposition, 55
apology as solution, 191
appeal process, 181
Appeal to the Parliament Concerning the Poor . . . , 38
arbitration, 2, 19, 25, 44–45, 57, 60, 64–65, 119, 177–79, 193
armbands, black, 75, 76

armed forces, refusal to be inducted in,
88
Armorer, William, 42
Arms Control and Disarmament Agency,
113
Association of Attorney-Mediators, 195
Attorney General, 55
Autenrieth v. Cullen, 102
avoidance of harm, 132
avoidance of serious contention, 59

bale dock, 36
Bar Association
American (ABA), 144
Maryland, 143, 195
Bar Committee on Character and
Fitness, 109
bar committees, ADR, 194
bar of Pennsylvania, law to admit lawyers
to, 55
Barbados, 34
Barclay, Robert, 26, 38
Barnett, Arthur, 82
barraters, 50
Bazelon, Judge David, 74–75
bedmaker, Fox's analogy of, 40
Bellers, John, 184
Bennet, Judge Gervase, 9
Besse, Joseph, 43
Bill of Rights, 60, 101, 106
Birmingham Meeting, 178
birth, 52
Bishop, George, 39
Black Dog Inn, 37
Black, Justice Hugo, 109
blacks, 80, 81
Blackstone, Sir William, 78
*The Bodie of the Common-Law of
England,* 40
Bok, Sissela, 162
Book of Cases, 43
Boston, 61
General Court, 62
Governor of, 63
Bouvier, Jean, 55
"bowles," 52

Bownas, Samuel, 63
boycott, of products made by slave labor,
18
Bradford, William Judge, 51
branding, 63
Brewster, Margaret, 63
Briggs v. United States, 97
Brinton, Howard, 24
Bronner, Edwin, 77, 100
Brooks, Arle, 98
Brown v. Board of Education, 82, 114,
187
Browne v. United States, 105
Budd v. Potts, 71
burial, 52
Burke, Richard, 138, 156, 159–60, 168,
169
Burlington County, 59
Burrough, Edward, 29, 32, 57, 178
Bushell's case, 35, 37, 45, 63, 199
Byllynge, Edward, 38, 60

Cadbury, Henry J., 107, 185, 198
Calow v. Wright, 71
Camm, John, 37
capital punishment, 3, 50, 72, 73, 92
Capitol Hill law makers, 111
career opportunities and travel rights,
adverse impact on, 75
Casper, Gerhard, 159
Catholic-Protestant conflict, 185
caution against going to law, 15
Ceely, Major, 16
Central Committee for Conscientious
Objectors, 95
charge to jury, 36
Chester County, 59–60
chicane, 54
child soldiers, 117
Children of Light, 19
Christian jurisprudence, 158, 168
Christmas Day, 31
Church of England, 32, 51
Church of the Brethren, 22, 89
City of Earth, 114
City of God, 114

civil disobedience, 3–4, 18, 24, 28–30,
    33, 34, 60–61, 63–64, 70, 88
civil rights, 45, 61, 72–74
Civil Rights Act of 1964, 81, 114,
    193–94
Civil Rights Commission, 114
civilian humanitarian service, 89
Civilian peace-builder corps, 116
civilian society, 90
Clark, Justice Tom, 96
clearness committee, 27
client confidentiality, 159
Coffin, Levi, 18
cognitive skills, 188
Coke, Sir Edward, 39, 41, 74
collaboration, 193
combatant service, 88
commands of the spirit, 29, 39
common law, 36
commonality of all persons, 112
common-sense solution, 94
Commonwealth v. Munson, 72
communal discernment, 27, 28, 83
communal silence, 112
communitarian justice, 64
community, 5, 12, 18, 23, 44, 48, 64,
    70, 112, 115, 133, 142, 170, 183,
    186, 197
community decision-making, 183
Community Relations Service, 193
compassion, 187
compelling interest, 105, 107
competition, 188
comprehensive peacemaking system,
    181
concern, 20, 26
    peaceful statement of, 75
confidentiality, 160
conflict, 136
conflict of interest, lawyers', 171
Congress, 25, 102, 113
Congressional hearings, 88
conscience, 17, 19, 29–30, 35, 39–40,
    52, 73, 79, 84, 88, 98, 105, 170
conscientious objection, 60, 72, 88–89,
    97, 105–06, 114, 117

conscientious objectors, 13, 23, 61, 95,
    97, 99, 108, 118
conscientious scruples
    against war, 73, 95, 104
    against killing, 108
consensus, 27, 112
Consonance of belief and action, 102
Constitution, 101–02
    persons under, 77
Constitutional Convention of 1776, 60
constitutional freedoms, 76
constitutional rights, 4, 108
constitutionality of statute, 77–78
consultation, Pendle Hill, 83–84
contempt of court, 33, 37, 82, 103
Conventicle Act, 30
convergence of belief and action, 11
convincement, 78
Corbett, Thomas, 43
Corinthians, 44, 58
Corporation Act of 1661, 32
corpse, 31
*The Corruption and Deficiency of the
    Laws of England*, 38
courage, 187
The Courage of Their Convictions . . . ,
    186
Court of Appeals, District of Columbia,
    74
court proceedings, truncated, 86
Cox, U.S. Solicitor-General Archibald,
    96
crimes
    capital, 51
    larceny, 50
    reduction of capital, 64
    satisfaction to victims of, 50
Cromwell, Oliver, 37, 69
Cromwell, Richard, 29
Cuba, 116
curfew order, 81
Curtis, Charles, 163

days and months, designation by
    numerals, 52
Dean, John, 162

death penalty, 51, 141
  abolition of, 114
debt, 71
decision-making, by community, 183
*A Declaration from the Harmless and
  Innocent People of God, called
  Quakers . . .* , 14
Declaration of Indulgence, 34
de-escalation of conflict, 116
defamation, 60, 71
Department of Defense Authorization
  Act, 93
Department of Justice, 194
Department of the Interior, 74
dependence, 102
dependent client, 168
deportation, 63
dichotomization, 189
Dickinson v. Bell, 93
Dickinson, John, 55
dictionary, of American law, 55
differences in Quaker respondents'
  practice with that of others, 148–49
disarmament, 114, 116
discernment, 23, 186
discharge, 75
disclosure of information, 75
discrimination
  legal standard, 83
  pattern and practice of, 81
disobedience, 29
disownment, 25, 58, 61
dispute resolution, 60
  alternative. *See* alternative dispute
    resolution (ADR)
  extralegal, 1
  multidoor approach to, 196
  process of, 178
disputes, intra-Quaker brought to court,
  58
distrain property, 32
distrained goods, 33
distraints, 41–43, 52
District of Columbia, 80, 92
District of Columbia Court of Appeals,
  74

divine guidance, 112
"divine lobbyist," 69, 200
dominant lawyer, 168
Douglas, Justice William, 78, 97,
  100–01, 107
Draft Act of 1864, 96
Draft Act of 1917, 96
due process, 79, 108
Duke of York, 50, 199
Duke of York's laws, 46, 48
Dwight, Timothy, 54
Dyer, Mary, 63

Earlham College, 98
ecclesiastical testamentary court, 31
Edward I, 33
effect of gender in respondents' answers,
  131
Elfbrandt v. Russell, 26, 78, 104
Elizabeth I (queen), 32
Elmira (New York) Friends Meeting, 75
empathetic sensibilities, 188
employment complaints, 193
Employment Division v. Smith, 85, 101,
  104
Empson v. Harlin and Way, 59
energy policy, 116
English Inns of Court, 31, 55, 57
English judiciary, 34, 42
English laws, conflict with, 3
English legal establishment, 30
enlightenment, 19
environmental protection, 113
Epistle of Tender Love and Caution to
  Friends in Pennsylvania, An, 99
Equal Employment Opportunity
  Commission (EEOC), 194
equal protection, 83, 108
equality, 12, 28, 38, 48, 52, 64, 70,
  79–80, 84–85, 103, 111, 142, 167,
  184, 186
  of speech, 17
  refusal to doff hats, 63, 71, 103
Eternal Light, 30, 70
ethical lawyering, 121
ethical stages, 189

evacuation orders, 81
Evans, Harold, 89
evidence, exculpatory, 81
evolvement, 19
exaggeration of claims and allegations, 41
exclusion from the bar, 108
exemption, 61, 88–89, 94
    certificates, 103
    fees, 61
    for conscientious objectors, 96, 107
    military, eligibility standard for, 97
expression of opinion
    benign and noncoercive, 75
    silent, 76
expression, protected, 77
extrajudicial dispute resolution, 167

fair justice system, 159
fairness, 121, 166
fairness doctrine, 91
Faith and Practice, 16, 20, 22–23, 121
federal budget, military-related portion
    of, 100
Federal Bureau of Investigation (FBI), 80
Federal Communications Commission
    (FCC), 91
Federal Conscription Act of 1863, 96
Federal Practice and Procedure
    Symposium, 86
Federal Rules of Civil Procedure, 86
Rule 56, 86–87
Federal tax laws, 101
fees, unjust, 54
Fell, Judge Thomas, 30
Fell, Margaret, 20, 24, 30, 33, 70, 87
"feminine" view of morality, 132
Fenwicke, John, 60
Fifth Amendment, 96, 102
financial aid, federal, 93
Finch, Atticus, 164–65, 170
fines, 52, 60, 62, 64
First Amendment rights, 70, 72, 74–77,
    79, 92, 106
First Day, 10
First Frame of Government, 48
first principle of ethics, 121

First Unitarian Church of Los Angeles v.
    County of Los Angeles, 79
Five Mile Act, 31, 42
foreign policy, of the United States, 116
forfeiture of inheritance rights, 33
Fort Sam Houston, 90
Fortas, Justice Abe, 76
Fourteenth Amendment, 76, 83
Fourth Amendment, 74
Fox, George, 2, 9, 11, 14–16, 23–24,
    28–30, 37–40, 42–43, 45, 48–49,
    63–64, 69, 77, 79, 83, 101, 111,
    114, 156, 160, 164, 167–68, 178,
    199
    story of Penn's sword, 89
    Worcester imprisonment of, 43
Frames of Government for Pennsylvania,
    79
freedom of religion, 77, 79, 84–85,
    107
Free Produce Association, 18
freedom of assembly, 73
freedom of religion, 73, 76, 109
freedom of speech, 73, 91
French and Indian War, 64
French v. Leeds, 71
French, Paul Comley, 89
Friends Committee on National
    legislation (FCNL), 22, 25, 69,
    111, 113–16, 119, 174, 200
Friends Conflict Resolution Programs
    (FCRP), 196
Friends General Conference, 89
Friends in Truth, 9
Friends Peace Committee, 75
Friends War Problems Committee, 111
Friends World Committee for
    Consultation (FWCC), 116
Friends, Religious Society of, 9
Fry, Elizabeth, 24, 115
Fugitive Slave Law, 18
fundamental law, 39, 48
fundamental rights, 77
Furly, Benjamin, 49–50

gambling, 115

Gandhi, Mohandas K. (Mahatma),
    110–11, 157, 177
gathered meeting, 26
General Assembly, 48–49, 51
general consultative status, 116
genocide, 110
genuine issues of material fact, 87
Gesell, Judge Gerhard, 93
Gestapo, 24
Glendon, Mary Ann, 140, 168, 171
God, 26, 28, 30–33, 39, 50, 59, 71,
    83, 85, 88, 91, 94–95, 103, 105,
    113–14, 131, 169, 193
God's law, 45, 48, 64, 71, 77
God's leadings, 28
going to law, 4, 70, 88, 118, 197
    caution against, 25, 65, 69, 186, 200
    caution against not absolute, 58
golden rule, 13, 19, 39, 42, 44, 48
Gonzalez v. United States, 97
good faith, 121
goodness, capacity for, 21
Gordon Hirabayashi Defense Committee,
    82
gospel order, 20, 25, 55, 57–58, 60, 64,
    119, 141, 178, 180–82, 197
gospel order, success of, 58
government surveillance, 73
governmental accommodation, 107
governmental interest, 85–86
great chain of being model, 169–70
Green v. FCC, 91
Greenham Women against Cruise Missiles
    v. Reagan, 93
Grotius, Hugo, 10, 162

hanging, 63
hard labor, 62
harmony, 2, 12, 15, 28, 44, 57, 60, 64,
    133, 184, 186, 197
hat honor, 17, 32–33, 38, 42, 142
Henry VIII, 32
Her Majesty's Commissioner for Trade
    and Plantations, 48
Higher Education Act of 1965, Title IV
    of, 93
Hirabayashi v. United States, 81

A Historical Description of the Province
    of Pennsylvania and County of West
    Jersey in America, 54
Hitler, Adolf, 15
Hobson v. Wilson, 80
holiday, 31
holistic approach, 192
Holmes, Jr., Justice Oliver Wendell, 70,
    166, 169
"holy experiment," 3, 46–47
honesty, 121, 157
Hookes, Ellis, 42
Horle, Craig, 44
House of Commons, 35
House of Correction, 62–63
House of Representatives, 60
House Ways and Means Committee,
    112
Howell, Sir John, 36
human brotherhood, 112
human rights, 116
humanizing influence, 133

Illinois Constitution, 108, 120
Illinois State Bar Committee on
    Character and Fitness, 108
immigrants, undocumented, 84–85
immigrants' rights, 73
immigration, 79
    control, 84
    Immigration Reform and Control Act
        of 1986 (IRCA), 83, 84
imprisonment, 30, 63
imprisonment at Worcester, 24
In re Petition for Rulemaking, 80
In re Summers, 108
independence of juries, 63
indictment, 36
individual discernment, 27
inheritance rights, forfeiture of, 33
inner light, 14, 20, 34, 38–39, 50, 72,
    105, 112, 199
Institutes of American Law, 55
Institutes of the Laws of England, 41
institutionalized fighting, 173
Instruction to Judges and Lawyers, 39, 40
integrity, 11–12, 28

intent or purpose, racially discriminatory, 83
Internal Revenue Service (IRS), 102
international arbitration agreements, 184
International Covenant on Civil and Political Rights, 118
international peacemaking, 185
Interregnum, 69
intervenor, 82
intimidation by court, 37
intimidation of juries, 34
Inward Light, 26
Inward Teacher, 21
Iran, 116
Iraq, 113
Irons, Peter, 78, 81
Ishiguro, Kazuo, 170

Jack, Dana Crowley, 140–41, 131–32, 165, 170
Jack, Rand, 131–32, 140–41, 165, 170
Jackson, Justice Robert, 87
Jamaica, 34
James, 13
James II, 34, 45, 50
James v. Board of Education, 104
James v. Board of Education of Central District No. 1, 75
Japanese ancestry, 81
Jenkins v. Commissioner of the Internal Revenue, 106
Jews, 15, 25
John, 20
judges, 130
    bribery of, 3
    king's control of, 35
    power of, 119
Judiciary Act of 1789, 104
juries, 35
    independence of, 37
jurisprudence, Anglo-American system of, 10, 169
justice, 5, 10, 30, 49, 54, 57, 69, 86–87, 109, 111, 115, 160, 180, 201
    as truth in action, 174
justiciable claim, 75
Justitiarius Justificatus, 38

Keeton, Judge Robert, 163
Kelyng, Justice John, 30
Kennedy, President John, 95
King Charles II, 3, 24, 30, 32, 37, 47, 50, 60
King v. Fearson, 72
King, Rev. Martin Luther, Jr., 174
King's Charter, 48
king's protection, loss of, 33
Kinsey, John, 55
kinship, 193
Kohlberg, Lawrence, 189
Korea, 70
Kosovo, 112

Lancashire, 30–31
land disputes, 57
land rights, 60
Lange v. United States, 80
Law and Lawyers of Sin, 39
law as battle, 172
Law of Freedom, 38
law of Maryland, Relief of Tender Consciences, in Relation to Oaths and Swearing, 63
law practice, 122
    effect of age on, 134
    effect of gender on, 134
    gender-differentiated styles of, 132
law school curricula, 166
lawsuits, advantages of, 187
law
    against Quakers, 62
    dictionary of American, 55
    District of Columbia, 80
    mistrust of, 54
    preamble, 41, 78
    testing of, 83
lawmakers, petitioning of, 69
Lawson, Thomas, 38
"lawyerhood," 2, 110
lawyers
    bitterness toward, 54
    conferences, 152
    fees of, 40
    practicing, 122
    professional morality of, 131

lawyers *(continued)*
    Quaker, 1, 3, 200
    regulation of fees of, 49
    responsibility of, 168
    role, 140
    rural and small town, 172
    true function of, 177
    urban, 172
leading, 21, 23, 26–27
leaflets, distribution of, 90
League of Nations, 116
least restrictive means, 105, 107
Lee, Harper, 170
legal counsel, Friends' engagement of, 41
legal defense organization, 43
legal education, 31
legal ethicists, 156
legal ethics, 2, 4, 121
    standards, 171
legal language, Pennsylvania, 48
legal reform, 2, 3, 4, 37–38, 64
legal system, 2
    domination of Pennsylvania's, 59
    goals of, 201
legislative priorities, 112
legislature, 70
liability, conspiratorial, 80
liberty of conscience, 24, 26, 32, 34, 51,
    70, 72, 77, 79, 106
life imprisonment, 33
light, 13, 19, 21–22, 87, 91
    God's, 79
    hold in the, 21
    measure of, 19–21
    of truth, 73
Lincoln, President Abraham, 173
linkages, 193
listening, 28
litigation
    alternatives to, 177
    paradigm, 188
Lloyd, David, 55
lobbying, 113
London, 36
London Yearly Meeting, 12, 23
Londonderry v. Chester, 72

long hair, 74
Lord Baltimore, 48, 63
Lord's advocate, 200
Lord's Day, 31
Lorrimore, Stephen, 32
Lowden, William, 58
loyal opposition, 33, 200
loyalty, 24
loyalty oath, 26
Lying, 162

Madison, James, 60
magistrate, 12, 71
Magna Carta, 36–37, 40, 45, 103
"malicious scaring phrases," 41
mandatory tithing, 32
mare, 71
marriage, 27, 31, 51–52, 71–72
marriage certificate, 27
Marshall, Justice Thurgood, 76
Maryland, 63
    boundary with Pennsylvania, 48
    State Bar Association, 143, 195
Massachusetts, 54, 61, 63–64
material fact, genuine issues of, 87
Mathewson v. Phoenix Iron Foundry, 72
Matthew, 13, 25, 29, 178–79
Mayer, Milton, 69
McCarthy era, 113
Mead, William, 3, 31, 33, 35–37,
    41–42, 45, 103, 199
means, least restrictive, 86
mediation, 2, 19, 25, 57, 118–19,
    177–78, 184, 191–93
    durability of settlements, 184
    peer-based programs, 195
medical supplies, 91
Meeting for Sufferings, 42, 61
    clerk of, 55
meeting
    for business, 18, 27
    for worship, 26, 80
    internal structure, 18
    unprogrammed, 3, 26
meetinghouse, 16
membership, 27–28

Mennonite Church, 89
Mennonites, 22
Metropolitan Police Department, 80
Middle East, 116
"military area," restrictions on persons
    in a, 81
military base, 90
military service, 117
military, not part of normal public
    community, 90
militia, 59
    refusal to pay for, 33
Minton, Senator Sherman, 90
minute, 105, 107
mistrust of law, 54
A Mite of Affection in 31 Proposals, 38
money, recovery of, 60
Monthly Meeting, 10, 18, 25, 79, 180
morality
    of law, 169
    moral choices, 170
    moral compass, 165
    moral distance, 131, 164
    moral integrity, 110
    moral responsibility, 163
    personal, 164
Moral Vision and Professional Decisions,
    164
Morgenthau, U.S. Attorney Robert, 96
Mosaic code, 39
Murphy, Justice Frank, 81

National Gazette, 54
Native American Advocacy Project, 115
Native Americans, 114–15
natives, 57
Nayler, James, 183
Nazis, 24, 110–11
need, calculation of, 80
Negroes, ban on importation of, 52
New Garden monthly meeting, 58
New Hampshire, 72
New Haven, 63
New Jersey, 77
    general assistance benefits, 80
    Supreme Court, 73

New Netherland (New York), 63
New York, 95
    State Constitution, 106
New York Times, 96
New York Yearly Meeting, 105–06, 119
Newgate Prison, 34, 37
Nicholas I, Czar of Russia, 185
Ninth Amendment, 106
Nixon, President Richard, 74, 92
Nobel Peace Prize, 15, 107, 198
noncombatant service, 88–89
noncreedal religion, 21
non-governmental organizations (NGOs),
    116
non-military related funds, 106
nonpayment of fines, 37
nonviolence, refusal to fight, 45
Noonan, Judge John, 160, 169–70
North Carolina, 61
Northern Ireland, 185
Norwich, 31
Nuremburg trials, 88

O'Connor, Justice Sandra Day, 153, 172
Oath of Allegiance, 30
oaths, 3, 11, 30–31, 38, 62–63, 72,
    77–79
oaths, loyalty, 70, 78
obedience, 29
obedience to the state, 23
Office of Foreign Assets Control, 91
officers of the court, lawyers as, 161, 166
Old Bailey, 31, 33–34
opposition to war, 103
oranges hypothetical, 193
Organization for Security and Coopera-
    tion in Europe (OSCE), 113
Orlando v. Laird, 102
overlapping needs and interests, 192
oyer, 36

pacifism, 14, 48, 70, 73, 88–89, 107,
    111
    refusal to be inducted in the armed
        forces, 70, 94
    refusal to bear arms, 63, 110

pacifism *(continued)*
    refusal to pay taxes for war, 14,
        99–100, 103, 105
    refusal to register for draft, 70
pacifists, 60, 61
Packard v. United States, 105
Packard, Rosa, 19
parish church, absence from, 32
Parliament, 31, 35, 40–41
Pastorius, Francis Daniel, 17
Paul, 44, 58, 178–79
    letter to the Galatians, 24
payment of taxes for war, 102, 105
peace, 5, 13, 61, 70, 108, 111, 115–16,
        183
    peace building, 113, 116–18
    peaceful resolution of individual, 110
    peacefulness, 111
    peacemaking, 57, 64, 14, 89, 91, 110,
        178
    testimony, 4, 14, 23, 28, 59, 64, 70,
        76–77, 88, 90, 97–100, 102, 107,
        112, 118, 173, 180
Peace Corps, 113
Pendle Hill, 83–84, 146, 152, 197
Penington, Edward, 179
Penn, William, 2–3, 23–25, 31, 33, 36,
        37, 39–41, 45, 47–51, 55, 58–61,
        64, 69, 101, 103, 114–15, 179,
        184, 199
    Penn-Mead trial, 35–36, 41–42, 45
    Penn's Charter, 47
    story of Penn's sword, 23, 89
Pennsylvania, 2, 25, 47, 49, 52, 57, 59,
        73
    Supreme Court, Chief Justice of, 55
    early penal system of, 51
    Frames of Government for, 79
Perry, Michael, 108, 169
personal lives, 2
personhood, 2, 110
Persons and Masks of the Law, 170
Phaedrus, 10
Philadelphia
    Monthly Meeting, 179
    police department, 75
    Yearly Meeting, 22, 55, 93, 119

*Philadelphia Yearly Meeting of the Reli-
        gious Society of Friends v. Tate,* 75
"philosophical map," 188–92, 190
Plain Dealing, 39
plain speaking, 11, 45, 157
plaintiffs, 70
planters, 57
Plato, 10
polarization, 189
Poor Peoples' Campaign, 80
population, ratio of lawyers to, 55
postconflict work, 117
poverty, 79
practice, large-firm private, 54
prayer vigil, 92
preaching, 31, 36–37
preemptive diplomacy, 118
preemptive strikes, 116
Presser, Stephen, 54, 169, 190
prison, 32, 37
pro bono, 95
pro se, 36, 104
professional duty, 170
property laws, 31
prophet, 84
"prophetic listening," 28
Proprietor, 57
Protectorate, 45
Provincial Council, 48
public assistance, recipients of, 80
Puritans, 61
Purvis v. United States, 97

Quaker Act of 1661–1662, 30, 32
Quaker Action Group v. Hickel, 74
Quaker docket, 60
Quaker Hill, 111
Quaker House, 117
Quaker lawyers, 1, 3, 200
    advantages & disadvantages of being,
        144–48
    respondents, 122
Quaker meeting attenders & members,
        122
Quaker peace and service, 15, 112, 185
Quaker testimonies, 136
Quaker United Nations, 116, 127

Quakers
    as percentage of English population,
    43
    of Philadelphia, 47
Quarterly Meeting, 10, 19, 181
    of Philadelphia, 51
queries, 22, 27
    questionnaire, 4, 122

race, 17
racial balance, 82
racial criteria, 83
racial discrimination, 81
racial equality, 26
racial integration, 73
*Reasons Against War and Paying for its
    Support*, 61
reconciler, 84
reconciliation, 117, 182
recovery of fines paid, 34
redemption, 50
reform, of prison, 37
reformist ideas, 158
refugees, 116
Refusal to certify for admission to bar,
    108
refusal to swear, 29–30, 45
registration, for armed services, 93
rehabilitation, 50–51, 65
relationship interdependency, 132
religion
    free exercise of, 101
    religious conscience, 105
    Religious Freedom Restoration Act of
        1993 (RFRA), 85, 99, 104, 106
    religious scruples, 71
    religious thinking, 121
    religious toleration, 34
    religious training and belief, 94
Remains of the Day, 170
Reno, Attorney General Janet, 187, 194
resolution, cooperatively devised, 190
respondents attempt to resolve tension,
    143
"responsibility to protect," 118
restitution, 50
restorative justice, 117

Revolutionary War, 61
Rhode Island, 61, 72
Richmond (Indiana), 111
Richmond Resolution, 89
rights and privileges, relinquishment of,
    90
rights
    against self-incrimination, 36, 102
    of free exercise of religion, 102,
        104–05
    of free speech, 76, 93
    of minorities, 114
    of symbolic free speech, 104
    to effective assistance of counsel, 104
    to freedom of association, 104
Riskin, Leonard, 188
Rodes, Robert, 158, 165, 167–68
role identification, 164
role morality, 164
role-differentiated behavior of lawyers,
    140
role-differentiated professionalism, 168
Roosevelt, President Franklin Delano, 89
Rudyard, Thomas, 41–42, 45, 50
rule changes, 159, 166
rules and powers, military, 90
rules of discipline, 58
rules of discipline and Christian advices,
    178

Sabbath, 31
sacredness of human life, 114
sanctions, 86
Scull v. Virginia, 82
*Seattle School District No. 1 v.
    Washington*, 82
*The Second Part of the Peoples' ancient
    and Just Liberties Asserted*, 41
Secret Service agents, 74
sedition, 70, 77
Seeger, Daniel, 95–97
Selective Draft Law Cases, 88
Selective Service Act of 1940, 108
    challenge to, 95, 99
Selective Training and Service Act of
    1940, 88–89, 96
    amendment to, 94

self-interest, 170
Senate Committee
　Judiciary, 113
　on Military Affairs, 89
　Select Committee on Indian Affairs,
　　115
Seneca, Lucius Annaeus, 10
sense of the meeting, 27
Shaffer, Thomas, 28, 165, 169–70
Shakespeare, William, 40, 41
Shawcross, Sir Hartley, 88
Sherbert v. Verner, 86, 105
silence, 26, 28, 34
silent witness, 76
simplicity, 12, 16, 48, 142
　early Quaker speech, 16
Sixteenth Fundamental, 49
Sixth Amendment, 104
slavery
　abolition of, 52, 79
　opposition to, 17
　slave labor, 18
Smith, John, 58
"so say and so do," 41, 77, 200
social justice, 111, 118, 158
Sophists, 10
Sophocles, 11, 131
South Carolina, 57
Southern Christian Leadership
　　Conference (SCLC), 80
Sparrow v. Goodman, 73
Speak Truth to Power, 69
Speaker of the Assembly, 55
Speaker of the House, 80
speaking truth to power, 24–25, 63, 69
Speed, Thomas, 35
The Spirit of Truth Vindicated, 39
Spirit, of God, 17, 21, 26, 112
spiritual values, 115
stand of conscience, 108
State v. Levine, 73
state, coercion by the, 78
Stevenson, Marmaduke, 61
Straut v. Calissi, 77
students, 77
sufferings, 32, 34
　county book of, 43

Sufferings, Meeting for, 43
summary judgment, 86–87, 104
summary proceedings, 85
　overuse of, 86
Summers, 110–11, 120
Sunday Observance Acts, 31
supremacy, 79
"Supreme Being," 94–95
　construction of, 96
Supreme Court, 76, 78, 81–83, 88, 94,
　　104, 106, 108, 119
　of New Jersey, 80
surveillance, 75
survey, 3, 121
　effect of gender in respondents'
　　answers, 131
　reasons for becoming lawyers, 123–26
　respondents who changed or left legal
　　practice, 149–50
　respondents' experience as Quaker
　　lawyers, 136
　respondents' mode of practice, 126
　respondents' pro bono work, 135
　suggestions for changes in legal system,
　　151, 153–56
　type of law respondents practice, 130
sustainable peace, 117
Swarthmore College, 102

Tatum v. Morton, 92
Tax Court, 106
tax levy on employees' salary, 101
tax protestor, 105
taxes for war, 59
tennis, 52
Test Act of 1673, 32
testimonies, 12, 13
Thomas, Gabriel, 54
Tinker v. Des Moines School District, 76,
　　118
tithing, mandatory, 32
Titus, 44
To Kill a Mockingbird, 164, 170
To the Parliament of the Comon-wealth of
　　England . . . , 38
tobacco, 63
Tolles, Frederick B., 69

trade laws, 31
Trading with the Enemy Act, 91
trespass, 71
The True Basis of Christian Unity, 22
Truman, President Harry, 98
truth, 10, 20, 27, 30, 32, 69, 70, 86,
   112, 116, 201
  search for, 160, 162, 167
  single standard of, 157
  truthfulness, 5, 28, 30, 157, 163, 166
  truth-telling, 3, 10, 11, 16, 38, 39,
    45, 59, 139, 156–57, 162, 201
Truth Exalted, 39
Truth Rescued from Imposture, 39

"un-American activities," 78
Underground Railroad, 18
undermining authority, 32
Unger, Roberto, 108, 169, 190
United Nations (UN), 113
  Charter, 115
  Economic and Social Council, 116
  Human Rights Council, 117
  Peacebuilding Commission (PBC), 117
  Study on the Impact of Armed
    Conflict on Children, 117
  Treaty on Law of the Sea, 115
United States v. American Friends Service
  Committee, 100
United States v. Baechler, 99
United States v. Cornell, 72
United States v. Crocker, 99
United States v. Flower, 90
United States v. Harper, 102
United States v. Hayworth, 101
United States v. Henderson, 98
United States v. Lansdowne Swim Club,
  80
United States v. Lee, 105
United States v. Nugent, 97
United States v. Palmer, 99
United States v. Peebles, 98
United States v. Philadelphia Yearly
  Meeting of the Religious Society of
  Friends, 101
United States v. Seeger, 94
United States v. Snider, 102

United States v. Wade, 162
United States v. Wilhelm, 103
unity, 27, 57, 112
Universal Military Training and Service
  Act, 88
unprobed affidavits, 87
unwillingness to be a soldier, 109
unwillingness to bear arms, 108

Vaughan, Roland, 42
Victoria (queen), 24
Vietnam, 70, 74, 76, 90–91, 102
Vietnam War, 80, 119
  peace agreement, 92
  moratorium, 75
  policy of, 92
Virginia, 61, 63, 64, 82
  Committee on Law Reform and Racial
    Activities, 82
  Department of Dispute Resolution
    Services, 195
  General Assembly, 82
Wagstaffe's Case, 34
Wald, Judge Patricia, 86
Waln, Nicholas, 55
war, 95, 108, 112
  alternative to, 119
  monetary support for, 99
  opposition to, 23, 103
  payment of taxes for, 102, 105
  protest, 77
  religious aversion to, 75
  role of, 76
  war-related portion of taxes,
    withholding of, 100
  wrongness of, 91
War Department, 82
Warr, John, 38, 40
Washington Peace Center, 80
Washington v. Seattle School District No.
  1, 83
Washington, state of, 82
Wasserstrom, Richard, 140–41, 168
Watergate hearings, 162
Welch v. Shultz, 91
welfare, 80
West Jersey, 49, 60, 71

Western Yearly Meeting, 98
White House, 74, 92
White House Counsel, 162
White, Justice Byron, 76, 162
Whitehall, 69
Whitehead, George, 41
Wilhelm, 104
William Say dispute, 179
Wingate, Edmund, 40
win-lose thinking, 188
Winstanley, Gerrard, 38
win-win, 189, 190
Wisconsin v. Yoder, 86, 105
Wither, George, 38, 40
women lawyers
    attrition of, 133
    care orientation of, 132
women, perspectives of, 125
Woolman, John, 12, 114
Worcester, 30
work of a lawyer, 109

World Conference on Women, 117
World War II, 81, 108
worship, 17, 27
Wright, Charles Alan, 86, 87
writ of certiorari, 76, 106, 108
writ of error coram nobis, 81
writ of praemunire, 33

yea and nay, 30, 31, 45
Yearly Meeting, 10, 19, 22, 44, 112,
    181
    Baltimore, 121
    London, 43, 185
    New York, 20, 22
    Philadelphia, 23, 25, 57, 79, 102
York, 30
York Castle, 32
Yorkshire, 30, 33
    justices, 29

zealous advocacy, 161, 166